URBAN PLANNING
Theory & Practice

URBAN PLANNING

Theory & Practice

M. PRATAP RAO
B.Arch., M.U.R.P., A.I.I.A., A.I.T.P., A.I.I.D.
Architect-Planner

CBSPD

CBS Publishers & Distributors Pvt Ltd

New Delhi • Bengaluru • Chennai • Kochi • Kolkata • Lucknow • Mumbai
Hyderabad • Jharkhand • Nagpur • Patna • Pune • Uttarakhand

Disclaimer

Science and technology are constantly changing fields. New research and experience broaden the scope of information and knowledge. The author has tried his best in giving information available to him while preparing the material for this book. Although, all efforts have been made to ensure optimum accuracy of the material, yet it is quite possible some errors might have been left uncorrected. The publisher, the printer and the author will not be held responsible for any inadvertent errors or inaccuracies.

URBAN PLANNING
Theory & Practice

ISBN: 978-81-239-0757-4

First Edition : 2001

Reprint: 2005, 2009, 2010, 2011, 2012, 2014, 2015, 2017, 2019, 2023

Published by Satish Kumar Jain and produced by Varun Jain for
CBS Publishers & Distributors Pvt Ltd
4819/XI Prahlad Street, 24 Ansari Road, Daryaganj, New Delhi 110 002, India
Ph: 011-23289259, 23266861 Website: www.cbspd.com
e-mail: delhi@cbspd.com
Corporate Office: 204 FIE, Industrial Area, Patparganj, Delhi 110 092, India
Ph: 011-4934 4934 Fax: 011-4934 4935 e-mail: publishing@cbspd.com; publicity@cbspd.com

Branches

- **Bengaluru:** Seema House 2975, 17th Cross, KR Road, Banasankari 2nd Stage, Bengaluru 560 070, Karnataka, India
  Ph: +91-80-26771678/79 Fax: +91-80-26771680 e-mail: bangalore@cbspd.com
- **Chennai:** 7, Subbaraya Street, Shenoy Nagar, Chennai 600 030, Tamil Nadu, India
  Ph: +91-44-26680620, 26681266 Fax: +91-44-42032115 e-mail: chennai@cbspd.com
- **Kochi:** 42/1325, 1326, Power House Road, Opp KSEB, Power House, Ernakulam, Kochi 682 018, India
  Ph: +91-484-4059061-65 Fax: +91-484-4059065 e-mail: kochi@cbspd.com
- **Kolkata:** 147, Hind Ceramics Compound, 1st Floor, Nilgunj Road, Belghoria, Kolkata 700 056, West Bengal, India
  Ph: +91-33-25633055-56 e-mail: kolkata@cbspd.com
- **Lucknow:** Basement, Khushnuma Complex, 7-Meerabai Marg (behind Jawahar Bhawan), Lucknow 226 001, India
  Ph: +91-522-4000032 e-mail: tiwari.lucknow@cbspd.com
- **Mumbai:** PWD Shed, Gala no. 25/26, Ramchandra Bhatt Marg, Next to JJ Hospital Gate no. 2, Opp. Union Bank of India, Noorbaug Mumbai 400 009, Maharashtra, India
  Ph: +91-22-66661880/89 e-mail: mumbai@cbspd.com

Representatives

- **Hyderabad** 0-9885175004
- **Jharkhand** 0-9811541605
- **Nagpur** 0-9421945513
- **Patna** 0-9334159340
- **Pune** 0-9923910676
- **Uttarakhand** 0-9716462459

Printed at Sanjay Printers, Sahibabad, UP, India

Preface

People migrate to cities in search of employment and for better prospects in life. Thus urbanisation has become an important feature in our modern life. Rapid growth of population and density of population in a given area are the main reasons for the multiplicity of problems in our cities. Under these circumstances some kind of planning, regulation and control of development is necessary in the cities in any kind of political set-up and in any kind of economy. Government policies leave a significant impact on the shape and size of our cities because through these policies we decide what type of life style we would like to have.

In this book, I have covered all aspects of urban planning in simple and concise manner to encourage the student to understand the importance of urban planning. Not only the theoretical aspects but practical case studies are included in each chapter for realistic understanding of the subject. I tried to cover the syllabuses of polytechnic, degree and postgraduate students of urban planning. They should find this book useful because I have given the latest information on urban planning. This book is also a good ready reference for professional urban-planners. I invite suggestions and changes, if any, from the readers to improve the content of the book.

M. PRATAP RAO

About the Book

Urban Planning is necessary, in any type of political set-up and economy, for organised growth and development. This book covers all the essential aspects of urban planning with case studies, specially with reference to Indian conditions. The chapters include Ancient and Modern urban planning, Planning legislation, preparation of Development plan, Housing, Traffic and transportation, Landscape design, Urban conservation and useful Planning standards. Most of the syllabus on urban planning has been covered for polytechnic, degree and post-graduate students.

It is also a good reference book for professional planners.

About the Author

M. PRATAP RAO is a well qualified practicing Architect-Planner at Hyderabad, Andhra Pradesh with eighteen years experience in the field of architecture and urban planning. He obtained Bachelors degree in Architecture from Jawaharlal Nehru Technological University, Hyderabad in 1977 and Masters degree in Urban and Regional Planning with first rank and gold medal from University of Mysore, Mysore in 1981. He was given Research Award for excellence in architecture by Indian Institute of Architects in 1991 and VSF fellowship of Vastu Shilpa Foundation, Ahmedabad in 1995. He participated and presented research papers in several seminars and published two books and twenty research papers in leading architecture urban planning journals.

He is an Associate member of Indian Institute of Architects, Institute of Town Planners India and Indian Institute of Interior Designers.

Contents

List of Figures

1

Introduction

Urban planning is basically a reflection of local peoples aspirations implemented within the prevailing politico-administrative system of the country. According to Lewis Keeble, a renowed urban-planner, it can be defined as 'the art and science of ordering the landuses and siting the buildings and communication routes so as to secure the maximum level of economy, convenience and beauty'.

I wish to clarify my views here on the different chapters, so that there is no ambiguity in understanding the text of the book. Vast literature is available on urban planning. I have tried my best to cover all the important aspects of urban planning, so that a student as well as a professional is equally benefitted by reading this book. The exhaustive literature is put in a concise manner without losing the essential content. The terms 'urban' and 'town' are used as synonyms in the book.

Each chapter is divided into two parts as theory and practice. The theory part explains the importance of each chapter and the practice part explains how it is practically implemented with the help of case study or case studies. I tried to cover wide variety of case studies so that the reader can get a better understanding of the subject.

Urban planning means dealing with people. All the projects, programmes and schemes are only secondary to people. Thus public participation assumes great importance in urban planning. In fact there is no urban planning without peoples participation. Urban development in India depends on the national and state government policies because the local-self governments like municipalities and municipal corporations are very weak in policy making. There is a need to strengthen these local bodies for efficient urban development.

Chapter 2 : Ancient Urban Planning

Ancient urban planning is divided into six topics as Ancient cities, Egyptian cities, Greek cities, Roman cities, Medieval cities and Renaissance cities.

Urban planning assumed importance in the history, only when the common man's interests were taken into consideration. This is possible in a democratic set-up. Thus conspicuous urban planning is visible only in ancient Greek cities, who invented the democratic form of government. Earlier Mesopotamian cities also cared for the common man revealing some kind of urban planning but the ruins are very very old making it very difficult to draw clear conclusions. We can say, serious urban planning in the world started with Hippodamus in planning Greek cities. Earlier civilisations can be appreciated but we do not have clear evidence to show their urban planning process except for brilliant isolated architectural monuments like temples, tombs, palaces and forts. Until the invention of democratic government by the Greeks, people lived under constant fear of war and displacement. They sought protection in gods and rulers, so the best of their skills and admiration was showered on them. This can be called as an age of survival for common people. Greeks and Romans built great cities because the development of human brain was given full encouragement during their periods. Human 'ego' reached great heights decreasing gradually the fear of natural calamities. This increasing intelligence led to further problems after the decline of Roman Empire with petty wars between small rulers. The disintegration again led to the fear of survival, not because of nature but due to the enemy attacks. Thus fortified cities were built which again brought the people under the control of gods and rulers. Slowly the fear of wars decreased with increasing trade and economic prosperity. The new merchant class became very powerful and encouraged renaissance in arts and culture, which changed the hierarchy of the society and brought new look to the cities. Money as a mode of exchange for goods and services started dominating the society. New colonies were established for trade and commerce. People became more independent and thoughtful with efficient transportation and communication systems. All these changes are reflected in the ancient cities.

Chapter 3 : Ancient Urban Planning in India

Ancient urban planning in India is divided into three topics as Ancient Indian cities, Ancient urban planning rules in India and

Indian cities during Mughal period.

Urban planning in India started with Indus Valley civilisation which is one of the oldest civilisations in the world. When compared to the age of this civilisation, very high and enlightened urban planning process took place during this period. After this period, urban planning details in India are available only in the ancient Vedic texts. There are two authentic texts available on ancient urban planning in India. They are Mayamata and Manasara. Manasara is as comprehensive treatise as the Mayamata. Both are similar in content and presentation. Arguably, both belong to almost the same period of South Indian School of Architecture. I have reproduced from the text of Mayamata translated by Bruno Dagens of Sitaram Bharathia Institute of Science & Research, New Delhi. I did not make any personal interpretations of the text because it may lead to biased opinion and distortion of the text. I have quoted from chapter 10 on towns (Nagara) because we are dealing an 'urban' subject in the book. There was no encouragement for urban planning during the Mughal period except for few isolated examples. When the British took over the Indian empire, they were interested in developing port cities like Bombay, Calcutta and Madras to improve their trade. They built exclusive cantonment areas to house their officials and army.

Chapter 4 : Modern Urban Planning

I have covered the topics on Industrial revolution and its impact, Modern urban planning initiatives, Modern urban planning concepts, Modern urban planning in India and important case studies.

I believe the industrial revolution has changed our life styles totally. Urban planning after the industrial revolution is totally different from earlier days. Thus it is very important to know, what changes the machine age has brought in our lives because our living and planning is purely based on these changes. It is also important to know, how people all over the world adopted to these changes before trying to understand our urban planning exercises in India. There are number of features we adopted from other countries. This is because, the impact of industrial revolution is similar all over the world, so the responses are also similar. The only difference is, socio-economic conditions and availability of technology. To cite an example, RCC, steel and glass are used universally for various purposes. Thus the machine age has brought problems, which are common to all people of all countries. The machine age challenge is universal but the responses could be different depending upon the local conditions, but each one is trying to learn from the others mistakes. This is the kind of progress we see in our urban planning ideas.

There are four thinkers who deeply influenced modern urban planning all over the world. They are Ebenezer Howard, Le Corbusier, Patrick Geddes and Doxiadis. Ebenezer Howard and Le Corbusier tried to create totally different worlds from the existing ones. Howard wanted to bring the good of both urban and rural areas in his new towns. Le Corbusier wanted to grow with the machine and take full advantage of its potential for speed and verticality. To certain extent both these approaches are adopted in modern urban planning. Patrick Geddes and Doxiadis has a more scientific approach to urban planning than Howard and Le Corbusier. Howard and Le Corbusier are conceptual in their approach whereas Geddes and Doxiadis are scientific in their approach. Geddes wanted to study the town to plan scientifically, and tried to adopt it to the changing needs slowly. He did not prefer large scale changes but wanted development to be done over a period of time giving place for all the activities performed in the city. The speed of machine age has no time to wait for Geddes type of planning, so he could not do much practically but left an indelible mark in the theory of modern urban planning. Doxiadis is a scientist and wanted the cities to grow in a planned manner. His vision is not limited to towns and cities but extends beyond the boundaries of the countries. Thus, his vision is practical and what we see happening all over the world. He advocates adoption to the changing needs of the society.

The foreign case studies, I have selected are Radburn layout, Greater London Plan and Brasilia. There may be many great cities all over the world which are not possible to cover in this text, so I have limited them to select few. The three case studies I have selected are important. Radburn layout in USA is unique and first of its kind in planning modern residential areas. It is based on super-block principle which is still followed in different modified forms for planning residential areas all over the world. Greater London Plan in Britain is the first comprehensive development plan in the world. It has all the ingredients we follow in modern urban planning anywhere. Brasilia is unique because of its monumentality, steel and glass structures and incorporation of automotive transportation in its planning. We see lot of road widening, fly-overs and expressways for efficient transportation in our cities today; but these roads form an integral part of the city in Brasilia. Thus the vision of the planners should be appreciated.

In India, I have chosen Chandigarh, Gandhi Nagar and NALCO Township at Talcher (Angul). All modern urban planning in India should begin from Chandigarh. It has become a model city of modern India. Whatever may be the criticism of its planning, it stimulated the urban planning activity in India. It is very important to know the basic planning principles of this city. Gandhi Nagar is built on similar lines but it was prepared by an Indian urban planning organisation and not by an individual, so the concept of the city is not as emotional as Chandigarh. The planners tried to build the city based on the practical requirements of the people. NALCO township at Talcher (Angul) is a fairly new development. It is an exclusive new town. There are two townships of NALCO, one is at Damanjodi and the other one is at Talcher (Angul). I have selected Talcher (Angul) because it has comparatively more existing development to be incorporated than Damanjodi in planning. The planning was conceived by Town & Country Planning Organisation, New Delhi which is an apex town planning body in India. It would be interesting to know how they tackled the problems as a team of professional town planners.

Chapter 5 : Urban Planning Legislation

Legislation is an important tool of planning in a democratic country. It curbs individual freedom for the betterment of the community. I have covered the topics on Evolution of urban planning legislation in India, Important committees, IDSMT scheme, Land acquisition act and case studies with a list of urban planning acts enacted in India.

The evolution of urban planning legislation is narrated since the first act of Bombay Improvement Trust Act in 1898. A general evolution of urban planning legislation process in India is given for an understanding. Under important committees, Barlow committee, Scott committee and Uthwall committee had a significant impact on modern urban planning exercises in India because Britain ruled India for a long time and took the initiatives in bringing out some important legislations. IDSMT is not an act, but in a way it is a national urban planning policy. Even though it is not comprehensive in content, it is a positive step in the right direction for planning our settlements. Knowledge of Land Acquisition Act is essential for an urban-planner because without land there is no physical development. Some important sections of the act are quoted for information. The government has full power to acquire a land in public interest after following a set of legal procedure. This fact should be known by everybody.

Under case studies, I have chosen Karnataka and Great Britain. The contents of Town & Country Planning Acts of all states in the country are similar with minor modifications. Thus the understanding of one state act is sufficient to give an understanding of other state acts. Town & Country Planning Act of UK is unique because it is an improved version of the present Town & Country Planning Acts implemented in India. Slowly in India also, we may adopt similar guidelines in future, so the contents are extremely useful.

Chapter 6 : Development Plan

Preparation of 'Development Plan' is necessary for the planned development of a city. I have covered the topics on Development Plan & its contents, important terms used in these plans with a case study of Delhi.

The need for the preparation of the Development Plan should be clearly understood. Any Development Plan of a city should have specific goals and objectives. The scope and contents of Development Plan are also described. The procedure for the preparation of Development Plan, its implementation and public participation should also be understood. General guidelines for the preparation of Development Plan are also given. Certain terms like zoning, density, sub-division and FAR are often used to express the various proposals in the Development Plan. These terms should be clearly understood because modern urban planning is mostly based on these tools for development regulation.

The Perspective Plan 2001 of Delhi is a good case study to understand the problems in the preparation of Development Plan. Delhi is our national capital and one of the leading metropolitan cities in the world facing number of urbanisation problems. When compared to other metropolitan cities in the country, Delhi has twin advantages of initial large-scale land acquisition and the importance of being a national capital. The large-scale land acquisition has given good control over land use planning, which cannot be expected in other cities because land acquisition is a major problem in any city. Except for these two advantages, most of the urban problems are similar except that they differ due to geographical location, size and magnitude. Thus one can draw many lessons from Delhi's experience. In fact, the first Comprehensive Master Plan in the country was prepared for Delhi in 1962. Its success inspired the preparation of Master Plans for cities all over the country. A brief summary of the

Master Plan is given because it may need another book to incorporate the details. This brief outline is sufficient to understand the way the problems are tackled.

Finally, urban landuse classification with graphic expression is given, which is based on the latest UDPFI guidelines of Govt. of India, August 1996.

Chapter 7 : Housing

Housing is a very important component of urban development. It comprises nearly sixty percent of the landuse of a city. The topics covered are the Importance of housing, Housing problems in India, National Housing policy, Housing agencies, Housing finance institutions, Neighbourhood concept, Residential layout planning and Slum housing with case studies.

The importance of housing need no emphasis. It is one of our primary needs of life. The housing problems in India are related to our socio-economic conditions. Our urban and rural housing is a result of these conditions. National housing policy gives the necessary thrust for housing. Our National Housing Policy of 1992 is a major step to give boost for the housing sector. Among the housing agencies, the public and private sectors have equal responsibility for providing quality housing. The private sector has a major share in housing, so it has to play an efficient and responsible role. The National Housing Bank established in 1988 gave the necessary lift for urban housing by providing housing finance on easy terms and conditions.

Neighbourhood concept is a significant step in organising residential areas. I have shown original idea of Clarence Perry and supported it with a case study, so that one can understand its importance even now. There are certain basic principles in planning a residential layout. I have shown 20 such design principles for efficient residential layout planning. Slum housing or poor housing is an important duty of the government in a welfare state because they constitute the majority of the population in the urban areas. There are some limitations to slum housing in a poor country like ours. When poverty is an integral part of our economy, we have to live and adjust with slums in cities. However, we cannot overlook the unhygienic conditions in the slums because they may spread diseases rapidly. Environmental improvement of slums is necessary to curb unhealthy atmosphere. I have included the case studies of Delhi, Mumbai, Calcutta and Chennai. Each city tried to solve the problem of slums in its own way depending upon the political party ruling at that time.

There is a lot that can be learnt from these experiences. There is no magic formula to eradicate slums, just like there is no magic to eradicate poverty on earth.

Chapter 8 : Traffic and Transportation

The development of any city depends upon the efficiency of its traffic and transportation system. The topics covered are Importance of transportation, National Transportation Policy, Important transport components, Characteristics of traffic, Transportation planning process, Surveys for transportation planning, Traffic control at intersections and Parking problems with a case study of Hyderabad city.

The importance of transportation system need not be debated because it forms the life of the city. The shape and size of the city depends on the transportation system prevailing in the city. The National Transportation Policy plays a crucial role in shaping the transportation system of the country. The rapid transit system is getting increasing importance in our metropolitan cities. Important transport components are described to have a clear understanding of the transportation system. Traffic forms an important component of urban planning. It is essential to know the characteristics of traffic for designing and planning traffic movement in the city. There is a common planning process for all kinds of transportation planning. Surveys are needed before taking up any transportation planning. Some important surveys which are normally used in transportation planning are described. Traffic control is a major challenge in our urban areas. Increasing fast and slow moving traffic on narrow roads is creating many traffic bottlenecks and prolonged traffic jams. Proper advanced planning and timely control is necessary to regulate traffic in our cities. As long as there is increasing production of vehicles, this problem will remain alive. Parking of vehicles in urban areas is another major problem. When the road width is insufficient for moving traffic, parking of vehicles on the roads aggravates this problem further. Space should be found for parking of vehicles for various needs. This is another vexing problem which needs to be tackled. Finally, the Hyderabad case study is described to show how they tackled these problems practically.

Chapter 9 : Landscape Design

Landscape design is the most neglected part in urban planning. By indiscriminate cutting of trees and other landscape features in urban areas we are losing precious natural wealth which can keep our biological existence in balance. The topics covered are Importance of landscape design, National Building Code of India, 1983, guidelines and Landscape design process with a case study of Chandigarh.

We should feel the increasing importance of landscape design because it can control pollution and improve our physical environment in the cities. Particularly planting of trees and organising parks is very important. NBC 1983 of India has provided certain guidelines in this regard, which are extremely useful in our urban areas for planning proper landscape. There is a procedure to be followed in landscape design. This will be useful for preparing landscape drawings and landscape maintenance. Chandigarh is a good example for landscape design even though it is not having a comprehensive landscape design for the entire city.

Chapter 10 : Urban Conservation

Urban conservation is a fairly new concept in our country. The demolition of historical buildings and areas led to the movement of urban conservation in Europe. It is slowly making an impact in our Indian cities also, particularly in metropolitan cities with historical background. The topics covered are pro and anti-urban conservation arguments with a case study of Hyderabad. It is sufficient if we get a basic understanding of this thought. The case study of Hyderabad elaborates the various aspects that should be taken into consideration for urban conservation.

Chapter 11 : Planning Standards

All planning standards should have some rational research basis. They cannot be based on individual opinion. I have incorporated the latest planning standards recommended by Government of India under 'Urban Development Plans Formulation & Implementation (UDPFI) Guidelines'. This study was conducted by Ministry of Urban Affairs & Employment, Govt. of India, New Delhi in August 1996. I feel these latest planning standards would be extremely useful for planners.

Chapter 12 : Urban Planning Terminology

There are several terms specially used in urban planning. I felt it would be useful to group these terms under one chapter for easy reference. I tried to cover as many terms as possible which are often used in urban planning. I hope the readers would find this chapter extremely useful for reference and easy understanding.

2

Ancient Urban Planning

City is a mirror of human civilisation prevailing at that particular period of time. It is not mere roads and buildings that make a city, but the prevailing culture which moulds the shape and size of a city. It is necessary to have a good understanding of the history of human civilisation to understand the cities of a particular period. It is not possible to cover the entire history under this chapter, so a brief understanding is given about some important cities.

A) Ancient cities

Major changes in human settlements occurred because of the adaption to the climate. People started growing plants and domesticating animals for food and survival. The growing of grain began in Southern Egypt and by 8000 BC agriculture was established along the river valleys of Nile, Tigris and Euphrates. Slowly the pattern of human activity changed. Permanent houses were constructed at a place near the fields encouraging the growth of towns and cities with complex social organisation. Large permanent human settlements appeared around 8000 BC.

Catal Huyuk in South-Central Turkey gives a detailed understanding of how a neolithic city functioned. This city covered an area of 32 acres. There were no streets but tightly clustered houses with an occasional courtyard, which served for dumping rubbish. Entry to the houses was by means of a hole in the roof, which also served as smoke outlet. The houses were built with timber frames. The panels between the posts and beams were filled with mud brick. The walls were plastered and often painted with figures. Many excavated quarters consisted of chambers devoted to shrines of mother goddess and a bull cult.

In the broad valley of Tigris and Euphrates rivers known as Mesopotamia (a Greek word means 'the land between the rivers') which is in Iraq now, the worlds first civilisation developed by 6000 BC and existed for 2500 years. Here writing, rituals, song and dance were developed for communication. Pottery vessels were made to store food grains. By 3500 BC larger cities were built along this river. The first of the large cities in Mesopotamia developed near the mouths of the two rivers. Though there are no records of a complete pre-planning of any city during this period, the cities appear to be laid for orderly growth. Building was a sacred activity undertaken by the priest-king. The only permanent buildings were temples, tombs and storehouses. Timber and stone were scarce, so the buildings were made of clay bricks, at first sun-dried and later kiln baked. The remains of this period are the great pyramid like mounds, which served as artificial mountains on which temples were built. The streets were narrow for pedestrain movement and joined one another at right angles but did not form a continuous grid iron pattern. This is a clear indication that there was no overall plan of the city. The houses had a central courtyard with bed rooms in the first floor and service rooms in the ground floor. All the bathrooms and latrines were built along the outer wall of the houses to drain directly into a sewer, which ran below the street.

B) Egyptian cities

Egyptian cities developed along the Nile river valley from 5500 BC. The soil was fertile because of the annual deposit of silt brought by the river. The perennial supply of river water has made Egypt into a prosperous agricultural belt. The people of Egypt took to farming and created canal system for regular water supply. The Egyptians worshipped several gods, but the Sun god was the most important for them.

The Egyptian King was called as 'Pharoah'. He was worshipped as god. People dedicated their lives for him. They believed in life after death, and felt that both body and soul existed in different forms after death. With this belief they preserved the dead bodies known as 'Mummies'. Food and luxury articles were placed in the tombs. The tombs of the Pharoahs are called as 'Pyramids'. Towns were built to construct these pyramids housing slaves and artisans. One such village was constructed at El-Kahun to house officials, craftsmen and labourers. Resident cells were constructed around a common courtyard. Narrow lanes served as pathways to houses and also as open drainage sewers. Walls surrounded the towns, which might have been built for protection from seasonal floods of Nile river. The

Egyptians sited their cities, villages and great temples on the banks of the river, which is the only water-way for transportation. The pyramids were located on the western bank of the river on the high lands to protect from the overflowing river. The 'Sphinx' is the most outstanding creation of the Egyptians. It is a huge sculpture with a lion body and human head. Monumental avenues, huge temples and pyramids stand as testimony to the luxurious lifestyle of Egyptian pharoahs. Many of these are found in Memphis, Thebes and Tel-el-Amarna; which were destroyed. However, there is no record of the history to describe the status of the ordinary people and their lives.

C) Greek cities

The ancient Greeks from 750 to 350 BC learned a lot from Egyptians but they shaped later a distinct art, architecture and town planning. The most important political contribution of Greek civilisation was the invention of democracy in Athens initiated by Pericles in 5th century BC. Laws, made by the people, were formulated to protect their interests. Democracy encouraged freedom of speech, community participation and development of philosophy, logic and science. This kind of atmosphere produced great men like Socrates, Plato and Aristotle.

A Greek city-state was called as 'Polis'. Polis was a community of families related by common ancestors. The ideal polis had 5000 citizens. Most cities were roughly of this size except Athens, Syracuse and Akragas which had over 20,000 people. Most cities grew around an ancient citadel built on an acropolis or high place. Athens is a good example. Acropolis sites were dedicated to various olympian gods with temples. At the base of acropolis, paths were laid to the surrounding farms with an agora or market place consisting of public buildings. Agora was the heart of a Greek city, where business and politics were conducted. Sports and recreation took place in the gymnasium. Drama and festivals were conducted in an open-air theater.

Greeks sought privacy in their houses. All the rooms in a house are designed for comfort according to the prevailing climatic conditions. All the rooms opened into an interior courtyard. The houses were simple and equal to all the citizens without any class distinction. Paving of streets, water reservoirs and underground drains were provided for houses, but sewage disposal and water supply distribution were not provided. Most of the towns were surrounded by protective walls.

Greek colonies were laid out from scratch. Persians destroyed Greek cities during 494 to 479 BC, which led to scientific method of town planning attempted first in Miletos. The new city of Miletos was designed by Hippodamus, who also designed the port city of Peiraeus and Rhodes. He was the first person to introduce the grid-iron pattern of road system in town planning. The site for Miletos was a levelled peninsula jutting into the sea at the mouth of the river. Hippodamus planned the grid-iron pattern of road system to the general direction of the peninsula rather than orienting it to the cardinal points of the compass. He divided the city into three distinct zones. To the north was the residential area, the Agora at the centre and another residential area of larger blocks at the south. The only missing area was a place for major temples. This may be because Milesian religious site of great Apollo sanctuary was located 14 miles to the south of the city. (see Fig. 2.1)

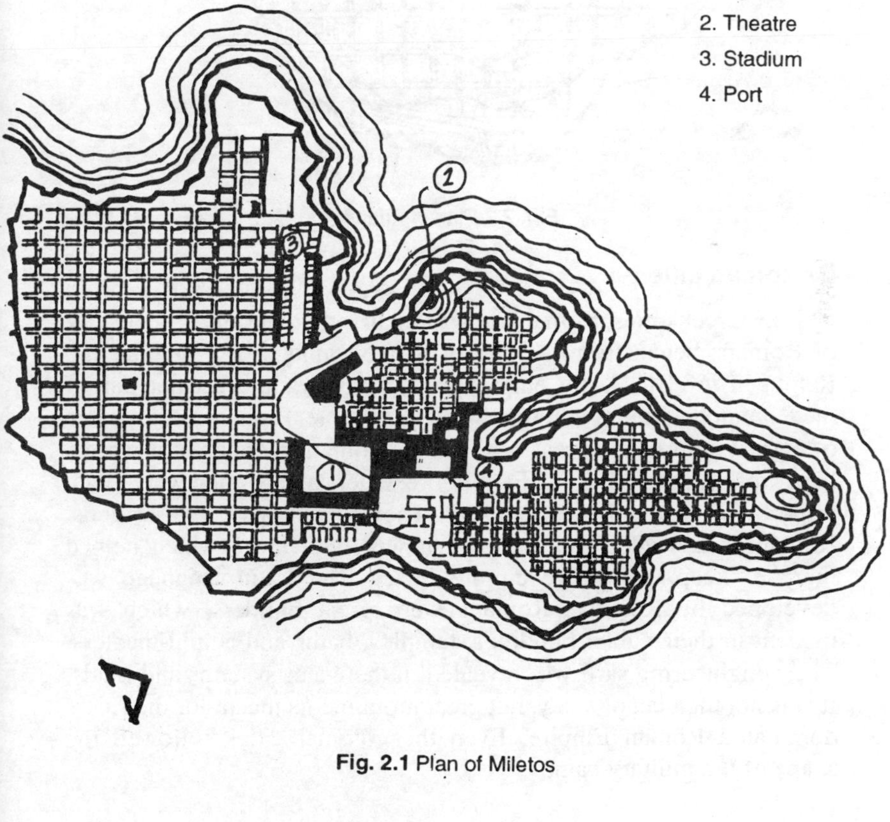

Fig. 2.1 Plan of Miletos

Priene, another city near Miletos, was rebuilt in the later part of the Fourth Century BC. Here also an orthogonal grid was used to a steep sloping hillside site with regular blocks of houses measuring approximately 120 by 160 feet. Six major streets ran east to west, fifteen minor streets were stepped and ran north to south. At the center was the rectangular agora. Over looking agora to the north was the temple of Athena and the theater. At the south edge of the city was the stadium. (see Fig. 2.2)

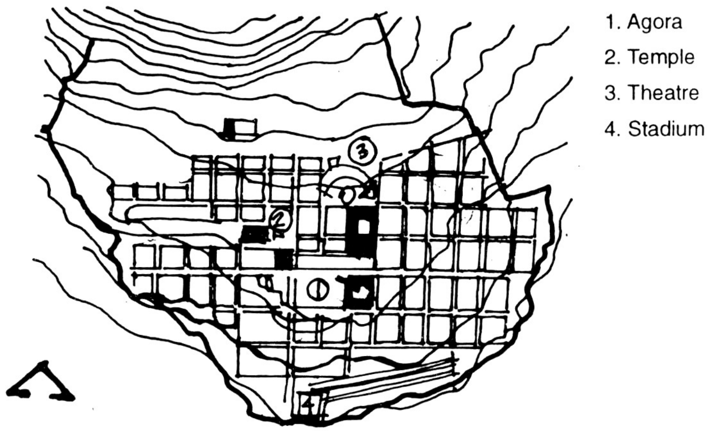

Fig. 2.2 Plan of Priene

D) Roman cities

Like Greek cities, Roman life was focussed on the city. The history of Romans began from the city of Rome founded by Romulus and Remus in 753 BC. As the empire grew, far away cities became part of the Roman empire for self rule by all the people. Rome was the centre of a great empire and great civilisation. Romans were great warriors, hard working and patriotic. Family life, elders and women were given importance in the Roman society. They worshipped several gods. Romans had well organised government with laws, which helped them to keep their large empire intact. The Latin language was developed by Romans. Romans were great builders, which was evident in their public buildings, temples, baths and amphi-theaters. Their engineering skill was revealed in the water systems and roads. It was not the plan of a city, but great monuments meant for the rulers dominated Roman Empire. Even the colonial cities followed the shape of the military camps.

Early Roman cities like commercial and resort town of Pompeii had streets forming irregular rectangles. As these cities expanded the blocks became more regular rectangles. At the heart of these cities was the 'Forum' (civic open space) lined with public buildings. The forum served the same function like the Greek agora. The forum in Pompeii was rectangular in shape and dominated by a temple of Jupiter at one end on the axis of the forum. (see Fig. 2.3)

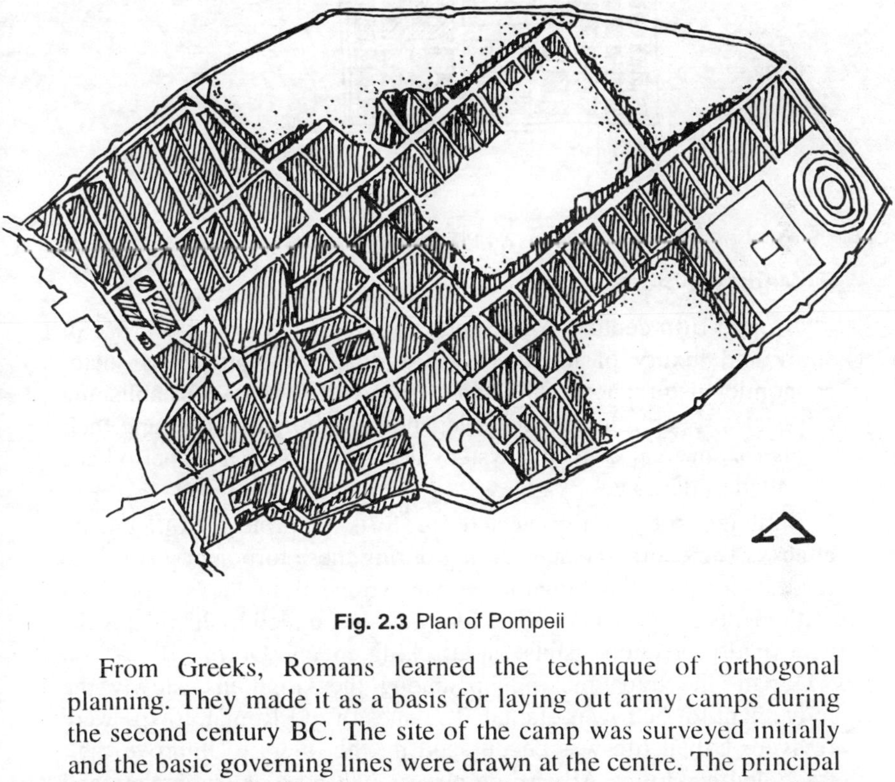

Fig. 2.3 Plan of Pompeii

From Greeks, Romans learned the technique of orthogonal planning. They made it as a basis for laying out army camps during the second century BC. The site of the camp was surveyed initially and the basic governing lines were drawn at the centre. The principal streets were marked from north to south and east to west. Beyond the camp walls, it was extended on larger scale in blocks. These large squares are equivalent to hundred small farms. Military camps became basis of many town plans in Roman empire. One good example which survived is Timgad in the Roman province of Namibia, which is Eastern Algeria now. It was planned in 100 AD to house the military for guarding a strategic place. This was laid out with rigid orthogonal grid but as it expanded the rigid grid pattern was gradually eliminated. (see Fig. 2.4)

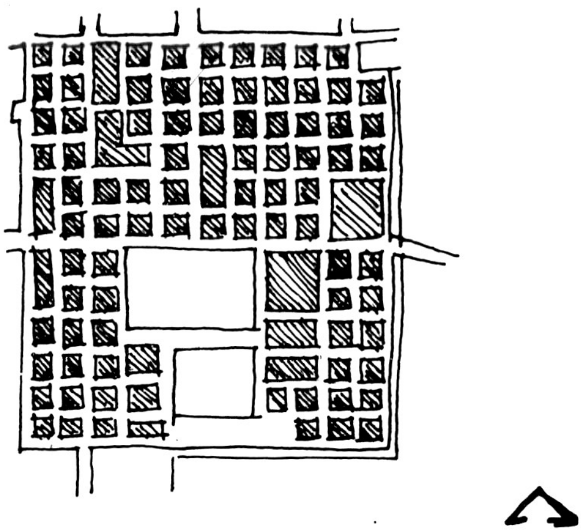

Fig. 2.4 Plan of Timgad

E) Medieval cities

Around fifth century AD Roman empire disintegrated because of show and luxury of its rulers. Cities lost importance and socio-economic disturbances followed. Cruel rulers started establishing city-states. People increasingly depended upon agriculture and their rulers for survival. A feudal system slowly emerged. This period can be called as dark ages.

Strategic sites were selected for forts to protect from enemy attacks. The church became strong during these turbulent years. The fortifications of the kingdoms were extended to the surrounding settlements for protection. The fort was surrounded by its own walls as a final protection against an attacking enemy. During 1000-1100 AD with the trade picking up among the kingdoms, slowly the movement to the towns started. The sites of old Roman towns were revived. Urban life was encouraged by the rulers to improve their trade and economy. All trading classes like masons, carpenters and weavers made rules and regulations to protect their trading practices. Thus wealthy trading class started emerging.

The early medieval town was dominated by church and the fort of the king. The space around the church became the market place. The public buildings were constructed near the market place. For protection, the town sites were located on irregular lands like hilltops or islands. The town roads and buildings were constructed to suit the topography of the land. The main roads radiated from the market square to the external gates with secondary roads connecting them. Few main roads were used for vehicular traffic. Rest of them were used for pedestrain movement. An irregular pattern of roads was deliberately derived to perplex the enemy entering the town. Hand fight with weapons was the main form of war between the enemies. As the town was restricted with the fortified walls, the houses were built in rows along the narrow streets. Open space behind the houses was used for domestic animals and cultivating gardens. The workshop, store and kitchen were located in the ground floor, where traders did their work. The living and sleeping areas were located in the upper floors. Windows were small and covered with crude glass. Streets were usually paved, but there was no facility for waste disposal. The workers lived in the homes of their employers. There was no distinction among different classes of people. (see Fig. 2.5)

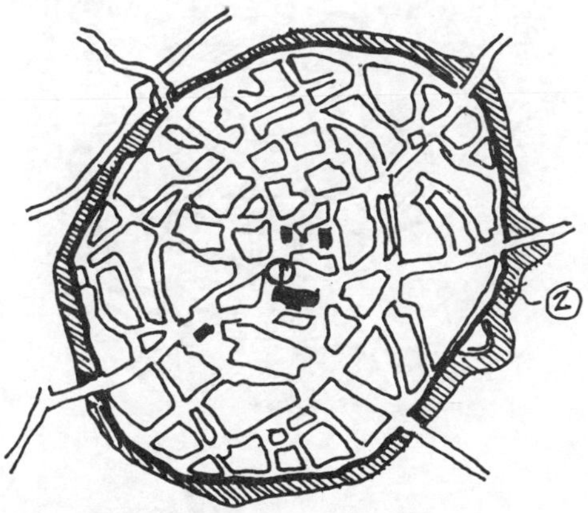

Fig. 2.5 Plan of Noerdlingen (Germany)

F) Renaissance cities

World travel and trading made people to gather around central places situated on main cross-roads. During 1400 to 1500 AD population grew rapidly in cities like Paris and Venice. The danger of wars decreased and trading prospered between towns and countries. The power of feudal lords declined and the merchant class slowly became powerful. Two important classes emerged, the wealthy merchants and the priests. The processing of goods and materials was taken over by merchants. The new economy centered around money flow. Increasing population within the fortified walls created congestion. Population density increased without proper water supply and sanitation. Vehicular traffic increased. The class distinctions increased between the rich and the poor. Disease spread rapidly in case of an epidemic. The first sewer system was introduced in London after the Black Death during the 15th Century.

During 1400-1500 AD gun powder and printing press were invented. In the late 18th Century long range war weapons were improved. The fortified walls and trenches became irrelevant. The size of the city increased. Broad main roads were built encircling the town. These new spaces separated the old town from the suburbs (see Fig. 2.6). The basic form of medieval cities did not change, but the

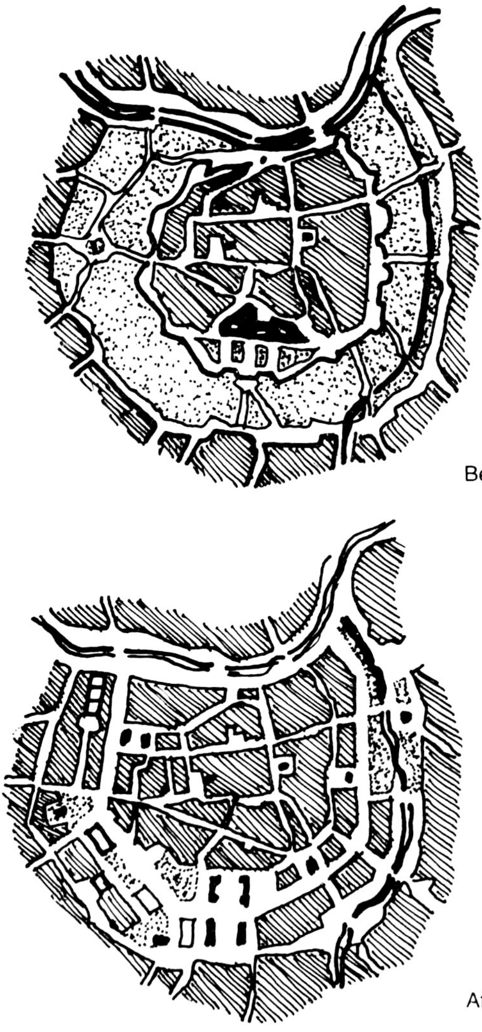

Before 1857

After 1857

Fig. 2.6 Plan of Vienna

structures were decorated with classic elements of Rome. In these renaissance cities, the basic concept was vista forming straight roads. Formal plazas were constructed at important places in the towns and given monumental scale and form. Lot of interest was shown to promote arts by merchants, priests and kings. Artists became professionals with versatility in different fields. Their services were highly applauded and encouraged. Bernini designed the huge plaza of St. Peters at Rome. Originally a narrow street led to St. Peters, but the new grand open space made the square very beautiful.

With the invention of mariners compass, new colonies were established during the 15th and 16th Centuries. Colonies were established in America by the Europeans who wished to have free new world of their own. The initial settlements were irregular, but most of the towns were plotted for allotment to new people. Initially the towns were small and within walking distance from all parts. The founding fathers of America selected a site along the banks of a river. This new city capital named as Washington DC was conceived on a grand scale within a pattern of geometrical order. Following their capital city, many cities in America adopted the radial plan with diagonal streets laid in grid iron pattern.

MODEL QUESTIONS

1. What are the major urban planning features in ancient cities?
2. Describe the nature of Egyptian cities.
3. Describe the importance of Greek cities with examples.
4. Describe the nature of Roman cities with examples.
5. What are the features of medieval cities?
6. What changes took place in renaissance cities?

3

Ancient Urban Planning in India

A) Ancient Indian cities

Urban planning in India started with Indus valley civilisation during 2500 BC. The valley of Indus was a vast rich fertile land, but now greater part of it is desert. The remains of this civilisation were found at Mohenjodaro in Sind and Harappa in Punjab; both these sites are now in Pakistan. These two cities had certain clear urban planning principles.

Agriculture was the main occupation of the people. The main food crops were wheat and barley. Animals like goats, buffaloes and elephants were in use. They were good artists and craftsmen. The bull with a hump, seen on the 'seals' of their kingdom, might have been considered sacred by them. They worshipped several gods and Siva must have been the main god. A common bathing ghat was found in Mohenjodaro. The seals of 'sailing ship' found in Harappa indicates that there was trade with Mesopotamia.

Mohenjodaro and Harappa were well laid out with broad roads and designed houses. Each one had its fortified citadel located on a place higher than the rest of the city. These cities were twin capitals of a large kingdom, which had a centralised government. There were waterways and clear script for communication. The citadel had a tank, storehouse, halls and residence of a high priest or the king. These cities were orderly planned along the river. Broad roads of 45 feet wide from north to south were crossed by minor streets at right angles. Each housing block was about 400 x 200 yards and subdivided by narrow lanes.

The houses were built with burnt brick in single and double storeys. Each house had rooms planned around a central courtyard, which had stairs to an upper floor. The houses were of different sizes indicating different levels of social status of the inmates. The conspicuous feature is that there were no windows on the outer walls of the house. All windows opened into the central courtyard. The doors opened onto the narrow lanes than the main roads. Every house had a bath-room and a well. Another major characteristic feature is that the streets and buildings were provided with brick drains with inspection holes. There were no decorative features on the blank walls of the buildings. (see Fig. 3.1)

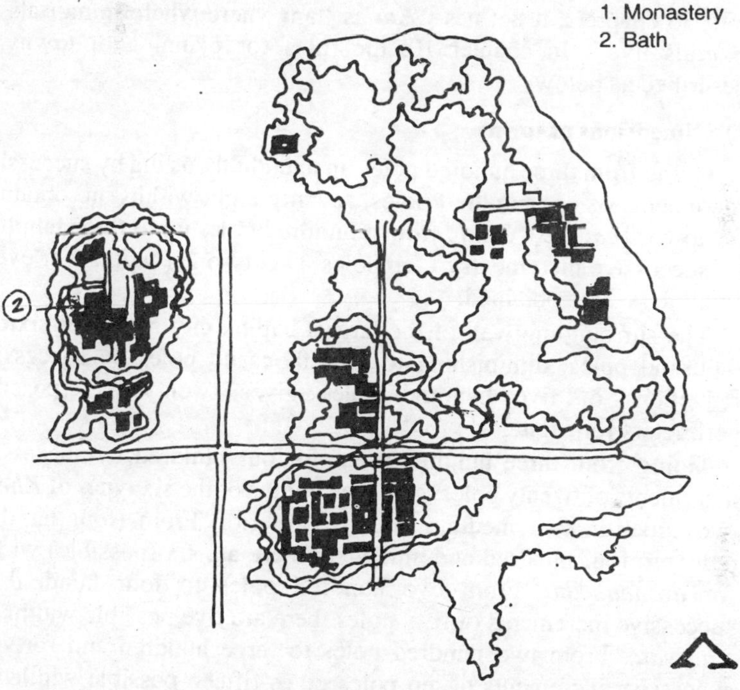

Fig. 3.1 Mohenjo-Daro

The Indus valley civilisation came to an end by 1500 BC. The decline may be due to the attacks by the Aryans or natural calamities. Indus valley civilisation was a glorious period in the ancient history of urban planning in India. After this civilisation, the information on ancient Indian town planning is available only from Vedic texts like Manasara and Mayamata containing clear directions on town planning.

B) Ancient Urban Planning rules in India

Mayamata expressed by Maya, the divine architect, is a general treatise, a *vastusastra,* written in Sanskrit but originating from Dravidian India, most probably from the Tamil area. The text must have been prepared between early 9th century and the late 12th century. The palmleaf manuscripts of the *Mayamata* are in Grantha (Tamil) script or in Telugu or Malayalam script. The aim of *Mayamata* is to organise the integration of the external manifestations of *Siddhanta Saivism* in a context which could be qualified as "non-sectarian Hindu". Comprising about 3300 verses and divided into 36 chapters, it defines *vastu* as "anywhere where immortals or mortals live". In chapter 10, the rules for planning of towns is described as below:

1) Dimensions of towns

Going from three hundred poles up to eight thousand by successive increments of one hundred poles, seventy-eight widths are obtained for towns *(nagara).* Going from a hundred poles up to three hundred by successive increments of ten poles, twenty-one (widths) for every small towns are obtained.

The surrounding wall of the largest capital city measures sixteen thousand poles; diminishing to four thousand poles by successive reductions of five hundred poles gives twenty-five (possible perimeters for capitals).

Going from three hundred poles to four hundred by successive increments of twenty poles, gives the widths of the six types of *Kheta:* two superior, two medium and two inferior. From (four hundred poles) to four hundred and ninety-six there are six (possible) widths for *dronamukha.* From two hundred poles to four hundred by successive increments of fifty poles there are five possible widths for *Kharvata.* From two hundred poles to three hundred and forty by successive increments of ten poles gives fifteen possible widths for *nigama.* From one hundred to five hundred poles by successive increments of one hundred poles gives five (possible) widths for *Kotmakolaka* and, according to the sages, these widths apply to the *pura* as well. The width of *vidamba* goes from two hundred to five hundred poles giving seven possible widths with a difference of fifty poles between each.

The dimensions having been indicated, here are the proportions : the length is double the width or one and a quarter times it, otherwise the length exceeds the width by a sixth or an eighth.

2) The surrounding wall

Square, rectangular, round, elliptical or perfectly circular, such are the five layouts for the walls. Their lengths may be seven tenths, six eighths, five sevenths, four fifths or three fourths of the perimeter (of the town?).

The thickness of the (bottom of the) wall is two, three or four cubits; its height is seven, ten or eleven cubits; its thickness at the top is two thirds what it is at the bottom. There is a moat all around the exterior and inside are the temples... etc.

3) Places to be avoided

Diagrams such as *pecaka* (with four squares) or *āsana* (with a hundred squares) or those between them should be used; the sage must avoid (building) on their lines and on other forbidden places.

4) Streets

A street should be planned there, or wherever desired, but starting at the north (or at the) east and according to the rules. From one pole to seven by successive increments of half a pole, there are thirteen (possible) breadths for the streets.

5) The royal capital

A heavily populated town situated in the middle of the kingdom and beside a river is an "ordinary" *(kevala)* town though if there is a royal palace there it is a "royal capital" *(rajadhani).*

A town is called "ordinary" when it has fortified gates at the four cardinal points and very large ramparts, when it contains shops as well as dwellings for all classes of people and temples for all the gods.

A town called "Royal Capital" is impregnable at the north and at the east; it is encircled by a wall beyond which is a glacis of earth; beyond that is a moat and lastly, farther away is a fortified garrison keeping watch in all directions, the royal guard facing to the east and to the south. This town has high gateways, various types of gallery (*mālikā*) and temples to all the gods. It is frequented by all sorts of courtesans and has a number of gardens. Elephants, horses, war-chariots and foot soldiers abound. People of all classes (live there). It has gates and posterns and contains a great number of dwelling houses as well as the king's palace. It is called *pura* or *nagara* when it is situated in forested country and when it contains houses for all classes, and shops.

6) Definitions

A *Kheta* is inhabited by sūdra; it is situated in the vicinity of a river or of a mountain. A *kharvata* is surrounded by mountains and is inhabited by people of all classes. A *janasthā-nakubja* is heavily populated and situated between a *kheta* and a *kharvata*.

A *pattana* is a town where products from other countries are to be found; it is inhabited by people of all classes; there are shops and an abundanc of merchandise such as precious stones, grains, fine cloth and perfumes; it is situated by the sea and extends along the coast.

Sages say that a *sibira* is situated in proximity to the realm of an enemy prince; it is provided with everything necessary for war and it accommodates the army and the commander-in-chief.

According to the sages a *senāmukha* is a place where people of all classes are mixed; it contains a royal palace and is provided with a well fortified garrison.

A *sthāniya* is a town founded by the king and situated beside a river or near to a mountain; it comprises a royal palace and a large garrison.

A town which extends (both) along the right and left banks of a river and which is frequented by traders of all sorts and inhabited by people of all classes is a *dronamukha*.

An inhabited place in the vicinity of a village is a *vidamba*. An inhabited place in the middle of a forest is a *kotmakolaka*.

A *nigama* is a town where the four castes are gathered, where people of all classes live together and where there are a number of artisans.

A *skandhāvāra* is near a forested region or a river; it is heavily populated and comprises a royal palace; that which is found next to it is a *cerikā*.

7) Forts

There are seven types of fort: the mountain fort, the forest fort, the water fort, the earth fort, the desert fort, the natural fort and the mixed fort. The mountain fort is built amidst mountains or on the side of a mountain or at its summit. The forest fort is situated in a dry place, hidden in a forest. The mixed fort unites the characteristics of the two preceding ones. The natural fort has only natural defences; the earth fort has (ramparts) of earth. The water fort is in the middle of a river or is in the sea. The desert fort is (situated in a place) devoid of trees and of water.

A fort should contain reserves of water, of food and of weapons; the ramparts are to be very big, very high and extremely thick; it should be impregnable at all points by virtue of its surrounding walls and it is guarded on all sides. Beyond the ramparts is a path, hidden in a forest, which is not waterlogged and is difficult of access.

There are fortified gates with stairways, some visible and others secret. Their doors have double leaves and are provided with four bars, with bolts and with a one cubit high clamp. (These gatehouses) are provided with a kind of bretesse (*minthaka*) which rests in the centre on a pillar and access (to which) is by a secret stairway. These gateways are in the form of pavilion, hall or *sāla*.

The enclosure walls may be built according to one of tweleve layouts: square, circular, rectangular, elliptical, *nandyāvarta* shaped or shaped like a cock or like the temporal bone of an elephant or like a coiled snake or square with curved sides, triangular, octangonal or semi-circular.

Brick ramparts are at least twelve cubits high and are twice as high as thick; the wall has a passable road at its base; inside the ramparts are all kinds of war machines set up at elevated points. All around is a moat and on its earthen bank are towers connected (with the wall); and beyond, and all around this, is a camp.

The fort is inhabited by people of diverse classes and contains the palace of the king. Present here are numerous elephants, horses, war-chariots and foot soldiers. it is abundantly provided with grain, oil and molasses, as with salt, medicaments, perfumes and poisons and with metals, charcoal, gut, ivory, bamboo and combustibles such as fodder and with leather, vegetables, barks and hardwoods.

A fort must be inaccessible, proof against attack and impregnable; it is constructed for defence and victory and must be impenetrable by enemies.

Indra, Vāsudeva, Guha, Jayanta, Vaisravana, the Asvin, Sri and Madirā, Siva, Durgā and Saraswati: these are the deities who are to be honoured within the walls and who should be borne in mind when a fort is built.

Such in the organization of forts as prescribed by the sages of old.

8) Town planning

Streets which go from east to west number twelve, ten, eight, six, four or two and the same numbers are suitable for those which go from north to south. In odd numbers ther are eleven, nine, seven, five, three or one streets (in each direction). According to whether the diagram is in even or odd numbers, the number of squares for Aja is two, three or one (?).

Streets are now indicated for all towns and cities. When there is one single street which is straight this is a *dandaka* plan; if (this street), at its centre, crosses another coming from the north, this is a *kartaridandaka* plan. If there are two paved streets starting from the east, this is a *bāhudandaka* plan. If there are gates at the four cardinal points and a large number of paved streets on either side of the main street this is a *kutikāmu-khadandaka* plan which is otherwise as above. When there are three streets towards the east and three towards the north the sages say this is *Kalakābandha-daudaka* plan. If there are three streets towards the east separated from each other by several alleys this is a *vedibhadra* plan suitable for all types of town. It should be known that the *svastika* plan is the same as for villages of that name; it comprises however, at most, six streets going east and six going north and, as has been mentioned above, the layout of the principal roads is that of a *svastika.*

When there are four streets going north, one around the place of Brahmā, and three paved streets towards the east it is a *bhadraka* plan which is suitable for all types of town.

When there are five streets going east and as many north as well as a large number of alleys this is a *bhadramukha* plan; when there are six streets going east and as many north as well as a large number of alleys this is a *bhadrakalyāna* plan. When there are seven streets from east to west and as many proceeding from the north, the rest being as above, this is a *mahābhadra* plan. When there are eight streets going east, eight north, twelve other streets and a great number of cul-de-sacs and alleys this is said to be a *vastusubhadra* plan. If a town comprises nine streets going east and nine north as well as gates, posterns, alleys and cul-de-sacs and a royal palace it is called *jayānga.* A town which comprises ten streets proceeding from the east and as many from the north, which contains a royal palace and where there are numerous alleys arranged according to the specific circumstances, such a town is named *vijaya* by the sages.

(In the *sarvatobhadra* plan) there are eleven streets from the east and eleven from the north; the king's palace is to be found, as is convenient, to the west of the place of Brahmā; in front of it is a huge empty yard; the queen's dwelling *(antahpura)* is in the chosen place and all that remains is arranged as expedient. Streets which proceed (from the place of Brahmā in the centre) towards the north and east are the royal streets; on either side of these are *mālikā* houses intended for the royal retinue; beyond these *(mālikā)* and on both sides is the quarter of the merchants and to the south of that the quarter of the weavers whilst that of the potters is to the north and, beside this, the quarters for each of the lower castes. The rest is to be as ordained above; this is the *sarvatobhadra* disposition.

Such are the sixteen varieties of town prescribed by the sages of old. A street should not be interrupted nor a crossroads established at the centre of a town plan. Anything which has not been laid down should be carried out by the sages in accordance with the wishes of the king.

9) Bazaars

Now I lay down the disposition for inhabited quarters and for bazaars *(antarapana)* appropriate to all types of towns. On the periphery is the chariot road and inside it is the merchants' quarter; to the south of this is the weavers' quarter and to the north that of the potters; a great many other artisans are installed along that road.

A street encircles the place of Brahmā and it is there that the bazaar for betel and similar produce, for fruits and for articles of value should be installed. Between the square of Īsa and the Mahendra gate is the bazaar for meat, fish, (dried) products and for vegetables; between the Mahendra gate and the square of Agni is the bazaar for solid and liquid foods; the ironmongers are between the Agni square and that of Grhaksata; between this last and that of Nirrti are the coppersmiths; between the square of Pitr and that of Puspadanta is the clothing bazaar; between this last and the square of Samirana is the bazaar for grains, rice and fodder. Between the square of Vāyu and that of Bhallāta is the bazaar for fabrics and materials of that kind and there is too the bazaar for food-stuffs such as salt and oil; between this and the square of Īsa is the bazaar for perfumes, flowers. etc. Such are the nine bazaars established in the centre and on the periphery (of the town). (see Fig. 3.2)

Along the streets leading to the centre is the bazaar where are found gems, gold, clothes, madder, black pepper, peepul seed and orpiment as well as honey, ghee, oil and medicaments.

Sāstr, Durgā and Laksmi should be worshipped at the places, (respectively), of Ārya, Vivasvant, Mitra and Prthividhara. Beyond this the temples are placed all around as in a village. Houses for people of all castes are installed a little farther away. The candāla and kolika huts must be two hundred poles beyond the town to the east and south-west.

Everything not indicated here should be arranged as has been prescribed for villages. A *pattana* has one straight road where no bazaars are to be found; for all other (towns) the bazaars should be established according to each specific case.

Sthāniya, durga, pura, pattana, kotmakolaka, dronamukha,

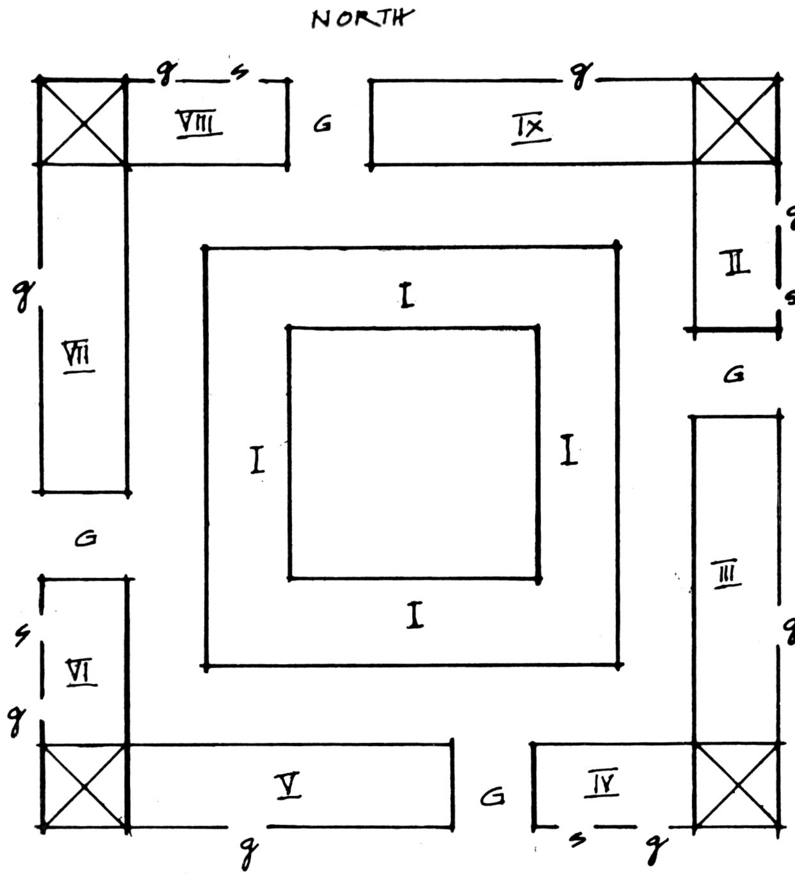

Bazaars : I : betel, fruits and valuables ; II : meat, fish and vegetables; III : solid and liquid foodstuff; IV : ironmongers; V : coppersmiths; VI : clothings; VII : grains, rice and fodder; VIII : fabrics, salt, oil .., IX : flowers.

Fig. 3.2. Town Layout (9.57 et sq. and 10.80 et sq.)
G : gates; g : small gates; s : sewage outlets:

nigama as well as *kheta, grama and kharvata* : these are the ten types of settlement established according to circumstance and they have been described by the sages of old.

The measurements, plans and streets suitable for villages and other setttlements are described according to the Tantra. These are intended for the classes, the first of which is the brahmin class, and for inferior castes.

The generous prince gives land and cows to the tetrad led by the architect and practised in work such as measurement. If he does this without reservation, riches in abundance will be his and his realm will stretch to the moon and stars as long as the world shall endure.

I) Case study : Madurai City in Tamil Nadu State

Many conditions laid down in Mayamata for a city are adopted in the site of Madurai. The layout of the central part of Madurai resembles the layout proposed in Manasara for Rajadhani class of cities. Madurai is a temple town with over 2000 years of history. It has also the credit of being a planned city since ancient days. The terrain of the city is on the south-west bank of Vaigai river, and slopes gently from south-west to north-west. This satisfies one of the conditions prescribed is Shilpa Shastras. The city is surrounded by fertile

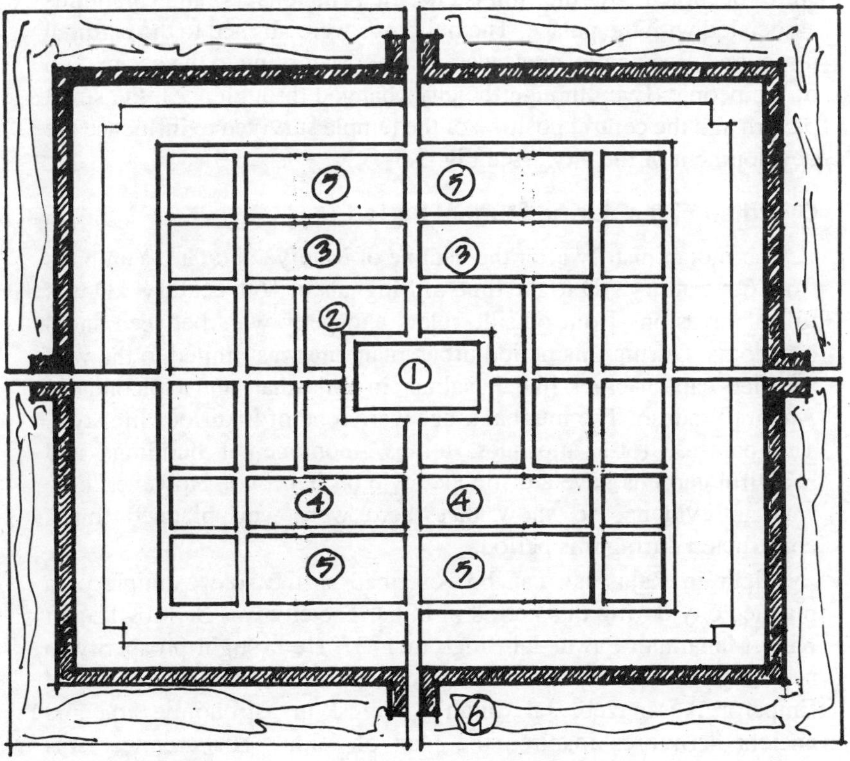

1. Temple
2. Royal palace
3. Kshatriyas
4. Vaishyas
5. Sudras
6. Moat

Fig. 3.3 Plan of Madurai

agricultural land from the beginning. The roads linking the ports passed through Madurai giving boost to its growth.

Madurai city was found around 1500 BC by Pandyas. It was ruled by Cholas, Nayakas and Moghuls. The British East Indian Company captured Madurai in 1801 AD and ruled for seventy five years before handing over to the British government. Industry, education and commerce were encouraged during the period of the British rule. The city was basically conceived as a religious and cultural centre.

The temple forms the centre of the city. Streets were laid around the temple. The palace was built in the north-eastern portion of the newly planned city. There were day and night markets along the two big streets. Commercial activities are also concentrated along the streets around the palace. The four streets around the kings palace were occupied by the ministers, rich merchants and brahmins associated with the palace. The buildings were aligned to the cardinal directions. Residential areas were planner according to the occupation of the people. Even though the city changed through ages, the street pattern and the central position of the temple survived to influence the development of the city. (see Fig. 3.3)

C) Indian cities during Mughal period

The Indian history after the decline of Maurya and Gupta empires from 6th century AD to the time of Mughals of 16th century AD was full of invasions from outside rulers and petty wars between small kingdoms. During this period urban planning was limited to the well fortified capital cities like Jaisalmer in Rajasthan and Golconda in Andhra Pradesh. The mughal kings were fond of luxurious life style. The palaces, forts, mosques, tombs, monumental buildings and beautiful gardens have a distinctiv style of their own. However there was no evidence to show that there were well planned towns constructed during this period.

Jaipur in Rajasthan can be described as the sole example of a planned city during this period in India. The city was built by Rajput King Maharajah Sawai Jai Singh in 1727. He brought prosperity to his kingdom by maintaining cordial relations with the Mughal Emperor Aurangzeb. Jai Singh's interest in astronomy, arts and ancient scriptures inspired the plan of Jaipur. His architect was Vidyadhar Bhattacharya, great grandson of the priest of the kings temple. The site was located in the valley formed by hills to the north and east. The city was designed on a grid-iron pattern with orthogonal clustering of square sectors. The major east-west road and three north-west roads divide the city into 8 district sectors known as 'chowkris'. One of them, where palace was located is twice the average sector area. Different zones of the city were planned in conformity with the Vastushastra. Brahmins were allotted areas in the north, Kshatriyas in the east, Vaishyas in the south and Sudras in the west. The close-knit urban structure reduces solar radiation. The house walls were thick with good thermal resistance. Minimum openings were provided on the external walls. All houses were provided with central courtyard, into which the windows open out. Pinkish stones were used for the building facades on the major roads, which brought the name of 'Pink City' to Jaipur. (see Fig. 3.4)

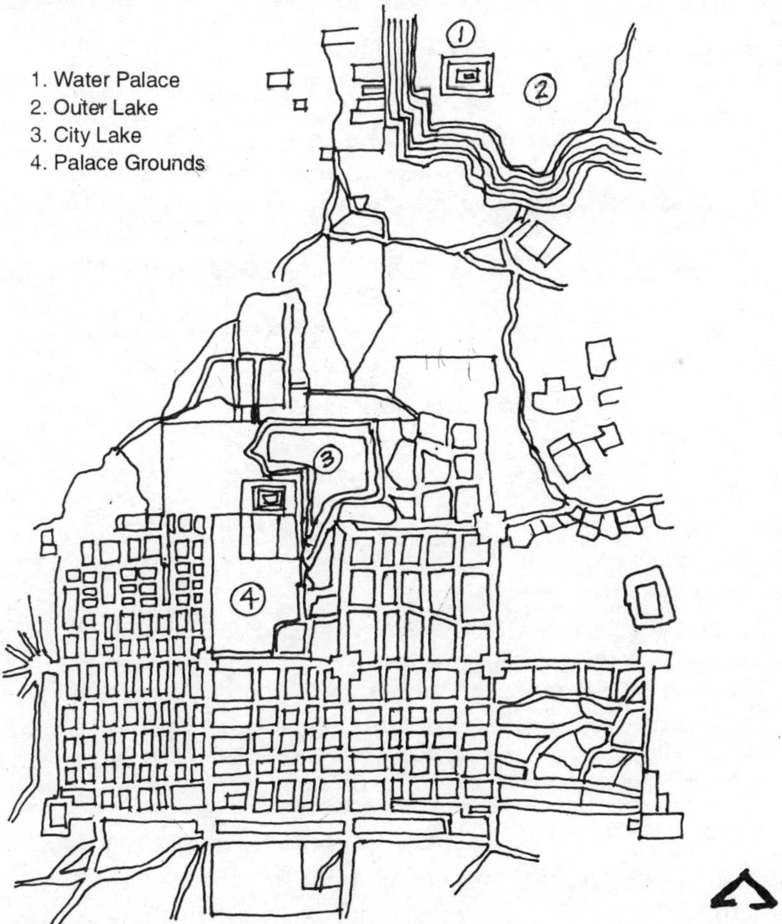

Fig. 3.4 Plan of Madurai

MODEL QUESTIONS

1. What are the major urban planning features of Mohenjodaro and Harappa ?
2. List out the important urban planning rules according to ancient vastushastra.
3. Describe the urban planning principles of the following ancient cities.
   (a) Madurai.
   (b) Jaipur.

4

Modern Urban Planning

A. Industrial Revolution and its impact

Industrial revolution from late 18th century onwards may be taken as a cut-off line between ancient and modern urban planning. Industrialisation was a boon to the growing population all over the world. Its affects like rising production and pace of life created chain reactions affecting both the natural and built environment. Inventions like elevators and automobiles have dramatically changed the shape and size of our cities. Industrialisation changed the production and consumption patterns in the society. The emergence of Economics as a science, the working class struggles, division of labour and dethroning of kings and dictators are the results of the changing life styles and political systems due to the industrialisation process. Professions and practices started specialising in the respective fields. Many departments and branches of various professions were opened in the cities without caring the integration of their activities for proper city development. This is visible in the misuse of land in the shape of buildings and roads. The profit motive and commercial outlook became part of the struggle for human existence. When compared to the rural society, urban society demanded more punctuality and precision to meet the obligations. This requirement forced the individual to be more rational. Money and brain, not spirit and heart, are the qualities needed for the urban resident for his survival. Science and logic became base of development and progress.

The invention of machinery to produce goods quickly than the human hand led to major changes in the nature of work and the duties of the work force. The textiles which used to be produced by hand at their looms or spinning wheel in the cottages were replaced by machines. Th introduction of mechanical power to drive several machines at a time needed the assembly of workers and machines in one building called as Factory. At first industrial development occurred on a small scale with little disturbance because the early machines were powered by water. Later coal was used for steam engines, which could drive many machines by means of drive belts. New settlements grew up near the coal mines. The emphasis shifted from the production of textiles to iron and steel, and then to manufactured goods as a result of technological development. These were aimed to cater to home as well as overseas markets. People flocked to the new industrial towns.

In the later stages other forms of power were developed which could be transmitted longer distances like gas and electricity. With this facility, anything could be developed anywhere, if the financial backing is available. Development was attracted to areas which already established as industrial centres because they offered skilled workers, infrastructure and the markets. Transport routes for distribution of goods became more important than producing near the source of raw materials because of the availability of the power grid. The new city work force may be classified as Primary, Secondary and Tertiary workers. Primary workers are those engaged in basic industries like agriculture and mining. Secondary workers are those involved in manufacturing. Tertiary workers are those involved in office and other service works.

There were also major changes in the nature of life styles. The changes occurred in the division of social classes, the family, the community and the relationship between home and work. All these reflected in the layout and zoning of towns and cities. The structure of society changed with new class divisions. New occupations emerged because of the technological inventions and changes in the economy. In the traditional rural society, a static feudal system existed. The inhabitants of a village basically consisted of the landowner and the peasants. People did not have any class but were born to certain status or family which shaped their life styles. With the industrial revolution, the social structure was transformed as many people moved from the villages and set up home in the new industrial cities. It became acceptable to classify people in terms of their work than with what they were born. Most significant development is the emergence of the new industrial working class. Changes occurred in the nature of work also. More people started working outside the home than in their own workshop or home. Workers were housed near the factory to work for set hours every day. In contrast, the traditional agricultural workers life is dictated by the seasons. The factories were clustered together with housing around for the workers.

Changes occurred in the family structure of the society. The traditional rural family was fairly large. Most of the people at present are brought up in a nuclear family consisting of husband, wife and their children. In pre-industrial societies, families were large consisting of the parents and their children, grand-parents, grand-children and also uncles, aunts and cousins living in the same house. During the industrial revolution, younger couples moved to the new cities leaving the older people behind. Birth rates were high during the initial stages of the industrial revolution with high infant mortality levels. As time went on families became smaller with reduced infant mortality rates due to the developments in medicine.

The problems arose mainly because of the concentration of working class people in poorly built housing near the factories and mills. They were located near factories for proximity and lack of sufficient money for commuting long distances. The transport systems also did not develop to the required extent. People were put together in poor accommodation near the place of work creating number of health and sanitary problems.

B. Modern Urban planning Initiatives

The industrial cities gradually became bad to worse. The environmental deterioration led to inefficient and unhealthy labour force affecting production. Thus the welfare of the masses became inevitable. Some leaders understood the problems of bad housing conditions. Many utopian plans were presented by industrialists. These plans were not executed but brought the attention towards the growing evils of the urban areas. Few model towns were executed in England, Ireland and USA between 1850 and 1900 A.D.

At the end of 19th century governments assumed more responsibility for the improvement of the cities in Europe. Around 1880 Sweden and Holland provided loans for public services. Then, Germany encouraged development of co-operative housing. British law empowered state and local authorities to build houses for rent to the working class. It was generally felt that good management is necessary to improve living conditions. In 1871 in USA, Boston Co-operative Company started a scheme of rental housing for workers with big plots, large rooms and less plot coverage. Some basic planning standards were laid out for ventilation, plot coverage etc., Many organisations were formed to improve housing for low-income workers and to make housing a profitable investment.

The industrial revolution brought people to the urban centres for employment. In England, urban population increased than rural population. In Germany also, it was the same. All industrial areas were congested. Land prices increased with the rapid growth of population. City expansion became difficult and land prices increased with higher concentration of population in selected pockets.

North America was divided into grids by early migrants. This grid-iron pattern formed the basis for planning cities ignoring other natural features. City planning was initiated in North America by using zoning regulations. In zoning regulations buildings to be allowed, height limits and prohibited landuses were prescribed. Public authorities were made responsible to regulate public services. Attempts to improve cities by planned decentralisation in the shape of new towns, urban renewal and planned development started. By the end of 19th century congestion increased in the cities. High land prices became common in urban areas. Multistoreyed buildings created additional problems. Social welfare schemes increased for the under previleged. As the density in the central areas increased, people moved out to the suburbs for better opportunities and clean environment. People became footloose with the availability of jobs in different cities. Rental flats met the temporary accommodation needs of the people and became popular. The invention and use of private cars changed the character of suburbs. They became segregated communities. The suburban environment provided all the urban amenities and services without the evils like congestion and pollution.

We shall discuss below some of the leading urban planning concepts which influenced modern urban planning, and also two important case studies to get an understanding of the modern urban planning process around the world.

1. MODERN URBAN PLANNING CONCEPTS

The concepts of four leading thinkers of modern urban planning had a significant impact in shaping the modern cities all over the world. They are Ebenezer Howard, Le Corbusier, Patrick Geddes and Doxiadis.

(a). *Ebenezer Howard (1850-1928):* Howard belongs to a period when there was severe protest against the growing ill-effects of industrialisation. Being a Town-Clerk and closely associated with the urban problems, he felt very bad at the growing disorder in the cities. He raised a voice saying that the worsening living conditions in cities is a decay of industrial civilisation and unless people raise to the challenge of creating a new order on a fresh ground, the base for the development of cities could never be laid.

His Town-Country magnet showing the combination of the advantages of both town and country led to the Garden City movement in England. Howard believed that the industrial revolution created overcrowding, bad housing and environmental problems; but it had many other benefits. Therefore he wanted to combine the best of the new industrial society with the best of the countryside in his ideal community named as 'Garden City'. Garden City was conceived as a powerful 'counter-magnet' to attract people from the over-crowded industrial cities and the poor villages. (see Fig. 4.1)

Howard planned garden cities of a population of 30,000 (approximately) each, divided into smaller neighbourhoods of 5000 to act as counter-magnets. He planned low-densities in the industrial areas with number of trees, private gardens, parks and other open spaces. He proposed a greenbelt around the city to be used by the people for agriculture. Howard was concerned not only with physical town planning but also social and economic characteristics of the community. He wanted the land to be owned co-operatively, but allowed for private ownership of shops and business. He wanted to incorporate co-operative house-keeping for running the city. In those days, there was poor State Town Planning system, so to realise his ideas he has to depend upon private investment and development. He started the process of setting up the first Garden City Company before the First World Warin Letchworth in 1903 and later in Welwyn in 1920 on the edges of London. (see Fig. 4.2)

Howards ideas influenced town planning a great deal such as the emergence of neighbourhood concept, the creation of hierarchical amenities and facilities, green belts, landuse zoning and provision of cycle paths. He was the first person to apply political intelligence to the problem of overgrowth and congestion of cities in a novel way to solve the problems. He wanted to replace the plansless expansion of the big city with planned expansion to accommodate the growing population. To achieve this, he proposed to build self-sufficient communities limited in size and density of population but big enough to sustain industries and to satisfy day-to-day needs of the people. Howards main contribution to town planning is his perception that there is a need to have a size for the community to have human identity. He felt that certain values missing in the overgrown cities could be brought back in these communities. His idea appeared rather

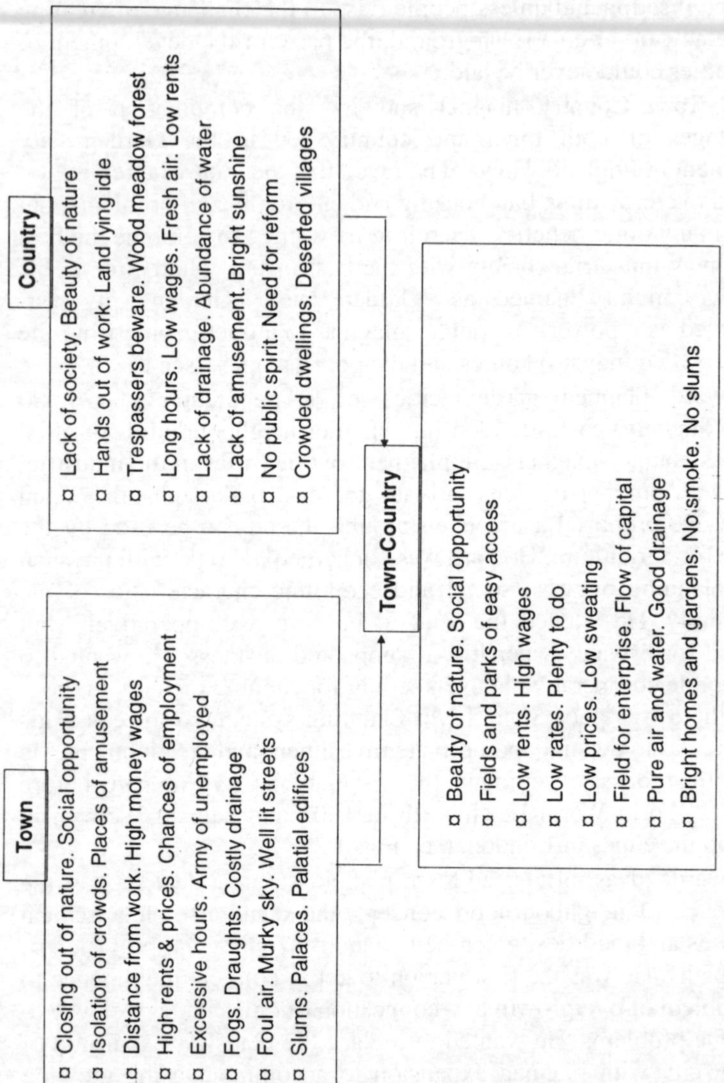

Fig. 4.1 Town-Country magnet *by Ebenezer Howard*

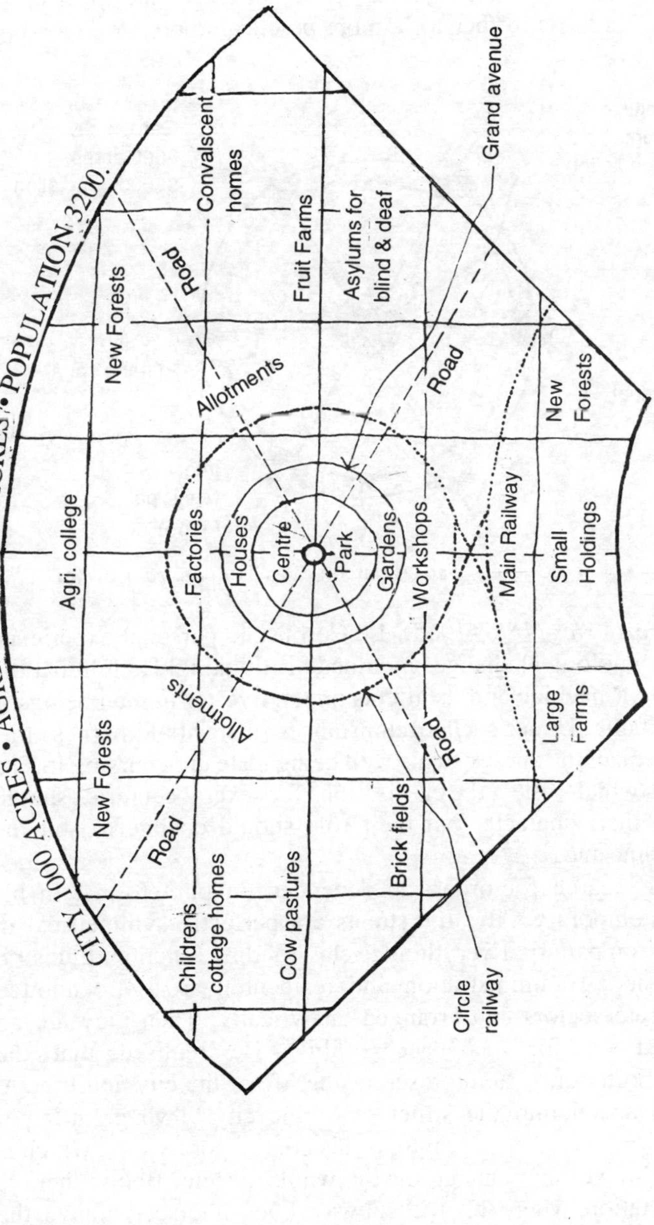

Fig. 4.2 Garden City Concept *by Ebenezer Howard*

emotional because the land and environment may be new but the people who come to live are not new. They bring their habits and beliefs into the town. This kind of criticism led to the thinking of improving his ideas further for a more practical approach. (see Fig. 4.3)

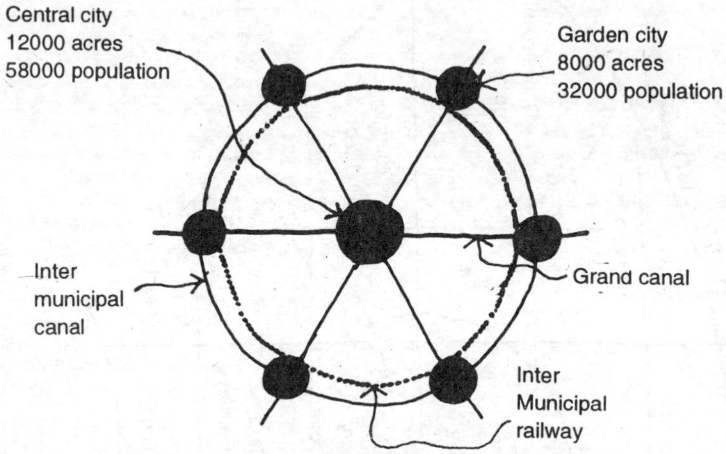

Fig. 4.3 The Social city with six garden cities by *Ebenezer Howard*

(b). *Le Corbusier (1887-1965):* Le Corbusiers personal experience of technological changes moulded his thinking. He felt that the need of machine and its affects on the lives of human beings is inevitable. Under such circumstances man should harness this huge machine energy to his well being instead of cursing it. The cities which reflect the civilisations for several centuries should keep their character but their role should change to suit the machine age.

In his search for order, he depended on pure forms. In his 'Contemporary City' the streets are perfectly symmetrical in grid iron pattern. Everything is classified by function. Industry, commerce, administration and residential areas are allotted separate sectors and arranged analytically. Then they are all linked up for easy accessibility. He realised that the transportation system preserves the life of the city and tried to build speed into the structure of the city. Two great super highways cross at the centre of his contemporary city, which is a multilevel interchange for the whole system. Below them is the station where all the subway lines intersect; above the highways, mounted on great street pillars, is the main railroad terminal. On the roof of this huge structure is a runway where planes can land. Surrounding the central terminal are 24 glass and steel skyscrapers each 60 storeys high. They have business centre. The streets are elevators, rising straight up instead of separating out. One skyscraper may have more usable space than a neighbourhood but it occupies only a little more ground than an old building. The rest is devoted to parks and gardens. (see Fig. 4.4)

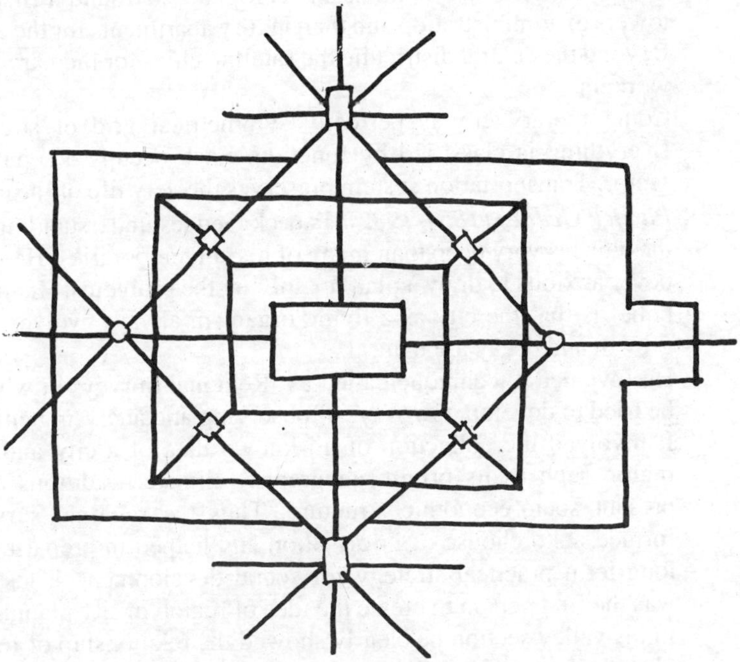

Fig. 4.4 Contemporary City by Le Corbusier

The Radiant city which he planned later was more daring and difficult synthesis of the contemporary city. He felt that for a better community life authority is required, which should be directed from the top according to one plan. The centres of life in the Radiant city are great high rise apartment blocks. The stress is not on the individual apartment but on the collective services provided to all by the residents. He says that a plan is necessary because the machine age requires conscious control.

Chandigarh in India is an application of Le Corbusiers town planning ideas. His challenges were the availability of low-technology and limited building materials like brick and concrete. The unique features of Chandigarh are the site near Himalayas, sector concept, separation of pedestrain and vehicular traffic, the grid iron pattern of the city and the artificial lake. Le Corbusier did not understand the problems of Indian cities in depth and his design was on western ideas. Inspite of such drawbacks Chandigarh inspired a bold planned urban development in the shape of new towns in India.

At the exact centre is the transportation interchange for automobiles, subways, trains and aeroplanes. Around it first 24 towers of administration and then luxury apartments for the elite Beyond the central district lie the satellite cities for industry and workers.

Contemporary city is perfectly symmetrical grid of streets. Everything is classified by function. Each occupy a separate sector. Transportation system preserves the very life of the city.

(c). *Patrick Geddes (1854-1982):* Patrick Geddes understanding of the cities is very deep than many of his contemporaries. He was never anxious to draw a plan for solving the problems. His firm belief is that the city as a living organism always evolves. Its growth and decay are natural.

He invented a technique called as 'Regional Survey' in which he tried to develop new ways of observing and analysing cities. It involved the collection of all known data of a city and its region such as its origin, geography, climate, traditions and present socio-economic structure. Thus the regional survey formed a storehouse of information and helped in preparing a long term practical strategy for social development. Thus he was the first person to create the idea of region in city planning. In his valley section he clearly showed the relationship of folk, place and work. He believed that an urban planner should be a generalist than specialist knowing fairly well about all the disciplines.

In his 'Valley section' he showed that all the natures occupations have a place. Starting from the head of the valley section the hunter and miner, the woodman, the shepherd, the poor and rich peasant and the fisherman have works which are closely related to their surroundings. The geographical space shapes the folk and the work, and the people with their work shape the environment. Thus there is a continuous struggle between environment and society. There are always problems in the cities which need immediate attention such as growing slums, increasing traffic, urban renewal etc., To deal with these relatively short-term problems Geddes developed special technique described as 'Conservative surgery'. Congestion is always high at the intersections. He wanted to create smooth traffic flows by pulling down carefully selected houses which are old and dilapidated. Public participation is another important concept which he stressed. Any city development programme is bound to be a failure without active public participation. He wanted 'Outlook Towers' to be established in all cities from where the citizens can view their cities to know the problems, Apart from this, the town planning exhibitions showing the various aspects of the city create awareness among the citizens. Patrick Geddes was not given many opportunities to plan in England because his thoughts were outside conventional planning practice prevailing in those days. Fig. 4.5

(d). *Doxiadis (1913-1975):* Doxiadis laid the base for the theory of human settlement planning, which he termed as 'Ekistics'. The five important principles which he discovered from the history are:

(a). *Optimisation of potential contacts:* Throughout the history of cities the main desire of man is to select the location which brings him close to the natural resources like water, fruits, minerals etc.,

(b). *Minimise the efforts to make the contacts:* Man spent least energy to make contacts which are easily accessible. He never tried to climb hills, he went round to make a route to spend least possible energy to make the contacts.

(c). *Optimisation of protective open space:* People can tolerate the crowded surroundings only for a certain length of time, and then he wants to enclose himself in a private room. This is an important principle which shows the privacy of space in human existence.

(d). *Best balance with the environment:* Man always tried to build his house, roads, gather food and fuel in such a way that his existence caused least harm to surroundings maintaining a balance with the nature. With the increasing industrialisation the natural environment is getting spoilt, the cities are growing and the accessibility is becoming

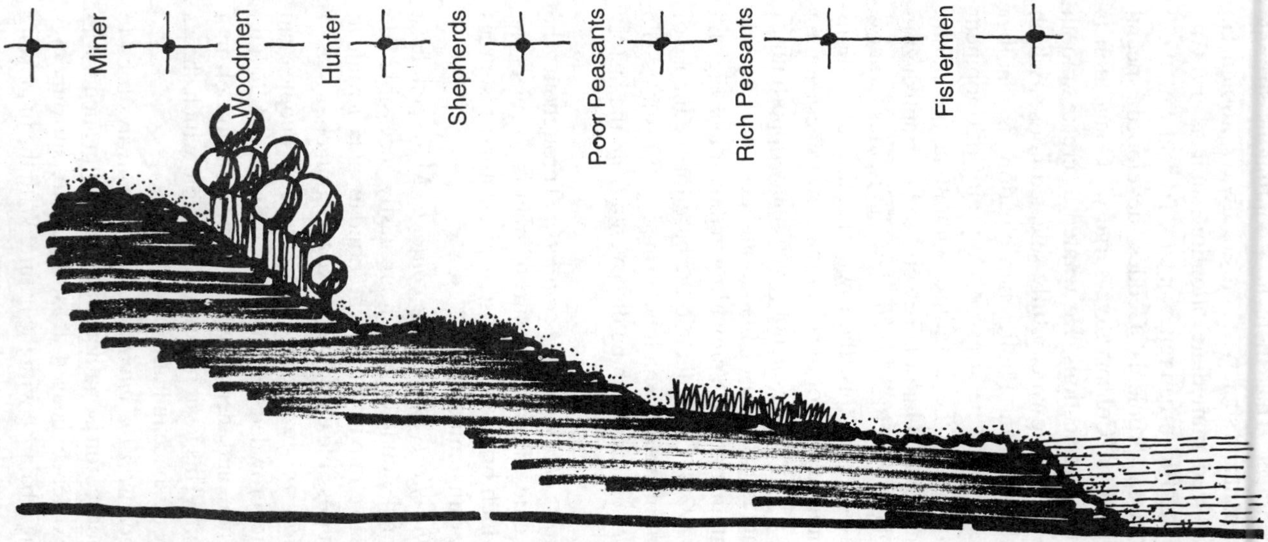

[in Geddes words "at the head of the valley section, first activity can be hunting, until woodman and miner comes in. Next to forest land comes the pasturages and its shepherds. Next on higher and poor soils comes the struggling peasant followed by rich peasant on deeper richer land down the valley. In the end we have the fishermen near sea". This is the evolution of human civilisation in the valley section. These simple occupations denote relationships of folk, place and work region by region. Understanding regions past history & present conditions helps for better socio-economic and cultural organisation].

Fig. 4.5 Patrick Geddes Valley Section

complicated. All these faults exist because our cities are not adjusting to the growing needs.

(e). *Synthesis of all the four principles:* Man developed doors to his house in order to achieve the maximum synthesis between third, and the first and second principles. He could maximise his contacts and open the door when he wished to be with his family and go out into the street and meet his neighbours with minimum effort.

The most important aspects of human settlement organisation are:

1. Nature,
2. Man,
3. Society,
4. Shells and
5. Networks

The harmonious relationship among these five elements leads to a better organisation of human settlement system.

Doxiadis feels that the city should expand and its growth should have the freedom but with a plan. The migration to cities cannot be stopped and it is wrong to decide the ultimate size of the population in a city. The migrants are neither drifting towards the attraction of the city lights nor they are refugees from a sudden disaster. They are a selected group of persons at the peak of their work power who have taken a decision about their future to live in the city.

Each community should prosper in its own way, and the beliefs and customs of the people should not be injured. The symbols of each community could be a church, a temple, a mosque or an outlook tower but every community lives in harmony with the beliefs of the neighbouring community. This is the concept of 'Entopia' which will spread over the entire world. Another aspect which he brings to light is the core of the city. The core of the city is always congested and encroached within a limited area. This he feels as the curse of the cities which causes several problems in the centre of the city. The centre of any dynamic city should be adapted to steady growth without encroaching on areas intended for other purposes. It should develop freely along a predetermined axis through the central nucleus of the city, taking into account its future development in one direction. According to Doxiadis the development of the city goes through four stages: from 'Dynapolis' (monocentric city developing in one direction) and 'Dynametropolis' (parallel development of several Dynapolises in different directions) through 'Dynamegalopolis' (giant cities) to 'Ecumenopolis'-the final stage of an urban formation connecting all giant cities. (see Fig. 4.6)

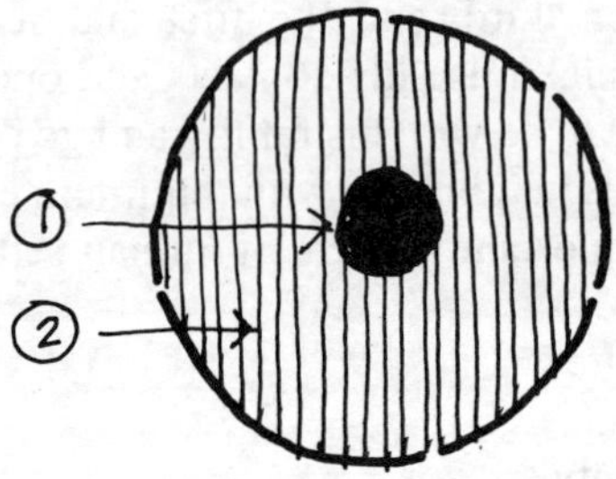

Existing City

Concentric city development with crowded centre and expansion all round the centre.

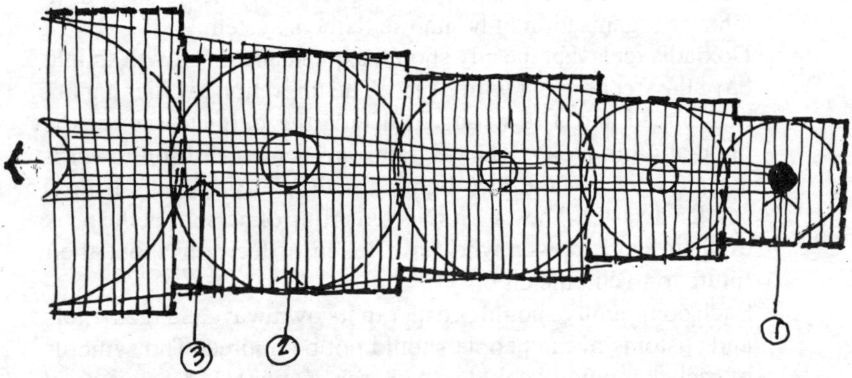

City development in one direction in parabolic or rectangular form.

Fig. 4.6 Dynapolis

There are two important case studies which influenced modern urban planning around the world. They are Radburn layout in USA and Greater London Plan in Great Britain. Brasilia is also another bold attempt of modern urban planning.

2. CASE STUDY 1: Radburn Layout in USA (1927-'29)

Radburn layout was inspired by the Garden City concept. It is located in New Jersey, which is within commuting distance from New York in USA. This layout was planned by Henry Wright and Clarence Stein. The concept of 'Super-block' of 30 to 50 acres was introduced in planning. In this layout, pedestrain and vehicular traffic are segregated. Single family dwellings were grouped around cul-de-sac roads. Kitchens and garages faced the rear road and living rooms faced the front garden. The access to the dwellings by car is from the rear courtyards, where the gargages are located. The pedestrain access is from the front side. Under passes reparated pedestrains and vehicular traffic. It has allocated space for industry, shopping and apartments but the green-belt concept was not incorporated. It is a well laid out safe and quiet area for the residents. It earned the name of 'Town for the motor age' and became a model for later layout planning of residential areas. (see Fig. 4.7)

3. CASE STUDY: Greater London Plan 1994 in Great Britain

Greater London Plan 1944 by Patrick Abercrombie was conceived during the Second World War period. London's major identified defects were traffic congestion, poor housing, inadequate open spaces and urban sprawl. A detailed survey formed the basis of the plan. The solutions covered not only physical defects but also the legal and financial defects. One of the major proposals was the redevelopment and decentralisation of the congested areas. New communities were planned to rebuild the bombed areas during the War.

The structure of the Greater London Plan was based on zoning in four rings. The Inner Ring contained the congested areas to be decentralised. The Suburbun Ring was a static zone for housing and industry. The Green Belt Ring allowed limited expansion of existing communities. The Outer County Ring was proposed for expansion in the shape of satellite towns.

The Plan proposed to relocate industries from the congested areas. It proposed creation of residential areas which could be divided into 'neighbourhood' units of 5000 to 10,000 people. Greater emphasis was placed on new open space standards. Higher densities of population were proposed. Flats were constructed in high blocks to keep the ground free. The road plan proposed outer ring roads, two inner ring roads, fast traffic ring roads and sub-arterial roads. Public services and markets were proposed to be built with revised planning standards. To achieve this; strict zoning, development plans and relocation of industries were suggested. (see Fig. 4.8)

4. CASE STUDY: Brasilia, capital of Brazil

Brasilia is the new capital of Republic of Brazil. The site located at 600 miles from Rio de Janeiro was selected in 1955. A linear type of design was proposed by architect Lucio Costa. With architect Oscar

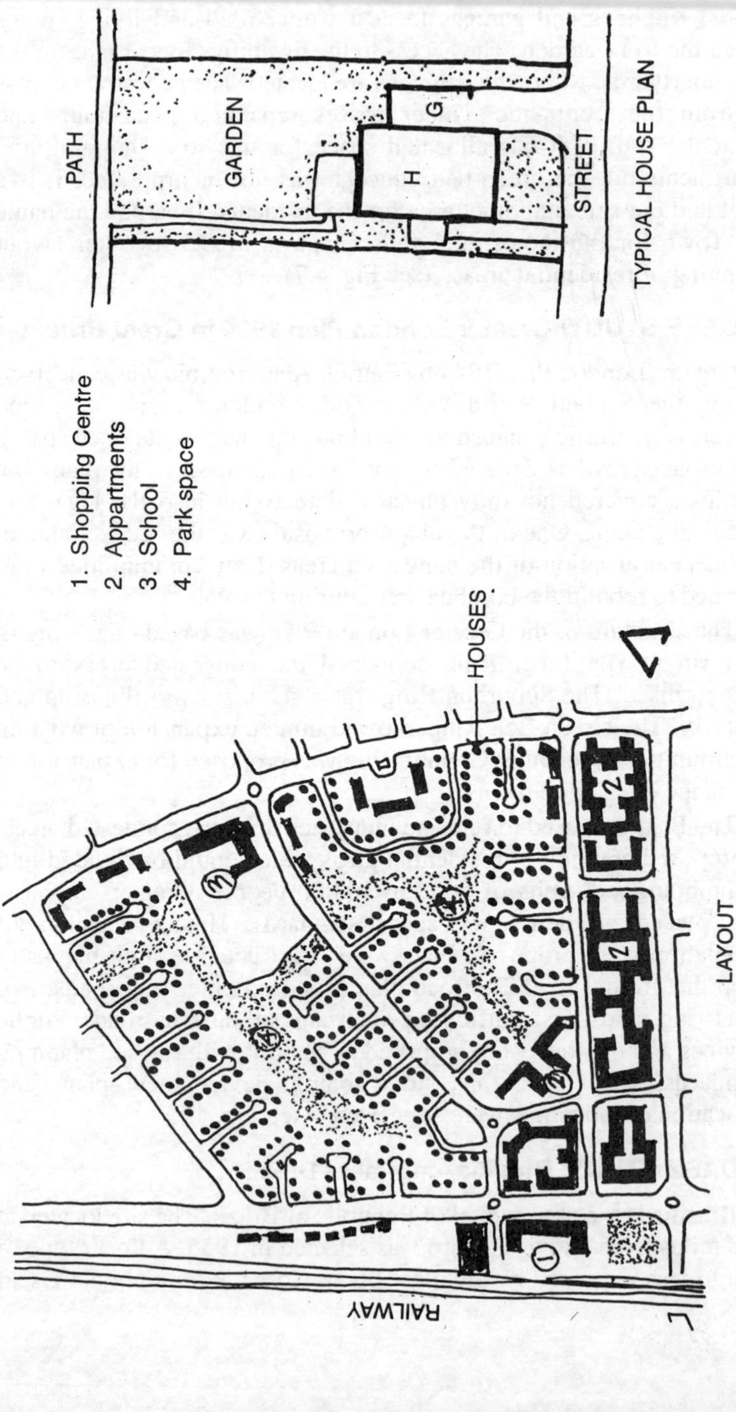

Fig. 4.7 Radburn Layout

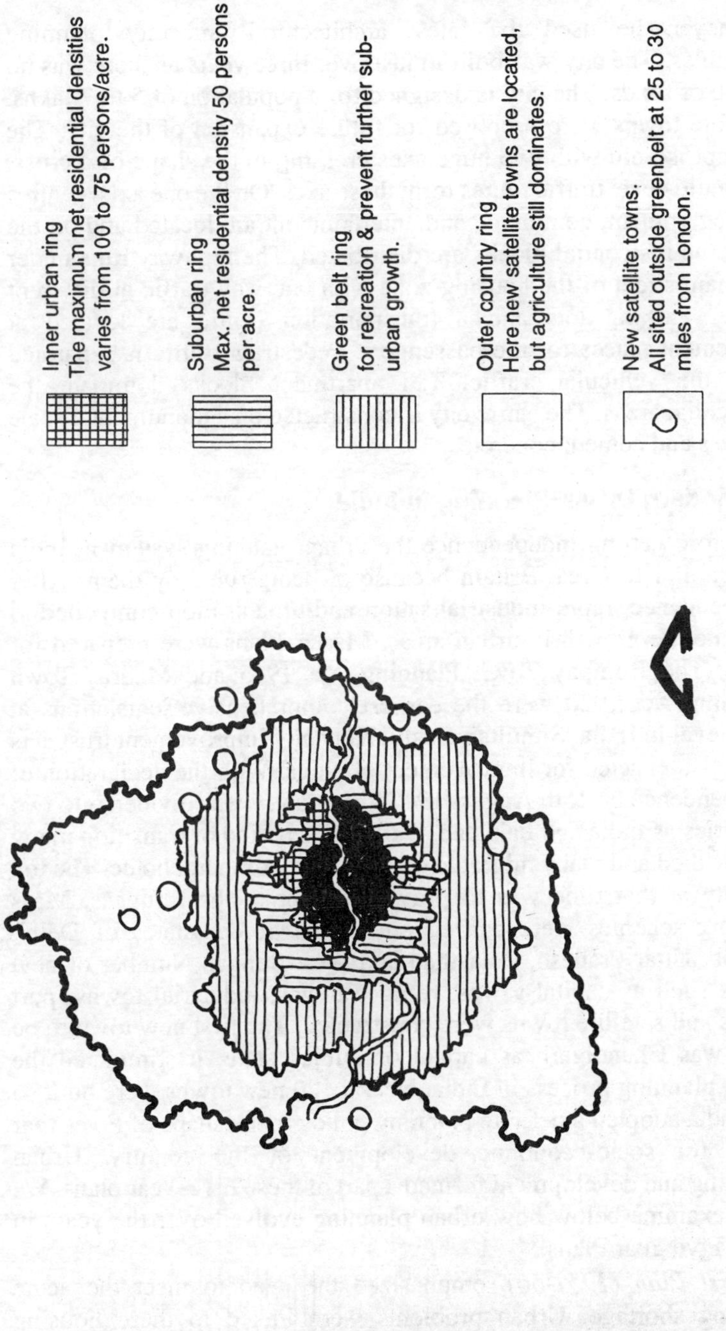

Fig. 4.8 Greater London Plan proposals

Niemeyer, he used the latest architectural and city planning principles. The city was built in just over three years as there was no dearth of funds. The city is designed for a population of 5 to 7 lakhs. Satellite towns were proposed for future expansion of the city. The concept is bold with two huge axes crossing in the shape of a cross. The multi-level traffic routes form these axes. On the one axis, centres for government, commerce and entertainment are located and on the other the residential blocks are distributed. The highway runs under the main street of the housing zone with one way traffic at different levels. Parking lots and a transportation centre are located at convenient places for the passengers. Pedestrain traffic is separated from the vehicular traffic. Tall apartment blocks dominate the residential areas. The entire city is constructed on a monumental scale in glass and cement concrete.

(C) Modern Urban Planning in India

Before getting independence the urban planning system in India was similar to Great Britain because of being ruled by them. After independence, rapid industrialisation and urbanisation compelled to regulate the growth in urban areas. Master Plans were prepared for cities. The Bombay Town Planning Act 1915 and Madras Town Planning Act 1920 were the earliest comprehensive legislations at state level in India. Simultaneously many city improvement trust acts were also enacted for improvement of cities. With the declaration of independence on 15th August 1947, the country was divided into two countries as India and Pakistan. During this period of transition many people died and many migrated to the country of their choice. The top priority at that time was to provide shelter to the refugees. Mass housing schemes were carried out in the border states of Delhi, Punjab, Uttar Pradesh, Rajasthan and West Bengal. Number of new towns such as capital towns, refugee towns, industrial towns, port towns and satellite towns were constructed. The first new town to be built was Chandigarh as capital of Punjab state. It stimulated the urban planning process in India. Nearly 120 new towns were built so far. India adopted a definite planning policy in the shape of Five-Year plans for socio-economic development of the country. Urban planning and development formed a part of these Five-Year plans. We shall examine below how urban planning evolved over the years in these Five Year Plans.

First Plan (1951-56), emphasized the need to meet the acute housing shortage. Urban problems were linked to these housing

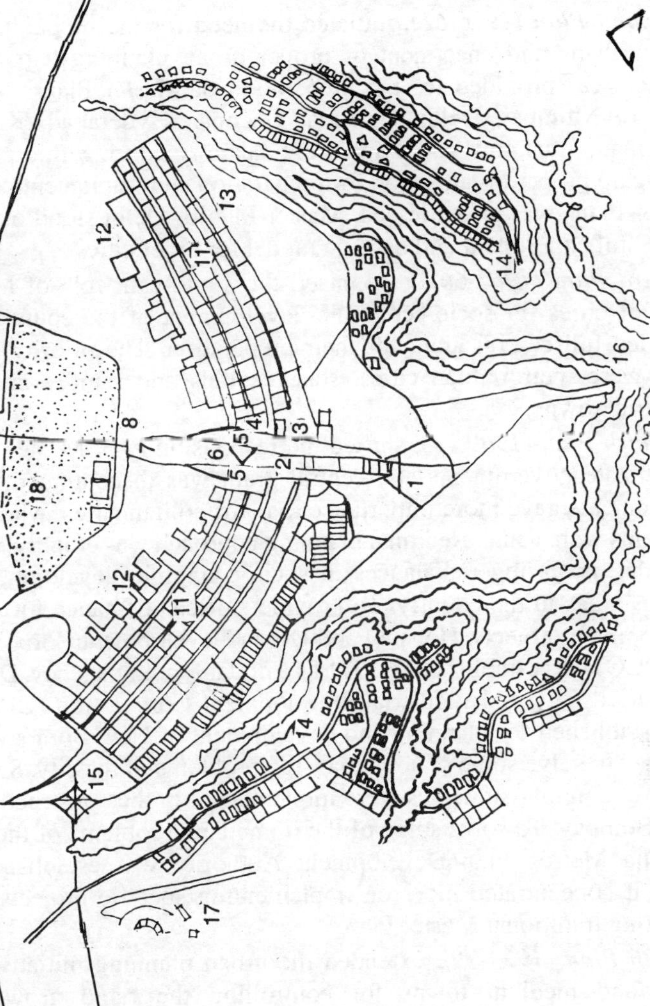

1. Govt. centre
2. Ministries
3. Banks & Offices
4. Shopping centre
5. Hotels
6. Broadcasting centre
7. Sports Complex
8. Municipal complex
9. Guards & Police
10. Rail terminal
11. Residential districts
12. Individual houses
13. Private residences
14. Suburban residences
15. Bus terminal
16. Presidents palace
17. Airport
18. Observatory
19. Food store house
20. Depot

Fig. 4.9 Brasilia Master Plan

schemes. Most of the urban planning concentrated on building new towns.

Second Plan (1956-61), initiated the need for the preparation of Master Plans and enactment of proper urban planning legislation. Finance was provided for the preparation of Master Plans. Master Plans of Mumbai, Delhi, Calcutta, Chennai, Hyderabad, Kanpur, Allahabad, Lucknow and Pune were taken up during this period. Setting up proper organisation for preparation and implementation of Master Plans was also stressed. Master Plan of Delhi stood out as a successful experiment and became model for other cities.

Third Plan (1961-66), recognised the significant role of Master Plans of cities for socio-economic development of the country and provided full central grant for their preparation. The priority urban areas were metropolitan cities, state capitals and rapidly growing industrial towns.

Fourth Plan (1969-74), shifted the responsibility of Master Plans to the state governments and central grant was discontinued. State governments gave more importance to metropolitan cities, where the problems were acute. Regional planning approach was emphasized to curb the increasing imbalances in socio-economic development of various areas in the country. To provide sufficient finance for urban development projects, Housing and Urban Development Corporation (HUDCO) was established in 1971 as a nodal funding agency. During this period City and Industrial Development Corporation (CIDCO) was established for planning and development of New Bombay near Bombay to solve some major expansion problems of the city. Several creative planning strategies were implemented in the construction of New Bombay. To solve some of the immediate problems of the city, Calcutta Metropolitan Development Authority was established in 1972. It concentrated more on implementing specific projects than preparing traditional Master Plan.

Fifth Plan (1974-79), extended the urban planning initiatives to small and medium towns for controlling the rapid growth of metropolitan cities.

Sixth Plan (1980-85), a programme of 'Integrated Development of Small and Medium Towns (IDSMT)' was introduced. This scheme was aimed to improve infrastructure in selected towns to make them act as regional centres for economic growth and arrest migration to bigger cities. Central assistance was given with matching contribution from state governments. Nearly 840 towns were identified for development in 25 states and 5 union territories.

Seventh Plan (1985-90), observed that urban development should be supported by economic development. Poverty alleviation became a dominant feature of the development strategy of the country. Emphasis was placed on improving the living conditions of the slum dwellers and schemes for employment generation of urban poor. National Commission on Urbanisation (NCU) was constituted in 1985 and submitted its recommendations in 1988. Eventhough all the recommendations were not implemented, a National Housing Bank was established in 1988 as a major step to encourage housing by extending finance through various financial institutions and banks.

Eighth Plan (1992-97), recognised the role of urban planning for poverty alleviation and to minimise unemployment. This plan stressed the need for regional spatial planning approach for socio-economic development. In the year 1992 two amendments known as Constitution (73rd) Amendment Act and Constitution (74th) Amendment Act were passed. These amendments made it mandatory for the state governments to devolve power of planning and decision making to the people through local-self governments. It established a system of local governance at urban and rural levels. They are Panchayats at rural level, Municipalities at urban level and Nagar-Panchayats in semi-urban areas. The 74th amendment provides constitution of two committees, District Planning Committee and Metropolitan Planning Committee to co-ordinate the plans submitted at lower levels for socio-economic development. These plans are consolidated further at state and national levels for comprehensive development of all parts of the nation.

Thus urban planning in India has come a long way since independence to develop urban areas and channelise the urbanisation process in the country. Two schemes which prominently helped for urban development are Integrated Development of Small and Medium Towns (IDSMT) and Environmental Improvement of slums (EIS). However, a comprehensive national urbanisation policy is lacking for balanced socio-economic development of both urban and rural areas.

1. CASE STUDY 1: Chandigarh, Capital of Punjab State.

Chandigarh is a classic example of modern town planning. Le Corbusier was involved in the designing of the new city of Chandigarh from 1951 to 1965. During the partition of the country in 1948, Western Punjab and the traditional capital of Lahore were conceded to Pakistan leaving Indian Punjab in need of a capital town.

Initial plan was drawn by Albert Mayer of USA. The chief engineer P.L. Varma and the state administrator of public works P.N. Thapar toured Europe in search of an architect-planner. On the word of British architects Maxwell Fry and Jane Drew, they turned to Le Corbusier. In 1961, in a small rest-house close to Chandigarh, the blue-print of the new capital was drawn in a few days.

Le Corbusier derived the concept of the city from the human body. Thus he conceived that the government buildings to form the head, the commercial centre as the heart, the university area as the brain, the industrial areas as hands, the leisure valley as the lungs and the roads as arteries.

The Master Plan of Chandigarh was designed for an initial population of 1.5 lakhs with an ultimate population of 5 lakhs on a site measuring 3600 hectares. It has been designed on super-block principle and termed as sector. Le Corbusier designed the four main government buildings known as 'Capital Complex' on the north side of the town consisting the Legislative building, the Secretariat, the High Court and the Governor's house. The south side was reserved for industrial development. The central sector contains civic centre and commercial buildings. The University and cultural centre are in the north-west side. (see Fig. 4.10)

Some of the important features of the Chandigarh Master Plan are:

1. Each sector is 1.20 km in length and 0.80 km in width. They can accommodate population ranging from 15000 to 25000 depending upon the area and density of population. There are usually three to four neighbourhood units in each block.
2. Each sector has a continuous green open space on the longer side and shopping street on the shorter side. The green open spaces has cycle tracks and pedestrain pathways, which are separated from the main road. The shopping street contains local shops and markets. Schools and essential services are located in the centre of the sector for easy accessibility without crossing the main roads.
3. As a principle, there is a clear segregation of pedestrain and vehicular traffic in the town.
4. The residential plots in all sectors do not have direct access to the main road, facilitating fast movement of traffic without any hindrance.
5. The dam of Sukhana Choe has created a lake on the north side of the town. It has been developed as a recreation place.
6. The industrial area is separated from the residential area by a

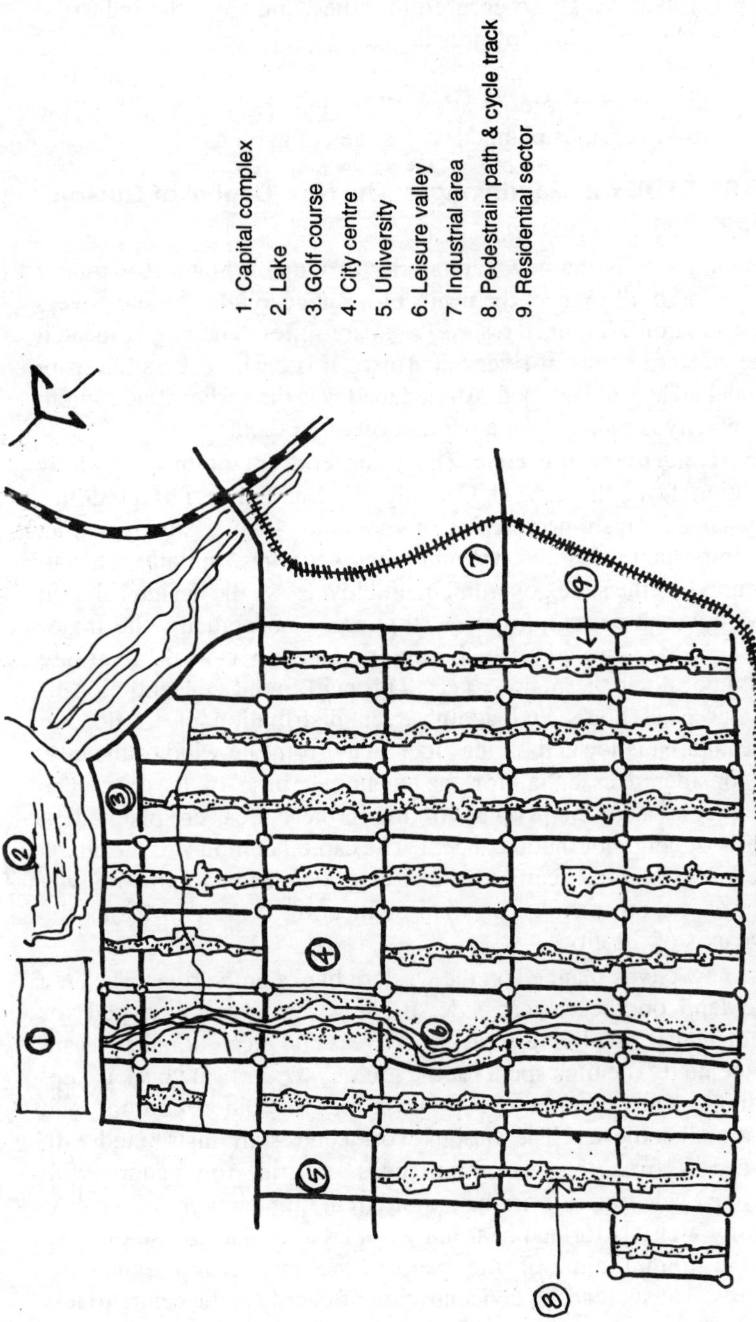

Fig. 4.10 Chandigarh Master Plan

green belt. It is also ensured that the wind from the industrial area does not blow towards the residential area.

7. Lot of emphasis has been given on landscaping and tree plantation and preservation. The leisure valley along the monsoon drain is planned with series of gardens.

2. CASE STUDY 2: Gandhinagar, The New Capital of Gujarat State

Gandhinagar is the new capital city of Gujarat State. It is totally planned and built to meet the needs of a state capital. The site covers a gross area of 5738 hectares or 21 square miles. The city is located on the western banks of river Sabarmati. It is easily accessible from Ahmedabad by rail and road. Ahmedabad was the earlier state capital. The new city is planned for a population of 3,00,000.

The concept of the city: The basic concept of the city drew inspiration from the city of Chandigarh. Gandhinagar is predominantly an administration centre of the state. It may slowly attract many important cultural, civic and allied activities. Initially it has to accommodate the state government employees, so the design is based on the government employment structure. Conceptually, the major work areas are provided in the centre and other work areas are distributed along the major roads. This will avoid concentration of traffic at peak hours and attains even distribution of traffic. An industrial area is located on the side, away from the wind of the city. It is considered essential for the economic base of the city. The residential areas of the people working in these areas are planned on the basis of neighbourhood concept. The capital complex of the city is located in the central sector of the city. It is connected to the railway station at the other end. The road connecting these two forms the central axis of the city.

The new city is planned on the western banks of the river. The area of the land on the eastern side of the river is not proposed for immediate use. The living areas, work areas and recreational areas are nicely related. The time spent for the journey to work and back is kept minimum. Thus people can spare time for other cultural and recreational activities. The various work centres are distributed with easy access from the residential areas. A grid iron pattern with exclusive cycle tracks form the major circulation network of the city. Primarily a city is formed near the work area. In due course of time, with the immigration of the people, the city grows expanding outwards. Thus it leads to concentration of people at the centre to less

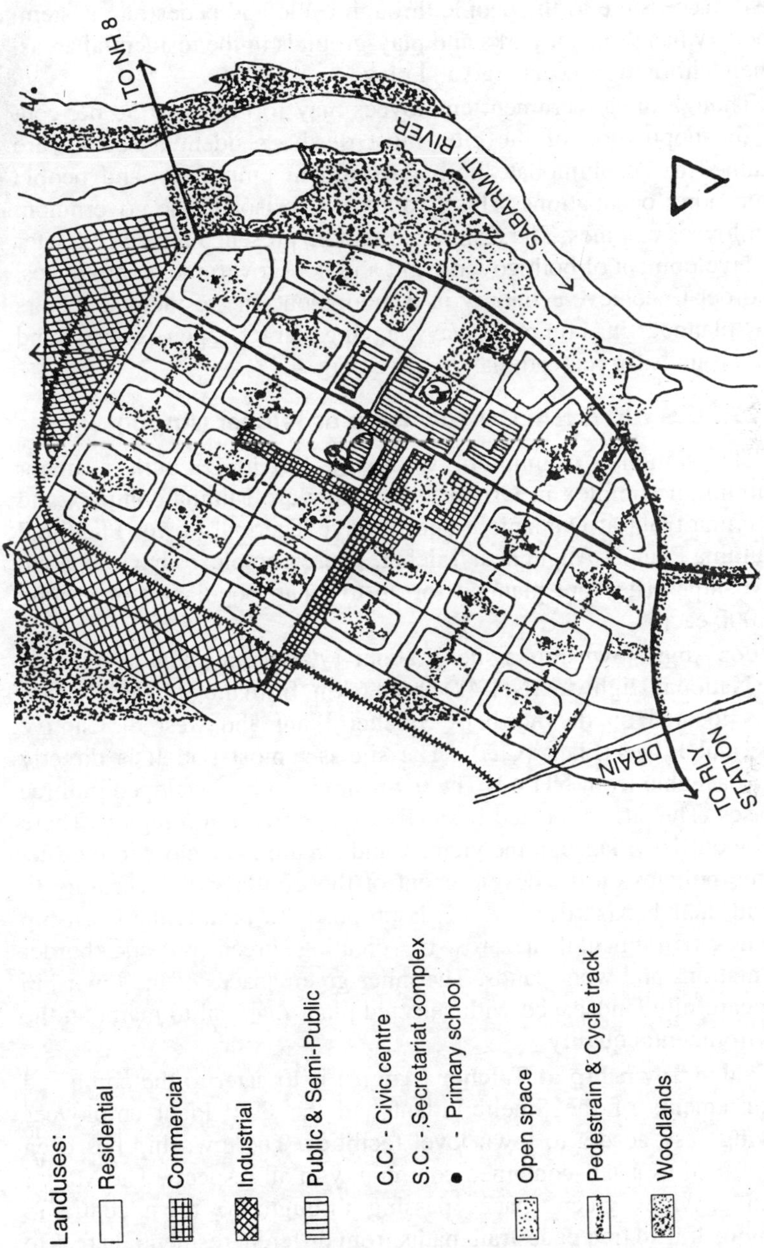

Fig. 4.11 Gandhi Nagar Master Plan

number of people at the periphery of the city. The riverside park is easily accessible to the people through cycle and pedestrain system. The city has series of parks and play-grounds in the residential areas, where children can easily go and play.

Though the government employees may form almost 50 per cent of the population of the city, most of the residential sectors are planned to accommodate both government employees and people from other occupations. This is done not to isolate the government employees colonies. The residential sectors present a mixed character of development of both government and non-government employees. In order to achieve economy in development, the residential sectors are planned in compact way leaving larger open spaces and playgrounds for recreational use. (see Fig. 4.11)

3. CASE STUDY: NALCO Township at Talcher (Angul)

The National Aluminium Company (NALCO) built a major aluminium complex in Orissa State. They are Minina complex and Alumina plant at Damanjodi and Captive Thermal Power Plant and Alumina Plant at Angul near Talcher. These complexes have separate townships. They are planned for an ultimate population of around 30,000 each.

For Angul township, a site of about 170 hectares was selected on the National Highway (NH-42) about 6 km. from the old Angul town. It is located on the north of Smelter Plant and west of Captive Thermal Power Plant (CTP). The site is almost flat. It is directly approachable from NH-42. The township is to be developed in three phases. The site is located basically in an agricultural region. There are about 16 villages in the vicinity and ten are quite close to the site. Some policies on the development of these villages is necessary to avoid their hapazard growth. It is proposed to protect the township from environmental hazards by creating green buffers, border plantations and wood lands. The inner green spaces of the township are carefully landscaped with selected plant material to maintain the environmental quality.

Nalco Township at Talcher (Angul) is to cater to the combined requirements of the Smelter Plant and the CTP Plant employees having easy access to town level facilities. The township has been conceived as a self-contained community in all respects. The Master Plan provides green spaces passing through the town centre to provide traffic free pedestrain paths from different residential areas to the town centre and other community facilities along these pathways.

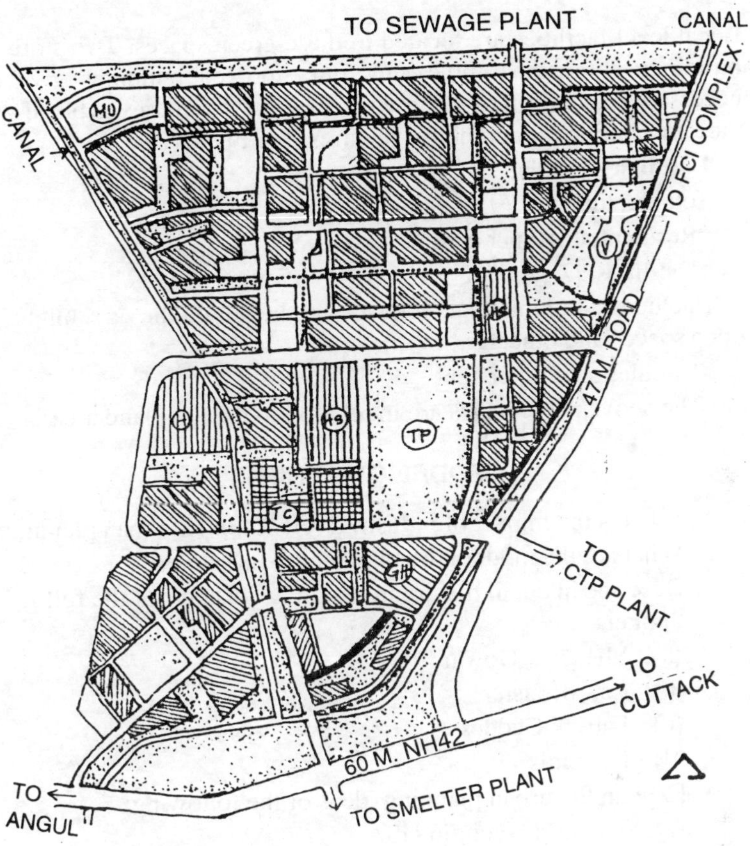

Landuses:

Residential → GH - Guest House

Commercial → TC - Town Centre
— - Weekly Market

Public & Semi-Public → H - Hospital
HS - Higher Secondary School

Recreation → TP - Town Park & Sports Complex

...... Pedestrain Path

MU - Miscellaneous uses

V - Existing Village

Fig. 4.12 NALCO: Township Talcher (Angul)

Local level facilities are located in these green spaces. Two storeyed buildings with some three and four storeyed buildings give the necessary urban form of the town. This urban form tries to blend with the surrounding topographical features (see Fig.4.12)

Landuse Details:

Total land area: 170 hectares.

*Residential: 59 per cent

*Facilities:27 per cent

(includes a commercial, educational, health public & semipublic, open spaces and others)

*Circulation: 14 per cent

(The above percentages are in relation to the total land area).

MODEL QUESTIONS

1. What is the impact of industrial revolution on urban planning?
2. What are the modern urban planning initiatives?
3. Describe in detail the urban planning concepts of the following thinkers
   (a). Ebenezer Howard
   (b). Le Corbusier
   (c). Patrick Geddes
   (d). Doxiadis
4. Explain the urban planning ideas of the following:
   (a). Radburn layout in USA
   (b). Greater London Plan
   (c). Brasilia
5. Describe the evolution of modern urban planning in India.
6. Explain the urban planning ideas of the following cities:
   (a). Chandigarh
   (b). Gandhinagar
   (c). NALCO township at Angul, Orissa.

5

Urban Planning Legislation

A. Evolution

The purpose of urban planning legislation is to prevent haphazard urban growth, slums and other kinds of misuse of land. Urban planning in a democratic country like India should be implemented within an appropriate legal framework to regulate the activities. Every individual should realise that his property rights are taken in public interest by a suitable law and not in an arbitrary way.

Legislations dealing with urban planning and development have been existing for a long time. These regulations vary in scope and content. Bombay took the lead by enacting the Bombay Improvement Trust Act 1898 under which the first Improvement Trust in the country was established in Bombay in 1898. This was followed by other states such as Mysore in 1903, Calcutta in 1911, U.P. in 1919, Punjab in 1922, Nagpur in 1936, Bangalore in 1945, Madras in 1948, Bihar in 1951, Orissa in 1956, Howrah in 1956, Rajasthan in 1959, Madhya Pradesh in 1960 and Karnataka in 1976. The main objective of these legislations has been the improvement of towns and cities through preparation and execution of improvement schemes by the Board of Trustees. These acts provide for the transfer of certain powers and property of the municipal bodies to the Trusts for implementation of schemes. The existing municipal bodies looked upon the Trusts as superimposed bodies resulting in conflict and friction.

Again Bombay took the lead in bringing about a comprehensive legislation at state level in the form of Bombay Town Planning Act in 1915. This was followed by Andhra Pradesh and Madras in 1920. The Bombay Town Planning Act of 1954 has made it compulsory for all the municipalities in the state to prepare Master Plans within a specific period for the municipal areas. This was followed by the

Assam Town Planning Act in 1959 and Mysore Town and Country Planning Act in 1961. During this period, the need for a comprehensive Town Planning legislation was felt by all the states, so the Town and Country Planning Organisation (TCPO) formulated the Model Town and Country Planning Law in 1960 to provide guidelines to the states. Some of the states revised their existing legislations and others enacted new legislations based on these guidelines. One such significant legislation is the Maharashtra Regional and Town Planning Act in 1966. This act provides the scope for the preparation of regional plans by the Regional Planning Boards and development plans and town planning schemes by the Planning Authorities. Another act on similar lines is the Tamil Nadu Town and Country Planning Act of 1971. It gives scope for the establishment of the Regional Planning Authority, the Local Planning Authority, the New Town Development Authority and Town & Country Planning Board at the state level to prepare regional plans, master plans, new town plans and detailed development plans.

In 1973, the Model Law prepared by TCPO has added the Model Urban Development Authorities Law providing for the creation of Development Authorities to undertake large scale development works. The idea of Development Authority was incorporated for the first time in the Delhi Development Act of 1957. The Authority is responsible for the preparation, enforcement and implementation of master plan and zonal development plans in the Union Territory of Delhi. Many other states made legislations on similar lines.

An important legislation, which was enacted by Parliament is the Urban Land (Ceiling & Regulation) Act of 1976. As per the act no person shall be entitled to hold any vacant land in excess of the ceiling limit in the various categories of urban agglomerations. Under this, the ceiling limit for Category A is 500 sq. mts; Category B is 1000 sq. mts; Category C is 1500 sq. mts and Category D is 2000 sq. mts. Other act enacted by Parliament and adopted by most of the states and union territories is the Water Pollution (Prevention & Control) Act of 1974 to prevent pollution of water. The Delhi Urban Art Commission Act of 1973 provides scope for setting up an Urban Art Commission to preserve, develop and maintain the aesthetic quality of Delhi. Some other important legislations pertaining to town planning and development are creation of Housing Boards, Slum Clearance Boards, Water Supply & Sewerage Boards and acts for controlling landuses. Most of these legislations are useful and good, but they created multiple agencies without a co-ordinating body. This ultimately led to the need for strengthening the local bodies like municipalities and corporations. As per the 74th Constitutional Amendment Act 1992 elections to municipalities and corporations should be held at regular intervals of five years, the finance commissions would review financial positions and committees should be constituted at ward, district and metropolitan levels. Thus this amendment facilitated peoples participation in planning and development.

B. Important Committees

The following committees had significant impact on the urban planning legislation in India.

1. **Barlow Committee:** In 1937 a Royal Commission was set-up under the chairmanship of Barlow to enquire into the distribution of industrial population and the social, economic and strategic disadvantages arising from the concentration of industry and working people in large built-up areas. The commission report published in 1940 contained recommendations for redevelopment and dispersal of population from the congested areas. This led to balanced industrial employment throughout Great Britain, and the establishment of a national authority to deal with these matters.
2. **Scott Committee:** The Scott Committee report in 1942, brought to light that good agricultural land represented a literally priceless asset, unlike most other factors of production. Once lost it was lost for good. Therefore, the report argued that the country should set up a planning system embracing the countryside as well as the town. This system should regard it as a first duty to preserve agricultural land. The concept of green belt started coming up after this report.
3. **Uthwall Committee:** The Uthwall Committee report in 1942 went on compensation and betterment aspects. It has two aspects, one is the problem of compensation and the other is betterment levy. The committee suggested that when a public body buys a land compulsarily, it should pay the current market value. But the complication is that the public body unlike most private buyers, might have helped to increase the land value it has to pay for. The word for this is 'betterment'. The betterment is charged to those who are beneficiaries of the development scheme taken by the planning authorities. The people affected by the scheme are given compensation.

C. IDSMT Scheme

The IDSMT scheme had significant impact on the planning and development of urban areas. During the sixth plan (1980-85) Government. of India introduced the 'Integrated Development of Small and Medium Towns (IDSMT)' scheme. Towns with population upto one lakh on the basis of 1971 Census were included for central loan assistance under this scheme. The scheme is aimed at increasing the growth rate of small and medium towns. This will enable them to act as growth and service centres for the surrounding region to check migration of rural population to the larger cities. Under the scheme, Govt of India advances a sum to each town and a matching amount is provided by the state Government. besides the share of the local agencies. In addition to the centrally sponsored schemes, development of small and medium towns includes state sector schemes to ensure integrated development of the various programmes at the local town level by various agencies. Following broad guidelines were given.

1) Components eligible for central assistance on matching basis

1. Land acquisition and development for residential schemes, and sites and services.
2. Traffic and Transportation for construction of roads and improvement of existing roads.
3. Development of mandies and markets, industrial estates and other services for the benefit of agriculture and rural development in the hinterland.

2) Components from state and local funds, which must form part of the integrated schemes.

1. Slum improvement, urban renewal and small scale employment generation activities.
2. Providing medical and health facilities.
3. Low-cost schemes of water supply, sewerage and drainage.
4. Parks and Playgrounds.

The IDSMT scheme was revised in the Eighth Plan (1992-97) with special emphasis to strengthen the economic base of the towns integrating them with the surrounding regions. The funding is split among Centre, State, HUDCO and other agencies and financial institutions. Towns upto the size of three lakhs population were included in the scheme.

D. Important sections of The Land Acquisition Act 1894:

***Section 4:** The proceedings for land acquisition commence with a preliminary notification by the Government. under section 4(1) which is issued, when it appears to the Government. that land in any locality is needed or likely to be needed for a public purpose. It is to be published in the official gazette. The Collector should give public notice of the substance of the notification at convenient places in the concerned locality. Subsequent to this notification, Government. officials can carry out survey of the land in question by giving a minimum 7 days notice to the occupier of any building or garden on the land in question.

***Section 5:** The compensation for any damage resulting from such survey is payable and the decision of the Collector on the amount payable is final.

***Section 5(A):** The next stage in the process is the hearing of objections against the proposed acquisition. Any interested person may within 30 days of the issue of notification file objections with the Collector against the acquisition. The Collector is to provide to the objector fair hearing either in person or by lawyer. After hearing the objections and making any enquiry, the Collector is required to make a report in respect of the land along with his recommendations on the objections. The decision of the Government on the objections is final.

***Section 6:** On considering the Collectors report if the Government is satisfied that the land is needed for a public purpose or for a company, a declaration to that effect is made by the Government. Different declarations will be made for different pieces of land. However, no declaration is to be made after the expiry of 3 years from the date of publication of the notification under section 4(1). The declaration has to give particulars for identifying the land by location or area and the purpose for which it is needed. This declaration is conclusive evidence that land is needed for a public purpose or for a company.

***Section 7:** After the declaration, the Collector has to take order for acquisition.

***Section 8:** Land should be marked out, measured and planned.

***Section 9:** After the declaration, the Collector notifies individually and publicly that the Government intends to take possession of the land and that claims for compensation may be filed with him by all persons interested in the land within 15 days.

***Section 11:** The Collector is then to hold an enquiry and make an award as to the compensation payable for the land acquired. Such an award is final subject to the fact that if any person requires the Collector to refer the matter to the court, he has to refer it.

***Section 12:** The Government. can take possession of the land on the award having made by the Collector and it is not necessary to wait for the decision of the court.

***Section 13:** Adjournment of enquiry.

***Section 14:** Power to summon and enforce attendance of witnesses and production of documents.

***Section 15:** Matters to be considered and neglected.

***Section 16:** Power to take possession.

***Section 17:** It empowers the Government. to expedite the procedure for acquisition in times of urgency. In the case of 'arable or waste land', when the urgency of the situation so demands, the Government. may direct that the stage of hearing of objections under section 5(A) need not be undergone.

In such a situation, the notification under section-6 may follow the notification under section-4 almost simultaneously without the intermediate stage of hearing objections under section 5(A). The Collector can take possession of the land without making any award during urgency.

***Section 18:** Reference to the court.

***Section 19:** The Collectors statement to the court.

***Section 20:** Service of notice.

***Section 21:** Restriction on scope of proceedings.

***Section 22:** Proceedings to be in open court.

***Section 23:** The following matters are to be considered in determining compensation.

1. Market value of the land at the date of publication.
2. The damage sustained by reason of standing crops etc.,
3. The damage sustained by reason of severing such land from his other land.
4. The damage sustained injuriously affecting his other property.
5. Change of residence or business charges should be paid.

Under the act, compensation is the market value of the land on the date of publication of the preliminary notification subject to certain conditions for various damages and a 15% solatium on the market value for the compulsory acquisition of land.

***Section 24:** The following matters are to be neglected in determining compensation.

1. Degree of urgency which has led to the acquisition.

2. Disinclination of the person to part with the land.

***Section 25:** Rules for the amount of compensation.

***Section 26:** Form of awards.

***Section 27:** Costs

***Section 28:** The Collector may be directed to pay interest on excess compensation.

***Section 31:** Payment of compensation or deposit of same in the court.

***Section 33:** Investment of money deposited in other cases.

***Section 34:** Payment of interest.

***Section 35:** Temporary occupation of waste or arable land.

***Section 36:** Power to enter and take possession and compensation on restoration.

***Section 37:** Difference to the condition of land.

***Section 38 to 48:** The act also empowers the Government. to acquire land for companies at their cost for purposes as specified and such acquisitions shall follow sections 38 to 44(B) in the act. No land will be acquired for the company unless the previous consent of the Government. has been obtained and an agreement in terms of section 41 has been executed by the company.

***Section 49:** Acquisition of part of house or building.

The Land Acquisition Act 1894, being a preconstitutional act, legislation was not required to satisfy the requirements of the constitutional provisions. It was enacted at a time when large scale acquisitions were not visualised by the legislature. Under the constitution 'Acquisition and Requisitioning' of property is placed in the concurrent list. In pursuance of this power, some states have enacted separate self-contained acquisition laws for application within their respective jurisdictions.

***25th Amendment to the Act:** Under this amendment the expression 'compensation' in article 31 was substituted by the term 'amount'. In other words, the amendment is directed to bar the jurisdiction of the court in the matters relating to compulsory acquisition of private property with a view to accelerate the pace of progress by rapid implementation.

E. Case study 1: Karnataka Town & Country Planning Act 1961.

The Karnataka Town & Country Planning Act 1961 is one of the oldest acts. Many of the aspects in the act are similar in other states, so it would be useful to study the important contents of the act.

1. Declaration of the local planning area by the State Government. and define the limits of such areas. Any disputes regarding amalgamation and finance will be decided by the State Government. after consulting the Board, Planning Authority and the concerned authorities.
2. Constitution of the Planning Authority after the declaration of the planning area. It shall be a corporate body. It shall have power to acquire, hold and dispose of the property under its control as per the act.
3. Planning Authority shall consist the following members.
   (a). Chairman appointed by the State Government.
   (b). Town Planning Officer appointed by the State Government.
   (c). Representatives of local bodies. One representative from each local authority nominated by the respective local authorities from among the members. The number should not exceed five.
   (d). Three other members appointed by the State Government. one of them may be appointed as Vice-Chairman.
4. It should prepare the present landuse map not later than two years after the notification from the State Government. A copy should be sent to the Director and another copy should be displayed for public information. An appeal from the public should be made to the prescribed Planning Authority within thirty days for any entry or correction or reentry of landuse.
5. Every Planning Authority not later than 2 years after its declaration of the planning area prepare and publish in the prescribed manner the Outline Development Plan (ODP) for such area a d submit to the State Government for approval through the Director. If it is not prepared within the specified period, the State Government may direct the Director to prepare and publish the ODP and recover the costs from the concerned Planning Authority. A copy of the ODP should be sent to the State Government through the Director and one copy shall be kept open for inspection by the public at the office of the Planning Authority.
6. Planning Authority shall declare the intention of making ODP in the official gazette inviting public suggestions within 2 months from the date of publication and also send a copy to the State Government. Such notification is not necessary if the

Director takes up the work. The Planning Authority can carry out surveys for the preparation of ODP and any such survey should be done after giving notice to the occupier.

7. Contents of the Outline Development Plan (ODP)
   (a). General landuse plan and zoning of landuse like residential, commercial, industrial etc.
   (b). Proposals for roads and highways.
   (c). Proposals for reservation of land for the purposes of Union, State and Local bodies or any established body by law in India.
   (d). Proposals for areas of special control and development control regulations like building line, FAR, architectural conservation etc.,
   (e). Such other proposals for public or other purposes as proposed by the Planning Authority from time to time.

   Upto 1 month after the publication of ODP public comments can be invited. It should get the approval of the State Government. through the Director and should be permanently displayed in the office. Immediately after the approval the ODP becomes statutory for implementation.
8. Permission for development of building and land should get the approval of the Planning Authority. The applicant should be intimated within 3 months, otherwise it is deemed to have been granted.
9. Any owner whose land has become incapable of reasonable beneficial use can request the Planning Authority to acquire the land. The Authority does so under genuine considerations in consultation with the State Government through the Director and acquires the land as per the Land Acquisition Act 1894.
10. For development of land, the owner or party should submit a copy of the proposal to the Planning Authority for sanction. The Planning Authority can sanction with or without modifications or refuse subject to the conditions of the Act. If any person does any work in contravention, the Planning Authority can stop after the enquiry and remove or pull down or restore land to its previous use. The concerned person should pay the expenses.
11. In the opinion of the Planning Authority that permission for a change in the use or development of any land or building can yield a better income to the owner may levy a prescribed fee not exceeding 1/3rd of the estimated increase in the value of the land. The affected party can appeal to the District court for final

decision if not satisfied by the decision of the Planning Authority.

12. Comprehensive Development Plan (CDP) shall be prepared not later than 3 years after the ODP publication. It should be submitted to the State Government. for approval through the Director. If it is not prepared within the specified period, the State Government. may direct the Director to prepare and publish the CDP and recover the costs from the concerned Planning Authority. A copy of the CDP should be sent to the State Government. through the Director and one copy shall be kept open for inspection by the public at the office of the Planning Authority. Surveys for the preparation of the CDP and related work can be carried out after giving notice to the occupier.

13. Contents of the Comprehensive Development Plan (CDP)
    (a). Comprehensive zoning regulations.
    (b). Complete street pattern indicating major roads, highways, traffic circulation etc.,
    (c). Areas reserved for agriculture, parks, playgrounds, public buildings etc., and areas reserved for such other purposes for new civic development.
    (d). Major road improvements.
    (e). Areas for new housing.
    (f). New areas earmarked for future development and expansion.
    (g). Stages by which the plan should be carried.

The CDP will supercede ODP. CDP will come into effect immediately after the State Government. gives approval. The CDP will be revised every 5 years.

14. Preparation of town planning schemes by the Planning Authority
    (a). Can make town planning schemes within the framework of CDP or ODP. It may make provision for laying or relaying of land, layout of new roads, streets, construction, alteration and removal, drainage, lighting, water supply etc.
    (b). They have the power to enter for survey and marking out land for the purpose.
    (c). After the intention to make a scheme, it shall be declared and published and send copy to the State Government. through the Director within 21 days. A copy should be kept

open for public exhibition.

(d). The draft town planning scheme shall contain the area, ownership, the extent of alterations in the boundary, details of the scheme, laying or relaying of the land and other particulars.

(e). Upto 1 month after the publication of the draft scheme, objections will be heard and considered. Then it will be submitted to the State Government. Within 6 months after submission the State Government will sanction the scheme with or without modifications.

(f). Joint planning schemes can be proposed in the case of contiguous areas.

15. The sources of finances include grants and loans by the State Government, and other fees and charges of the Planning Authority. The Planning Authority should maintain accounts and audit regularly as per the rules.

F. Case study 2: Town & Country Planning Act of U.K. 1971

The Town & Country Planning Act of United Kingdom in 1971 is unique in its approach to solving the urban problems. It would be extremely useful to have an understanding of this Act because most of the legislations in India are similar to Great Britain. In India also, we may slowly adopt similar guidelines for urban planning and development.

The purpose of this Act is to present policies and proposals for the development and other use of land in an area. While the focus of the plan like 1962 Act, is on physical development but policies and proposals are not simply to be expressed in landuse terms. A range of other considerations have been brought into the Development Plan. They are spatially integrated to landuse and transportation planning, measures for improving the physical environment, the implementation of regional planning, capital resource availability and other social considerations. Development Plan consists of Structure Plans and Local Plans.

1. **Structure Plans:** It consists of a written statement and key diagram. It may incorporate a supplementary regulation and plan for urban areas.
2. **Local Plans:** It consists proposals, maps and written statements for areas within the Structure Plan. Local Plans could be District Plans, Action Area Plans and Subject Plans.

The emphasis is more on the development of ideas of corporate policy making, frequently called as corporate planning. It represents an attempt to strengthen the policy making and review function throughout the authority and put policy on a more corporate, less departmental, sector or service basis.

POLICY FRAMEWORK

Structure Plans

Programmes (topic by topic) | Local Plans (area by area)

Another concept is that of a community plan. It is a policy statement embracing all kinds of Government control in the community including the local authorities powers and services, and policies of local, central and public authorities.

1. **Structure Plan:** The Structure Plan will cover the whole or substantial part of the authority's area. It consists of a written statement, key diagram, illustrations or descriptive matter explaining or illustrating the proposals in the plan, and the Secretary of States notice of approval of the plan.
   The written statement fulfills 5 main functions as policy statement.
   (a). **Interpreting national and regional policies:** Local authority policy may be set in regional development policies, co-operatively between local and central governments. It is given expression in an adopted regional strategy. Both national and regional policies will be generalised but specific expression is given in relation to local circumstances.
   (b). **Stating objectives and strategic policy:** A statement of local authority political objectives for the area. The strategic policies for environmental change adopted for these objectives should be stated.
   (c). **Stating policy norms for regulatory decisions:** Some important executive decisions and actions will derive guidance directly from the Structure Plan in response to strategic issues. The Structure Plan contains some direct expressions of desired relations for these issues to be secured by the local authorities.
   (d). **Providing a framework for detailed policy statements:** The Structure Plan can indicate the kinds of topics or areas

for which detailed policies under Local Plans and Programmes will be needed, and the relationship between these and the strategic policies.

(e). **Bringing major issues and policies before the public and the Secretary of State:** The opportunities for participation and objection are provided with Structure Plans and the necessity of obtaining approval from the higher authority of the Secretary of State for the Environment. It brings the authority's perception of environmental issues and their policies before the public for debate and independent assessment.

All the provisions recognise that administrative areas may not be the most appropriate areas for expressing planning policy. They may be better related to parts only of an administrative area or to the area of two or more planning authorities. In general terms the basic areal unit of the Structure Plan is most usefully the subregion. It is an area of closely related policies on functional and locational issues including transport policy where it is not possible to demarcate clearly, greater reliance must be placed on the regional context of the plan or on the development of an agreed subregional framework.

The total field of environmental policy embraces all five policy fields of infrastructure, function, environmental quality, location and movement, and rate of change. Policy matters within this field are appropriate to the Structure Plan. The Structure Plan policy broadly expresses for a period of 20 years ahead, but without a fixed end date applicable to all its policies.

(f). **Programmes:** One of the main functions of the Structure Plan is to provide a framework for the further development of more detailed policy in other kinds of policy statements. The distinction between Local Plans and Programmes in the environmental policy are two fold. Firstly, while Local Plans relate essentially to a sub-area expressing policy on a range of topics. Programmes are concerned with one topic throughout the whole area of the local authority. The former has an areal basis, the later a topical basis. The second distinction is more clear, Local Plans are statutory policy statements whereas Programmes are non-statutory.

Functions of Programmes:

(a). **Applying the strategy of the Structure Plan:** The Structure Plans comprehensive statement of objectives and strategic environmental policy will have clear implications for particular programmes.

(b). **Stating detailed programme area policies:** In each Programme a more detailed statement of policy will be developed for that particular topic.

(c). **Detailed resource implications of programme area policy:** The framework of programme areas and the policy statements for them shall be linked with resource management, financial, manpower and annual budgeting.

The preparation of Programmes is done either by County or District depending upon the programme areas.

2. **Local plans:** The Local Plan, with the exception of the Subject Plan, is a comprehensive policy statement for a restricted area. Local Plans are predominantly the concern of the districts. Authority to prepare Local Plans will rest with both counties and district. An agreement known as development plan scheme must be reached between them regarding their respective responsibilities.

(a) **Plan Area:** Local Plans are for areas smaller than those covered by Structure Plans. There is no statutory obligation or practical necessity for a complete coverage of the Structure Plan area by subsequent Local Plans.

The District Plan intended as a statement of comprehensive policy for relatively large areas, usually where change will take place in a peacemeal fashion over a long period of time. The Action Area Plan is intended as a statement of comprehensive policy for intensive change over a short period of time. The Subject Plan is concerned with a particular class of change and extends spatially as far as that class does.

Example

**District Plan* - Town centre : an inner housing area renewal etc.,

**Action Area Plan* - A new highway development, a country park, expansion of shopping centre etc.,

**Subject Plan* - Land reclamation project, landscaping motorway corridor or etc.

(b) **District Plans:** District Plans are intended as comprehensive policy statements embracing all the topics with which planning policy is concerned. The larger plan areas and longer time spans of the District Plan provide a means of expressing policy statements.

Thus a District Plan for a town would likely to contain policies relating to the functions of that settlement, particularly the changes in employment chances envisaged there. Its impact on the local economy and its place in the settlement hierarchy as envisaged in the Structure Plan. Most District Plans contain policies related to its infrastructure, size, structure and the housing stock.

Districts will also be large enough for significant locational changes. As a policy statement it must present the local issues and policies to the public in a meaningful way and serve as a basic guide to all issues arising from environmental change within the district.

Like Action Area Plans, they are detailed tactical policy statements concerned with fairly specific locations, activities, attributes and times. A proposal map is shown with the boundary of the district local authority proposals. This would be accompanied by a written statement of policies. District Plan policies will be less specific than Action Area Plans because of lesser importance of the authority's promotional role and the greater time scale.

(c). **Action Area Plans:** Action areas are intended to serve as comprehensive policy statements for areas of intensive environmental change. They may be concerned with any of the matters specified in the regulations like population, employment, housing, transportation, industry, commerce etc.,

Action Area Plan can be for the development of a major shopping centre on a virgin site, but the policy decision should be in the Structure Plan. Action Area Plan should deal essentially the changes in infrastructure and the environmental quality of the area. It gives clear amounts and qualities of accommodation to be provided and also the kind of external environment created by the development. Action Area Plans are prepared for the short and medium terms of 5 or 10 years only. They are largely concerned with policies of physical development in which the local authority has got a major role. The basic document contains the proposals map marking the boundaries of the area and the local authority proposals. This will be accompanied by a written statement explaining how it will be carried out.

(d) **Subject Plans:** The Subject Plan is essentially for bringing the characteristics of development plans to topics of limited areal extent.

For example, landscaping of a motorway corridor or the recreational use of a river valley. The need to put them under the Subject Plans has two main reasons. One, the statutory rights of participation and objection are accorded to the community. Secondly, their status within a formally adopted Subject Plan might be comparatively greater. The choice depends largely on the policy.

g) Existing Urban Planning Acts in India

S. No.	State	Name of the Act	Year of Enactment
1.	Andhra Pradesh	Andhra Pradesh Urban Areas (Development) Act	1975
2.	Assam	The Assam Town and Country Act	1959 as amended in 1985
3.	Bihar	Bihar Town Planning and Improvement Trust Act	1951
4.	Goa	Goa, Daman and Diu Town & Country Planning Act	1976
5.	Gujarat	Gujarat Town Planning and Urban Development Act	1976
6.	Haryana	(i) Punjab Scheduled Roads and Controlled Areas Restriction of unregulated Development Act	1963
		(ii) Haryana Urban Development Authority Act.	1971
7.	Himachal Pradesh	Himachal Pradesh Town and Country Planning Act	1977
8.	Jammu & Kashmir	(i) J & K Town Planning Act	1963
		(ii) J & K Development Act	1970
9.	Karnataka	(i) Karnataka Town and Country Planning Act	1964
		(ii) Bangalore Development Authority Act	1976
		(iii) Bangalore Metropolitan Regional Development Authority Act	1985
		(iv) Karnataka Urban Development Authority Act	1987

(Contd.)

10.	Kerala	(i) The Travancore Town and Country Planning Act	1945 as amended in1947 and 1975
		(ii) The Travancore Town Planning Regulations	1932 as amended in 1960
		(iii) The Madras Town Planning Act	1920 as amended in 1971
11.	Madhya Pradesh	Madhya Pradesh Nagar Tatha Gram Nivesh Adhiniyam	1973
12.	Maharashtra	(i) Maharashtra Regional and Town Planning Act	1966 as modified upto 1988
		(ii) BMRDA Act	1975
		(iii) MHADA Act	1976
		(iv) Maharashtra (Urban Areas) Preservation of Trees Act	1975
13.	Manipur	Manipur Town and Country Planning Act	1975
14.	Meghalaya	The Assam Town and Country Planning Act	1959 has been extended to Meghalaya w.e.f. Jan., 1989
15.	Mizoram	The Mizoram Urban and Regional Development Act	1990
16.	Nagaland	The Nagaland Town and Country Planning Act	1966
17.	Orissa	(i) The Orissa Town Planning and Improvement Trust Act	1956 as amended in 1976
		(ii) Orissa Development Authority Act	1982
18.	Punjab	(i) Punjab Town Improvement Act	1992
		(ii) Punjab Scheduled Roads and Controlled Areas (Restriction of Unregulated Development Act	1963
19.	Rajasthan	Rajasthan Urban Improvement Act	1959 as amended in 1991
20.	Sikkim	(i) Gangtok Municipal Corporation Act	1975
		(ii) Bazar Committee Act	1969
21.	Tamil Nadu	The Tamil Nadu Town and Country Planning Act	1971
22.	Tripura	The Tripura Town and Country Planning Act	1975

(*Contd.*)

23.	Uttar Pradesh	Uttar Pradesh Urban Planning and Development Act	1973
24.	West Bengal	Town and Country Planning Act	1979
Union Territories			
1.	Chandigarh	(i) Capital of Punjab (Development and Regulation) Act	1952
		(ii) Punjab New Capital (Periphery) Control Act	1952
		(iii) Chandigarh Trees Preservation Order	1952
2.	Dadra and Nagar Haveli	The Goa, Daman and Diu Town and Country Planning Act	1974 extended by a notification of the Ministry of Home Affairs
3.	Daman and Diu	The Goa, Daman and Diu Town and Country Planning Act	1974
4.	Delhi	The Delhi Development Act	1957
5.	Pondicherry	The Pondicherry Town and Country Planning Act.	1969

(*Source*: Institute of Town Planners, India Journal, June 1993.)

Model Questions

1. Describe the evolution of urban planning legislation in India.
2. What is the importance of the following committees?
   a) Barlow committee
   b) Scott committee
   c) Uthwall committee
3. What is IDSMT scheme?
4. Describe some of the important sections of The Land Acquisition Act 1894.
5. What are the major laws in Karnataka Town & Country Planning Act 1961?
6. What is the novelty of Town & Country Planning Act of UK 1971?
7. Describe the nature of Structure Plans and Local Plans in the Town & Country Planning Act of UK 1971.

6

Development Plan

(A) The Need

A human settlement is a living organism. It has an origin, growth, decay and regrowth. It is not a static but dynamic entity. The settlement is subject to various types of forces like physical, social, economic and political, which influence its form and structure. It is necessary to channelise these forces in a planned manner to create the total environment; which is healthy, efficient and satisfying for working, living and recreation. The development plan is an instrument to achieve these objectives.

The city is a corporate entity. The local government of the city has a great deal of influence on the nature, extent and manner of development of the city. The various utilities, services and facilities provided by the Centre, State and Local Governments affect the urban environment, The local government has to co-ordinate the various decisions which affect the physical development of the community. The local government needs some technical guidelines in making its decisions. It requires a legal and technical instrument for long-term and short-term policies, programmes and strategies for the orderly development of the community. The Development plan provides such an instrument.

(B) Goals and Objectives

It is basically a policy document. It provides the basis for a programme to accomplish certain aims and objectives, and to satisfy the aspirations of the community. The Plan should aim:

1. To create an environment which is functional, efficient, healthy and aesthetically satisfying for human activities.
2. To promote the larger interests of the community as a whole.
3. To serve as a policy framework to fulfill the needs and

aspirations of the community.

4. To co-ordinate the physical, economic, social and political forces that govern the structure of the community and the technical means to regulate it.
5. To formulate long-term and short-term action programmes with a view to injecting long-term considerations into short-term actions.

(C) Scope and Contents

There seems to be no agreement among the planners regarding the scope of the Development Plan, whether it should encompass all aspects of the community and its development and redevelopment or it should be confining itself only to those aspects which have a direct bearing on physical development. However, a broader scope for planning seems to be inevitable and a stress on inter-disciplinary approach is necessary.

The basic elements of a Development Plan are:

Landuse: The Development Plan should indicate areas designated for residential, commercial, industrial, socio-cultural, recreational, administrative and other uses.

2. **Circulation**: The roads, streets, railways, waterways, airways, terminal facilities, transit systems etc., for the movement of people, goods and services.
3. **Utilities, services and facilities**: The Development Plan indicates the desirable location, size and other particulars regarding public utilities like water supply, sewerage and power, municipal services like transport and fire fighting and community facilities like education, health and recreation.
4. **Civic design**: The Development Plan should depict the design of important elements in the city such as civic centre, the central business district, shopping centres and cultural areas. The civic design proposals should improve the aesthetic quality of the urban space.
5. **Open Spaces**: The Development Plan indicates the location and extent of desirable open spaces for parks, playgrounds, stadiums, gardens, crematoria etc.
6. **Special problems**: Cities do not have identical problems. By virtue of its location, size, structure and form each community has some special problems and unique characteristics of its own. The Development Plan should highlight the distinctive features and suggest solutions to the special problems.

(D) Procedure for preparation

The preparation of a Development Plan takes considerable time ranging from about a year for a small town to about two to three years in case of a medium-size town. The actual period will depend upon, the area and size of the community, the staff and funds available. 'Interim Development Plan' is prepared to avoid land speculation and undesirable developments during the initial period, when the Development Plan is under preparation.

There are several methods suggested for getting the plan prepared. Some of the methods normally followed for the preparation are :

1. **Planning department of the local government**: Some belive that the planning department of the local government is best suited to prepare the plan as it is familiar with the problems and potentials of its community. It has the extra advantage of combining both plan making and plan implementing functions.
2. **Specialised planning organisation**: Some feel that the plan should not be prepared and also executed by the same organisation to avoid preconceived ideas and prejudices. They also fear that the local body cannot effectively resist local pressure from vested interests. They suggest that a specialised and independent 'Planning Authority' should prepare the plan.
3. **A Consultant**: Many cities do not have the capacity to undertake the complex task of preparing a plan. They find it convenient to engage a consultant to prepare the plan within the broad framework of policies and guidelines determined by the concerned authority.
4. **State Town Planning Department**: In most developing countries the Town Planning Department of the State Government prepares the plan for the Planning Authority.

There are several other ways of getting the plan prepared. Whatever may be the method, the importance of securing active public participation in all stages of the planning process indicate the desirability of making the local government serve as an instrument of planning.

(E) Plan Implementation

Plan making and plan implementation are inseparable. The tools for the realisation of the plan should be built into the plan as integral parts of the process of planning. Several cities have more than one plan but few of them are systematically implemented. The failure of the plan is often due to the lack of support in the form of appropritate land policies and town planning legislation. Some of the plans have not been backed by zoning regulations, improved building bye-laws, sub-division regulations, fiscal programmes and long-term budgets.

(F) Public Participation

The success of a plan depends on the active participation and co-operation of the people. Planning agencies have a vital concern with citizen reaction to planning proposals because ultimately the plans are realised by the people through their various building activities. A wide range of voluntary organisations and institutions such as youth clubs, colony associations, chambers of commerce, womens councils and professional bodies may be involved in the planning process. The mass-media such as newspapers, journals, radio, television and cinema can be effective in educating the public on civic problems and planning. Town planning exhibitions can also serve as a useful means of communicating planning ideas and stimulating public interest. Well presented monographs, booklets, handouts, pamphlets, manuals, guides etc., go a long way in stimulating civic interest in planning.

(G) General Guidelines of Development Plan

1. Historical setting

(a) The origin and growth of the city.
(b) Significant landmarks in its evolution.
(c) The historical and cultural heritage of the people and their values, attitudes and aspirations.

2. The land

(a) The city in the regional, state and national contexts.
(b) The city in its geographical setting. Location, terrain, vegetation, rainfall, temperature, humidity and wind direction and velocity.
(c) Physical extent of the city and its urban form.
(d) The geological conditions, nature of soils and building materials available locally.

3. The people

(a) Trends in the growth of population of the city.
(b) Present population characteristics like age structure, sex ratio, literacy, education levels, religious sects, occupation pattern, employment, wages, vital statistics, marriage and fertility rates.

(c) Family and household size.
(d) Trends in the migration to and from the city, its causes and consequences.
(e) Population projections, demographic characteristics and density pattern.

4. Physical setting

(a) The extent of government and private land; which is vacant, developed and developable.
(b) Present landuse and its analysis for various uses like residential, commercial, industrial, administrative, recreational, roads etc.
(c) The structure of the central area of the city, its problems and potentials.
(d) Assessment of future land requirements of the city and its land values.
(e) The housing situation in the city. The existing housing stock, its quantitative and qualitative assessment. Types of dwellings, size, occupation ratio, structural condition, repair and maintenance, type of construction, local building materials, architectural design, ownership, rents and taxes, future housing needs.
(f) Slum improvement, its scope and limitations.
(g) Urban image, its aesthetics and landscape.

5. Physical infrastructure

(a) *Traffic and Transportation system:*

1. The existing network of roads and streets in the city, its functional classification, hierarchy, road geometry etc.
2. Existing number of vehicles in the city, its types and trends.
3. Movement of people, goods and services. Intra-city and inter-city flow of passengers. Goods traffic by highways and railways. Correlation between landuse and traffic.
4. Flow of vehicular traffic, traffic volume, composition, directions, speed and other variables.
5. Origin-Destination surveys, delays and accident surveys.
6. Parking survey, demands, indices, deficiencies, projections etc.
7. Mass transportation availability in the city.
8. Traffic regulation and control. Existing situation and improvements
9. Terminal facilities like motor parks, bus depots, railway stations etc.

10. Projection of traffic volumes for the next 20 years.
11. Proposals to impove road geometry, traffic flow and outline circulation plan.

(b) *Water Supply*

1. The sources of water, its quantity, quality, per capita consumption, demand, supply and deficiency.
2. Water filtration, storage and distribution system.
3. Estimation of future requirements of water for civic, domestic, commercial and industrial purposes.

(c) *Drainage, sewerage and solid waste disposal:*

1. Existing drains, septic tanks, gradients, flow, outfall points, composition of sullage, water pollution etc.
2. Solid wastes both organic and inorganic, dumping grounds etc.,
3. Need for comprehensive sewerage scheme.

(d) *Others*

1. Electricity system, telephone system, fire fighting system, post and telegraph system etc.

6. Social infrastructure:

(a) *Education facilities:*

1. Existing schools, colleges and other educational institutions in the city. Their types, numbers, locations, spatial and structural conditions, sphere of influence, facilities and deficiencies.
2. Correlation between population, density and number of existing schools.
3. Future requirements of education facilities and desirable locations.
4. Adult literacy.

(b) *Health facilities:*

1. Common ailments in the city and the surrounding area. Number of in-patients and others treated for various ailments.
2. Existing medical and health hospitals, clinics and nursing homes. Their types, numbers, locations, condition of sites, buildings, land availability for present and future needs, accessibility and deficiencies.
3. Estimation of the future need and proposals.

4. Medical facilities for specialised treatments such as T.B, leprosy, cardiology and other infections diseases.
5. Availability of veterinary hospitals and their need.

(c) *Recreation facilities:*

1. Present status of parks, playgrounds and other open spaces, clubs, hotels, cinema halls, auditoriums, community centres, fairs and festival grounds. Their location, size, quality, utilisation and other related issues.
2. Needs for the next 20 years and location with respect to other landuse elements.

(d) *Cultural facilities:*

1. Existing libraries, museums, churches, mosques and other sociocultural institutions. Their number, location, accessibility, utilisation and patronage.
2. Present deficiencies, future needs and location with respect to residential and other areas.

7. Economic base

(a) *Industrial base*

1. Existing manufacturing industries, classification, employment, power, inputs, performance, location, access, use of water and power. Industrial effluents like smoke, dust, heat, noise, odour vibration and glare.
2. Small scale industries, handicrafts and other service industries.
3. Sites for location of new industries in future and land requirement

(b) *Commercial base*

1. Retail and wholesale markets in the city, commodities, turnover, location, site and building conditions and service areas.
2. Commercial offices.
3. Land requirement for the future new markets and improvement of existing markets.
4. Marketing centres and co-operative stores.

(c) *Tax base*

1. The local bodies and their tax receipts, finances and public expenditure.

(d) *Agriculture, forestry and fishery base:*

1. Contribution of agriculture, forestry and fishery as primary occupations to the gross product. Location and extent of agricultural fields. Forest reservations. Fish ponds and their conservation, development and utilisation. Supply of food and fuel to the city.

8. Implementation:

(a) *Financial implications:* Fiscal programming and long-term budgeting for the realisation of the plan. Phasing the plan priorities in the implementation of the plan. Sources of finance for implementing the plan.

(b) *Legal implications:* Legal basis for preparation and enforcement of the plan. Development control, zoning and sub-division regulations and building bye-laws.

(c) *Planning administration:* The existing administrative set-up for Town & Country Planning at the state and local levels. The city Planning Authority and its set-up, status, functions and limitations. Administrative machinery needs for implementing the Development Plan.

(d) *Public participation:* Public participation methods in the preparation and implementation of the plan at all stages.

H) Important Measures in Development Plan

The following important measures are taken into consideration in the preparation of the Development Plan.

1. Zoning regulations
2. Density of population
3. Sub-division regulations
4. Floor area ratio (FAR)

1. Zoning regulations

The zoning regulations and their administration is a major tool in carrying out the landuse part of the Development Plan. In order to promote public health, safety and general moral and social welfare of the community, it is essential to regulate the use of land and buildings. This is to ensure that the most appropriate, economical and healthy development of the city takes place as per the landuse plan. For this purposes, the city is divided into a number of 'use zones' such as residential, commercial, industrial, recreational etc. Each use-zone has its special regulations because a single set of regulations cannot be applied to the entire city because each zone varies in character and functions. In this respect, zoning regulations differ from building codes. Building codes are applicable uniformly to all land or building of similar use, wherever they may be located whereas zoning regulations are not to be used for nuisance control and human segregations into income or caste groups for certain areas.

The preparation of zonal development plans for new areas is comparatively easy than old and built-up areas of the city, where detailed study and data collection are required. Zonal Development plans for the old areas should form part of a comprehensive urban renewal and redevelopment programme. In the meantime, community facilities may be provided on an adhoc basis. It is important to improve the circulation in the older parts of the city. Slum improvement is more sensible than demolition and redevelopment.

Zoning protects residential areas from the harmful effects of commercial and industrial uses while promoting business and industry by ensuring planned and orderly development. The open spaces around the building provide adequate light, air, fire protection etc. It prevents over-crowding in buildings and continued adequacy of water, sewerage, transportation, schools, parks and other facilities. It does not prohibit uses of lands and buildings which were legally established before the zoning regulations are enforced. If these uses are contrary to the regulations in a particular use zone and would not be allowed as new uses, they are termed as 'non-conforming' uses.

(a) *Non-conforming uses:* The provision regarding non-conforming uses comes into effect with respect to industrial and other landuses mentioned. For the rest of the non-conforming uses the provisions will come into effect only after the preparation of the zonal development plans because they determine the siting of local facilities like shops etc. All existing places of worship and burial grounds shall not be considered as non-conforming uses.

(b) *Discontinuance of non-conforming uses:* Industrial non-conforming uses are those that do not conform to the landuse shown in the Development Plan. They will have to be shifted in gradual stages in industrial areas earmarked in the plan. In allocating new industrial sites, the demands of the non-conforming uses will have to be given priorities by the authorities for expediting the shifting. This can be in the shape of providing extra land needed for expansion by the industry at the new site allowing the present owners to develop the land from which they are shifting in accordance with the landuse by providing loans etc. It should also be noted that the shifting of industry according to the plan will be possible only if suitable land for the purpose is available.

The non-conforming industries should be given suitable time to shift from their present site. A time schedule should be worked out for their shifting. This process must be governed by the fact that there should be minimum amount of production and the workers should not be put to undue hardship. In the case of industrial non-conforming uses, additions to the building or machinery should not be allowed but the use of existing machinery and building for a different line of manufacture may be permitted provided it is not noxious.

(c) *Contents of the Zonal Development Plan:* The Zonal Development plans shall show the broad outlines of the following:

1. Appropriate boundaries of the neighbourhoods with gross residential density.
2. Major internal roads and services.
3. Community centres.
4. Appropriate location of high schools and primary schools.
5. Neighbourhood parks.

The pattern of self-contained Planning Division is conceived from bottom to top. The lowest tier in the urban complex will be the 'Housing Cluster' containing 750 to 1000 population. These clusters roughly correspond to the traditional 'Mohallas' found in Indian cities and towns. It will have as its nuclues a nursery school with a tot-lot. These housing clusters are grouped around a primary school and convenience stores with a small park will form a 'Residential unit' containing a population of between 3500 to 5000 people. However, for wider range of community activities the 'Residential Planning Area' of 12000 to 15000 population containing nearly 3000 families should be planned. It will have for its focal point a high school, a community hall with adequate neighbourhood shopping for the day-to-day needs. For the provision of additional facilities such as a health centre, library, cinema, shopping, recreation, three residential planning areas are grouped to form a 'community centre'. Seven of these community centres form a 'District' with a

'District Centre'. This will have a composite retail shopping centre with commercial and service areas. In some cases, they will have a small area for Govt. offices and an industrial work centre to provide employment. This will serve a population ranging from 150,000 to 250,000, In the Zonal Development Plans the community centres, high schools, primary schools, parks and other facilities should be shown. The District Centres alone can be shown in the Landuse Plan.

(2) **Density of population**

For calculating density in the residential zones, one dwelling unit is presumed to have 5 persons in India. The density shown in the Landuse Plan for a particular area shall be followed in considering layout plans for the area till such time as the Zonal Development Plans are finalised to achieve the overall density prescribed for the area. However, a variation upto 15 percent of the gross density prescribed for the area. However, a variation upto 15 percent of the gross densities may be allowed. The community facilities should be planned on the basis of the actual gross density achieved. In calculating gross residential density, all land meant for community facilities like local shopping, parks, playgrounds, schools, roads and other facilities should be included. Incidental open spaces left around and in between two buildings should be included.

(3) **Sub-division regulations**

The purpose of these regulations is to guide the development of the new areas in accordance with the Landuse Plan. As long as this is done along sound planning principles with adequate space standards, the future of the city is assured. This will avoid the necessity of costly corrective measures needed if sub-standard growth is allowed to take place. While the requirements regarding water supply, sewerage, grading and surfacing of streets, street lighting etc., will be governed by municipal by-laws, the sub-division regulations will be confined to standards for street width and community facilities which are laid down as a sliding scale according to the density.

The sub-division of land refers to the division of land into two or more parcels for the purpose of sale or building development. It is essentially a process of converting raw land into building sites. In many countries this process is controlled by local laws, which regulate the manner and location of sub-division and the provision of improvements such as roads and drainage systems.

The sub-division regulations require a prospective developer to submit a plan of his proposed scheme to the Planning Authority before he proceeds to make improvements or to divide and sell his land. The approval of the Planning Authority compels the developers to comply to the rules. Sub-division or selling of lots in an unapproved scheme renders the developer liable to civil and criminal penalities. In this way, sub-division regulations can exert a significant influence on the location, manner and timing. Sub-division regulations are a useful legal tool for taxation, registration of plans, accurate land records etc.

(4) **Floor Area Ratio (FAR)**

It is also known as 'Floor Space Index (FSI) It is the quotient obtained by dividing the total covered area on all floors by the area of the plot.

FAR (or) FSI = Total covered area of all floors/Plot area.

For example, a Floor Area Ratio of 1:1.5 means that the total area of all the floors in a building cannot be greater than 1.5 times the area of the plot. If all the floors in a building have same area, then a building consisting of five floors will have on each floor an area equal to 0.3 times (1.5/5 = 0.3) the area of the plot in each floor. If the building consists of ten floors, each floor will have an area of 0.15 times (1.5/10 = 0.15) the area of the plot in each floor. It is also related to building height regulations. Thus FAR controls the density of built-up area on a given plot.

(I) Factors to be Considered in Development Plan

The following factors should be taken into consideration in the Development Plans of the cities.

1. Urban population growth cannot be prevented, it must be planned and accommodated.
2. The form of cities is determined by individuals and organisations rather than by governments. Private sector will continue to play dominant role in city development.
3. There are certain limitations on the abilities of governments to intervene effectively in the urban development. Government interventions have produced unintended and undesirable results in many cases. A more realistic approach would be to distinguish between the need for government intervention and private sector encouragement in the development of cities.

4. A more realistic affordable standards of services for the poor should be derived and adopted.
5. The planning process cannot be a sequence of survey-plan-action. These stages need to be pursued concurrently. Plans need to be flexible and incremental rather than rigid.
6. The limited ability of planning authorities to enforce regulatory systems of development control should be realised. Hence there is a need to identify alternative ways of land development like developing infrastructure.
7. Plans should take into consideration the political agendas and political processes within which an implementable plan programme must be developed.

(J) Case Study: Master Plan for Delhi, Perspective 2001 (MPD-2001)

The Perspective Plan-2001 ensures an appropriate balance between the spatial allocations for the distribution of housing, employment, social infrastructure, shopping centres, public and individual transport and adequate arrangements and reservations to accommodate different kinds of physical infrastructure and public utility systems. The perspective plan thus comprises a set of co-ordinated policies concerned with all aspects of development in the city accompanied by a series of maps. The concept behind the perspective plan is as follows:

(a) *Delhi is to be planned as an integral part of its region:* Major urban problems of the metropolitan city of Delhi originates outside and their solution is also beyond its territory. Rapid growth of population and employment can be restricted through restructuring of the settlement pattern and the transportation network in the region, and through legal and fiscal measures to operate at inter-state level.

(b) *Ecological balance to be maintained:* Delhi has two distinct features. They are the ridge which is the rocky outcrop of Aravilli hills and the river Yamuna. Some parts of the ridge have been erased in the central city area. No further infringment of the ridge is to be permitted. River Yamuna is to be made pollution free through various measures. The river is to be made an integral part of the city, physically and visually, by developing recreational areas along its banks.

(c) *Central City Area to be treated as 'Special Area':* The walled city and its extension and Karol Bagh, has a special mixed landuse pattern of development which is different from other areas. This area, which cannot be developed on the basis of normal planning policies or controls, has been given the status of 'Special Area' to be treated in a different manner.

(d) *Urban heritage of Delhi to be conserved:* The plan emphasises modernisation with conservation. Some of the old historic areas have been designated as controlled conservation areas. Special plans are to be formulated for the conservation and improvement of these areas.

(e) *The city centre to be decentralised:* The central city areas constitute a strong business centre bringing lakhs of workers and others everyday to these areas. Development of district centre for each district and directional freight complex would be effective in creating a completely new pattern and city foci.

(f) *Mass transport system to be multi-model:* The intra-urban transportation is related to the regional transportation. The new railway line to avoid through traffic from Delhi is to be constructed in the region. The ring rail to be fully utilised for intra-city passenger movement by 2001. The landuse long ring rail is to be restructured and Mass Rapid Transit System (MRTS) to be introduced on higher density corridors. The goods traffic is to be intercepted at the periphery of the urban areas.

(g) *The urban development to be 'Low-rise high density':* In case of the existing urban area the transportation system, and the physical infrastructure are to be restructured to accommodate additional population upto 3 million by the year 2001 and upto 4 million ultimately.

(h) *Urban development to be hierarchical:* Its hierarchical cellular structure with nuclei to contain essential facilities and services at different levels. The hierarchical structure is to be in five tiers.

(2) **Regional and sub-regional frame**

Delhi population is growing at a very rapid pace, creating complex problem of urban development and management, if part of this growth could be channelised into other cities, the smaller ones, it could provide relief to the core city and will prove to be a source of strength to the smaller settlements. In this context, for the balanced regional development The National Capital Region Planning Board is co-ordinating through a plan for the National Capital Region (NCR) which includes some parts of Haryana, UP and Rajasthan besides the Union Territory of Delhi.

At sub-regional level Delhi Metropolitan Area (DMA) including the Union Territory of Delhi, should be considered as one urban agglomeration for the purpose of planning. Thus in the regional context the DMA & NCR concepts and plans have become more important today than they were during the preparation of first Master Plan of Delhi in 1962. In the plan the policies for the balanced development of the NCR have been stated and the Delhi Metropolitan Area has been re-defined, taking into consideration the urban settlement at the doorsteps of Delhi and the ridge in the south which extends to Haryana.

(3) **Population and Employment**

At present the rate of growth of Delhi population by the year 2001 would be 144.26 lakhs in urban areas and 5.27 lakhs in rural areas. Though regional development has lagged behind, but considering the positive actions which would be taken in this respect, population for the Union Territory of Delhi has been assigned as 121.73 lakhs in urban areas and 6.37 lakhs in rural areas. During the course of the implementation of the plan an attempt should be made to restrict the population of the Union Territory at a lower level of 12 lakhs.

The present employment of about 19 lakhs would increase to about 49 lakhs by the year 2001.

Land and infrastructural provision would be required to accommodate this employment and rapid growth of population. Only essential Central Government offices which serve the Ministries of the Government of India and only the liasion offices of the undertakings should be located in Delhi. The Quasi-Government employment needs to be judiciously distributed in the regional towns and the counter magnets, which are part of the National Capital Region.

Also to contain the trend of increasing employment in industrial sector, only non-polluting industries employing not more than 50 workers should be allowed in Delhi Urban Area.

To accommodate the assigned urban population by the year 2001 a two-pronged strategy has been recommended.

(i) To increase the population holding capacity of DUA-81.

(ii) Extension of urbanisable limits to accommodate additional population.

4. Shelter

Emphasis should be both on the development of new housing areas as well as on conservation, improvement and revitalisation of the existing residential areas. About 16.2 lakhs new housing units are required in the next two decades.

Housing co-operatives in Delhi, which are an overlapping sector between public and private, have been a reasonable success and should be further encouraged.

Earlier the plan had proposed general public housing in the form of two family development alongwith multi-family (Group Housing). Recently the two family plotted development has been permitted a third family unit on the Barsati floor. Surveys and studies have indicated that plotted development for a long time remain only single storey built and also that group housing in the overall study design has a very marginal intensive use of land. Further relating housing to (i) Affordability, (ii) Efficiency of land utilisation (Landuse intensity), (iii) Equity (Social distribution of land), the most appropriate type of general housing would be partially built plotted housing on individual plots of 70 to 80 sq.m. Part of housing could be provided in the form of three family plots developed into work-up dwelling units, generally varying from 150 to 250 sq.m and multi-family housing co-operatives for general housing. Co-operative for general housing should be given a bigger role and small co-operatives with individual housing on plotted basis could also be introduced.

(a) *Resettlement colonies:* Immediate need of resettlement colonies is provision of individual services i.e., water, sewerage and electricity. Non-Government organisation should supplement social action of Govt. departments and income supplementation programmes specially for women should also be undertaken. Regular sewerage may not be possible immediately in many areas because of non-availability of connecting line or financial constraints. In such cases the low-cost sanitation through two pit method on individual or collective basis should be adopted. For construction of dwelling resettlement colonies by individual families, system of institutional financing for this category is needed.

(b) *Unauthorised colonies:* Unauthorised colonies are generally the result of lack of discipline and serious shortage of housing. The house owners of such colonies which have been considered for regularisation could be asked to form societies and come forward with plans for improvement of the target group.

(c) *Urban villages:* These old settlements should be provided with basic services and amenities while preserving to the extent possible their traditional life style.

5. Conservation, Revitalisation and Environmental Improvement

Conservation and revitalisation is required in case of traditional areas like the walled city. This requires (i) shifting noxious and hazardous industries and trades, and delimitation of non-residential activities, (ii) upgrading of physical and social infrastructure, (iii) Introduction of transport modes of medium capacity and speed and management and regulation of traffic, (iv) conservation and restoration of historic building, (v) revitalisation of organic residential areas.

6. Industry

According to the existing regulations, a large number of existing industrial units are non-conforming as these are located in the residential and commercial use zones. Thus the overall question of conforming, non-conforming and overall compatibility of industries has been studied and recommendations have been made for different types of industries in this regard.

7. Trade & Commerce

(a) *Retail trade:* To accommodate requirements of shopping-cum-commercial offices and other related activities like cinemas, hotels and ancillary facilities, the five tier system of commercial areas ranging from CBD to Convenience Shopping Centre with some modifications has been retained. Beside the CBD in the old city, Connaught Place and Karol Bagh, two sub-CBDs one in the Trans-Yamuna area and other in the urban extension are proposed. Besides 5 district centres are already in different stages of development, 2 new district centres have been envisaged, 14 in the existing urban limits and 8 in the urban extension.

(b) *Informal sector:* The significant roie of informal sector in commercial activity has been recognised and guidelines have been provided for planned developed.

(c) *Wholesale trade:* For wholesale trade, four regional wholesale markets in different directions have been proposed. The wholesale markets have to be integrated with freight complexes, so that wholesale business could be operated more efficiently and in a better environment. To effectuate decentralisation, 11 regional-cum-local wholesale markets as secondary wholesale markets are recommended to be developed in different planning divisions.

8. Transportation

Keeping in view the physical forms obtainable in the existing urban areas like Old Delhi, New Delhi and contemporary development, as also the projected rate of trip generation, a multi-mode transportation system consisting of electrified ring rail, light rail and bus transport inter-linking various parts is proposed.

New modes proposed for the intra-city passenger movement is the light railway. In the existing urban area and in the urban extension about 200 km. of light rail would be required by the year 2001.

For the central congested areas of the walled city, re-introduction of moderate capacity medium speed transport system along select number of routes is recommended. However, this should be supported by a restraint on the use of private modes of transport and provision of parking at interchange points.

To provide safe environment for. bicycle movement in certain corridors, fully segregated cycle tracks need to be provided by adjusting existing road sections and making use of land available by the side of nullah.

For inter-city passenger movement four metropolitan passenger terminals on major rail linkages have been recommended. All these metropolitan passenger terminals would have one inter-state bus terminus each and would be linked with different parts of the city through MRTS and bus transportation. Another bus terminus has been proposed near Dhaula Kuan/junction of ring road and National highway no. 24

(a) *Goods movement:* For the integration of goods movement through road and rail, freight complexes consisting of wholesale markets warehousing, trucks and rail transport terminals have been recommended on four major rail-road links close to the proposed metropolitan passenger terminals.

(b) *Metropolitan Transport Authority:* To run a multimodel complex transportation system for Delhi on rational lines, Delhi needs a unified single transport authority on the line suggested by National Transport Policy Committee.

9. Physical infrastructure

(a) *Water supply:* Delhi would need additional water supply to the extent of 671 million gallons per day (MGD) by the year 2001.

This is expected from Tehri Dams in Himachal Pradesh and through exchange of water with Haryana. The supply system would require enhancement of the existing four water treatment plants and construction of a new treatment plant.

(b) *Sewerage:* To serve entire population with sewerage the existing sewerage capacity of 118 MGD would be required to be augmented to 900 MGD with the availability of water. This would require enhancement of the capacity of existing sewerage treatment plants and construction of three new sewerage treatment plants including Rithala plant which is in the process. The areas where immediate regular sewerage is not possible intermediate low-cost sanitation system should be adopted as a short range provision.

(c) *Power:* Delhi's requirement of power by the year 2001 is estimated to be 4000 MW. For additional requirement it would have to bank upon the northern power grid. To meet the targetted demand of 4000 MW by the year 2001 the power distribution network would be required to be taken over to 400 KV grid from existing 220 KV grid.

(d) *Solid waste management:* Solid waste generated in different parts of Delhi would increase from 2300 tons per day in 1981 to 6735 tons per day in 2001. Considering the nature of solid waste and the economy of its disposal major part of solid waste has been proposed to be disposed off in sanitary land fill. No new site for compast plant has been proposed. It is recommended that the experience of the existing two compost plants with MCD and NDMC be reviewed in 1994 and if necessary policy could be modified.

10. Social Infrastructure

(a) *Health:* Two-tier system in the form of general hospital and health centre earlier proposed did not satisfy the full requirements of health needs, thus a six-tier system has been evolved consisting of: (i) General hospital (500 beds), (ii) Intermediate hospital category 'A' (200 beds) (iii) Intermediate hospital category 'B' (80 beds), (iv) Poly-clinic with some observation beds, (v) Nursing home and child welfare and maternity centre and (vi) Dispensary.

(b) *Education:* Besides land reservation for normal educational facilities, land would also be reserved for technical and professional education institutions and also for central and integrated schools and for the schools of handicapped to overcome the present shortcomings.

(c) *Telecommunications:* Reservations of land for telephone exchanges has been proposed so as to increase the telephones per hundred population from 3.37 in 1987 to 10 in the year 2001. Revised standards have been worked out for infrastructure (social) including postal facilities, police, milk distribution etc.

(d) *Facilities and service centres:* To accommodate facilities in groups in the existing urban areas facility centres have been proposed. Similarly, to accommodate the additional need of repair and service shops service centres concept has been evolved.

11. Environment

(a) *Natural features:* Two major natural features in Delhi area are the ridge and river Yamuna. Though part of the ridge in Delhi has been erased the total ridge area since available is about 7777 ha. This should be conserved with utmost care and should be afforested with indigenous species with minimum of artificial landscape.

River Yamuna flow has a high level of pollution, which is mainly from the untreated sewerage and waste from industrial areas. Strict enforcement of Water Pollution Act is needed to keep the river clean. Channelisation of the river as proposed shall provide scope for a major river front development scheme.

(b) *Long Spaces:* Areas reserved for parks are to be developed for intensive recreational activities. Atleast 30 percent of the district parks area should be developed as woodland for ecological stability. Due emphasis is given on the development of sports facilities for all age groups in the form of neighbourhood play area, district and divisional sports centres.

(c) *Replantation:* There are large number of trees in parks, which have completed their full span of life. This is specially true of the trees in New Delhi area. Replantation as a cyclic process is recommended.

(d) *Urban design:* Urban aesthetics and conservation of city's past is necessary. Delhi has tradition of urban design, which has been lost in recent past. Four pronged policy— (i) identification of areas of significant natural and built environment for special treatment, (ii) visual integration of various parts of the city, (iii) conservation of city past, (iv) policy for tall buildings and major urban projects has been worked out to revive the same.

The central part of Delhi has well developed social and cultural institutions. With the increasing population additional areas for social and cultural activities have been earmarked. Areas along Central Vista from Janpath to National Stadium needs to be continued to be reserved for social and cultural institutions.

(e) *Water and air pollution:* Water and air pollution based on available studies, is increasing. In case of water pollution, diversion of discharge of waste water from major drains into the sewerage system to be followed by adequate waste water treatment has been recommended. Six areas have been identified as 'Pollution Control Areas'.

12. Special Area

The walled city and its extension and Karol Bagh and the area in between has been earmarked as special area for the purpose of development. This area cannot be developed on the basis of normal regulations. Special regulations have been worked out for this area and incorporated into the Development Code.

13. Rural area

The rural area of Delhi being in the periphery of major metropolis has a special significance.

This area is also attracting migrants, 26 percent of rural Delhi households are migrant households, mainly from Haryana and UP. The area needs to be provided with a reasonably high level of infrastructure and good road linkages with the city. Based on the population, linkages and growth rate certain villages have been identified for the location of major health facilities, markets, schools and rural industries.

14. Modernisation and city's personality

A city belonging to this age should have— (i) efficient transportation and communication system, (ii) convention and exhibition centres, (iii) shopping arcades, amusement parks and, (iv) places for comfortable living for the visitors. The city should provide all these and should also reflect its traditions and heritance, its culture and its warmth to the visitors and its inhabitants.

15. Landuse plan

The existing landuse plan has been modified on the basis of the following:

(i) Policies enunciated for different sectors
(ii) Requirements of additional physical and social infrastructure, transportation and employment centres
(iii) Restructuring of landuse along the ring rail
(iv) Modifications in the landuses already approved
(v) Restructuring in landuse based on the studies for the Perspective-2001 and considering inter-relationship of urban activities and their effect on the environment and image of the city.

16. Mixed landuse

Concept of mixed landuse has been introduced in the plan by:

(i) Providing special regulations for the central old build-up areas.
(ii) By permitting non-residential activities on residential premises, taking into consideration its community need, traffic and parking provisions.
(iii) As an intended mixed use in new developments by permitting non-residential activities on the ground floor and residential activities on the floors above.

17. Zonal (Divisional) Plans

The Union Territory of Delhi is divided into 15 zones (divisions). The zonal (divisional) plans would provide further detailed policy of the plan as necessary and act as a link between the layout plan and the Master Plan.

18. Development code

It is systematic code to decide the use activities (uses) in two levels. They are:

(i) Conversion of use zone into use premises (layout).
(ii) Permission of use activities in the use premises.

It also gives regulations for sub-divisions of use zone into use premises and control of buildings within use premises.

19. Plan monitoring and review

(a) *Plan monitoring:* No long range urban development plan can be implemented unless it is responsive to be the emerging socio-economic and other forces during the plan implementation period. Time lag between the happenings and emerging socio-economic forces and the plan responses creates accetuating conditions of unintended growth. The respective plan to check the unintended growth needs a scientific monitoring frame. Monitoring frame is required for :

(i) Evaluating the achievement of physical targets prescribed in the plan.

(ii) Identification of physical and soci-economic changes to review the plan policies.

(b) *Plan review:* The plan monitoring would provide sufficient material for any modification required in the plan. Any other aspects out of emerging socio-economic and physical forces could be taken up for study to review the plan proposals. A comprehensive review encompassing all aspects should be taken up in 1994.

(c) *Constant study and research:* Policies indicates directions and detailed development projects ultimately create environment. During the plan implementation all the aspects of development *i.e.*, housing, transport, work centre, recreation, infrastructure, etc., need constant study and research to make the plan effective in providing high quality living environment. The DDA should constantly do the studies, research and monitoring work to make planning a firm instrument for the development of the city. (see Fig. 6.1)

(K) Urban Landuse Classification

N	A-N	Use Zone	N	A-N	Use Zone
1.	R	Residential	11	R-1	Primary Residential Zone
			12	R-2	Mixed Residential Zone
			13	R-3	Unplanned/Informal Residential Zone
2.	C	Commercial	21	C-1	Retail Shopping Zone
			22	C-2	General Business and Commercial District/Centres
			23	C-3	Wholesale, Godowns, Warehousing/ Regulated Markets
3.	M	Manufacturing	31	M-1	Service and Light Industry
			32	M-2	Extensive and Heavy Industry
			33	M-3	Special Industrial Zone Hazardous, Noxious and Chemical
4.	PS	Public and Semi-Public	41	PS-1	Govt./Semi Govt./Public offices
			42	PS-2	Govt. Land (use undetermined)
			43	PS-3	Educational and Research
			44	PS-4	Medical and Health
			45	PS-5	Social Cultural and Religious
			46	PS-6	Utilities and Services
			47	PS-7	Cremation and Burial-grounds

(Contd.)

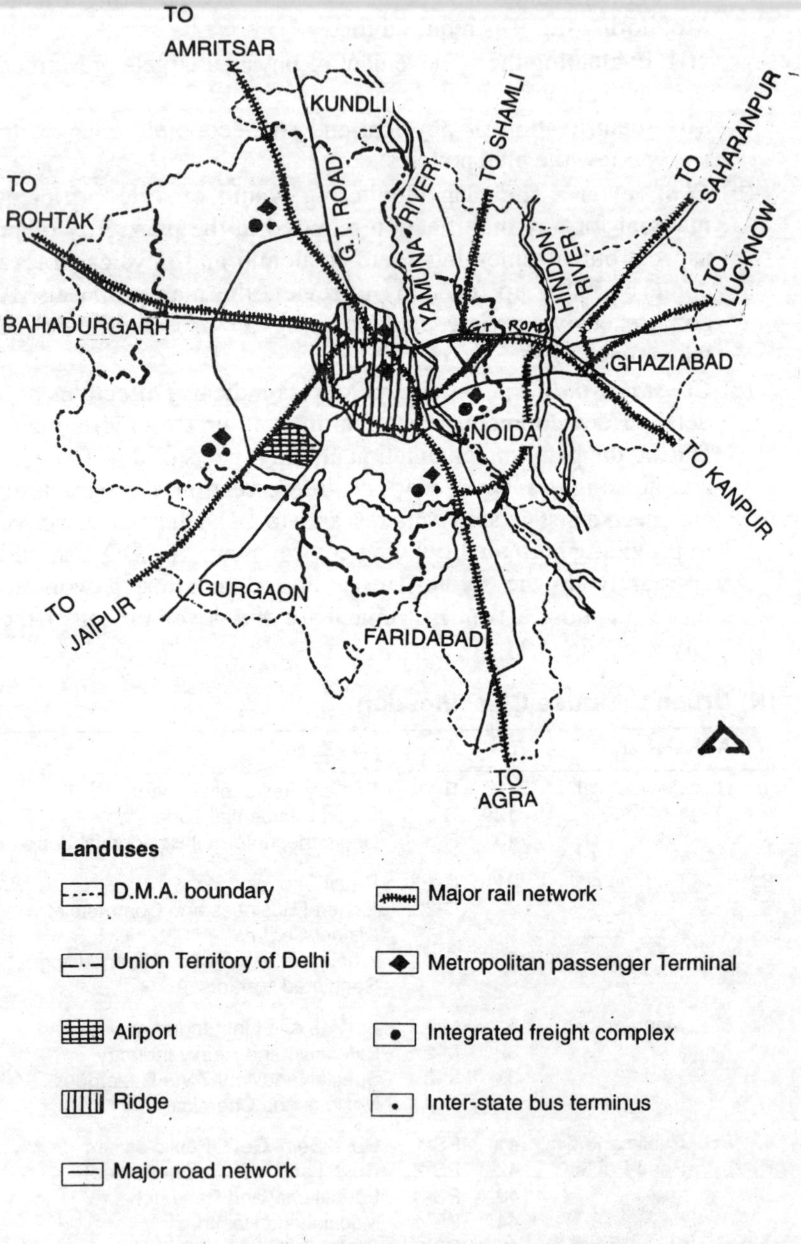

Fig. 6.1 Delhi Metropolitan Area

5.	R	Recreational	51	P-1	Playgrounds/Stadium/Sports Complex
			52	P-2	Parks & Gardens - Public Open Spaces
			53	P-3	Special Recreational Zone - Restricted Open Spaces
			54	P-4	Multi-Open Space (Maidan)
6.	T	Transportation and Communication	61	T-1	Roads
			62	T-2	Railway Stations
			63	T-3	Airport
			64	T-4	Seaports and Dockyards
			65	T-5	Bus Depots/Truck Terminals and Freight Complexes
			66	T-6	Transmission & Communication
7.	A	Agriculture and Water Bodies	71	A-1	Agriculture
			72	A-2	Forest
			73	A-3	Poultry and Dairy Farming
			74	A-4	Rural Settlements
			75	A-5	Brick Klin and Extractive Areas
			76	A-6	Water Bodies
8.	S	Special Area	81	S-1	Old Built-up (Core) Area
			82	S-2	Heritage and Conservation Areas
			83	S-3	Scenic Value Areas
			84	S-4	Village Settlement
			85	S-5	Other Uses

N: Numberic Code A-N: Alpha-Numeric Code

(L) Graphic Expression

Code				
N	AN	Use Zone	Notation	Colour Specification
I	R	RESIDENTIAL		YELLOW
II	R1	Primary Residential Zone		Yellow
12	R2	Mixed Residential Zone		Orange
13	R	Unplanned/Informal Residential Zone		Brown
2	C	COMMERCIAL		BLUE
21	C-1	Retail Shopping Zone		Blue with A-N Code
22	C-2	General Business & Commercial District/Centres		- do -
23	C-3	Wholesale, godowns		- do -

(*Contd.*)

3	M	MANUFACTURING		PURPLE
31	M-1	Service & Light Industry		Purple with A-N Code
32	M-2	Extensive & Heavy Industry		- do -
33	M-3	Special Industrial Zone Hazardous, Chemical & Noxious		- do -
4	PS	PUBLIC & SEMI-PUBLIC		RED
41	PS-1	Govt./Semi Govt./Public Offices		Red with A-N Code
42	PS-2	Govt. Land (Use Undetermined)		- do -
43	PS-3	Educational & Research		- do -
44	PS-4	Medical & Health		Red with A-N Code
45	PS-5	Social Cultural & Religious		- do -
46	PS-6	Utilities & Services		- do -
47	PS-7	Cremation & Burial Grounds		- do -
5	P	RECREATION		GREEN
51	P-1	Playgrounds, Stadium, Sports Complex		Green with A-N code
52	P-2	Parks & Gardens (Public Open Space)		- do -
53	P-3	Special Recreational Zone (Restricted Open Space)		- do -
54	P-4	Multipurpose Open Space (Maidan)		- do -
6	T	TRANSPORTATION & COMMUNICATION		BLACK
61	T-1	Roads		Black with A-N Code
62	T-2	Railways		- do -
63	T-3	Airports		- do -

(*Contd.*)

64	T-4	Sea Port & Dockyards		- do -
65	T-5	Bus Depots Truck Terminal & Freight Complexes		- do -
66	T-6	Transmission & Communication		- do -
7	A	AGRICULTURE		LIGHT GREEN
71	A-1	Agriculture		Light Green with A-N Code
72	A-2	Forest		- do -
73	A-3	Brick Kilns & Extractive Area		- do -
74	A-4	Water Bodies		Light Blue
8	S	SPECIAL AREA		EDGED IN BLACK
81	S-1	Old Built-up Areas		Dotted line with A-N Code
82	S-2	Heritage & Conservation Areas		- do -
83	S-3	Scenic Value Areas		- do -
84	S-4	Village settlement		- do -
85	S-5	Other Uses		- do -

(*Source* : UPDFI Guidelines; Govt. of India; August 1996)

MODEL QUESTIONS

1. What is the importance of a Development Plan?
2. What are the goals and contents of a Development Plan?
3. What are the different measures to prepare and implement the Development Plan?
4. List out briefly the guidelines of Development Plan.
5. What is the importance of the following regulations?
   (a) Zoning
   (b) Density
   (c) Sub-division
   (d) FAR or FSI
6. What are the major features of Delhi Master Plan 2001?
7. List out the major urban landuse classification.

7

Housing

A. IMPORTANCE OF HOUSING

There are three basic needs for human survival. They are food, clothing and shelter. The fight for all these three basic needs goes on simultaneously. Each one of them is special in its own way. Food can not be grown everywhere unless the land is fertile. Clothes cannot be made without the basic raw material. Shelter is needed near the place of work with services for survival, and give protection from different climatic conditions. To certain extent, we tried to satisfy our need of food and clothing. However, the problem of shelter is not totally explored. In rural areas, the problems of housing are related to land and building cost only, whereas in urban areas in addition to these, the density of population is a major problem. The need to accommodate more number of people at one place poses several problems. Thus, the importance of housing in urban and rural areas is different because of the growth and density of population.

Well planned housing can create conditions, which are hygenic and environmentally conducive for healthy growth of human civilisation. On the contrary, bad housing can lead to unlawful and unhealthy environment. Thus there is a need to create a healthy housing atmosphere. It may be permanent or temporary or low-cost housing, but its aim should be to create healthy environment. In rural areas, if the houses are constructed in an order leaving sufficient space for the road, light and ventilation then services can be easily provided. Similarly, in urban areas if the local building by-laws are adhered, then many disputes can be avoided. Every citizen has a responsible role to play in constructing a house in a city than in a village. Thus urban housing assumes greater importance because of the various complex problems prevailing in urban areas.

B. HOUSING PROBLEMS IN INDIA

The prevailing housing problems in India can be briefly summed-up as below:

1. Poverty and Migration

All major problems in India are related to poverty and high growth rate of population and housing is not an exception. India is the second most populous country in the world after China. Recently, there is an increasing emphasis on restricting the family size to control the growth rate of population. There is a large scale unemployment in rural areas. A family which used to depend on agriculture for survival, cannot do so any longer. Increasing family members cannot be supported by division and cultivation of agricultural land alone. They have to find alternative ways of employment to make a living. There are limited employment opportunities in rural areas, so people migrate to cities to make a living. This leads to concentration of population in few selected cities and towns for employment.

2. Slums and Squatters

The rapid pace of urbanisation in India created slums. They have become the most complicated problem in our cities. Some of the worst slums in the world are found in India. Urban slum is not a physical problem, it is a physical manifestation of deeper socio-economic problems prevailing in the country. People living in slums render certain essential services in urban areas. They are important part of our city life. The migrants not only create unhealthy slums but they also deteriorate the urban centres. It is impossible to solve this complex problem without preventive measures. Housing the urban poor is a major challenge of modern cities.

3. Dearth of Land

There is a dearth of developed land for housing. One of the major obstacles for this is the Urban Land Ceiling Act 1976. This Act provides the right for compulsory acquisition of land in bulk. It is felt that through this Act better distribution of urban land is possible for middle and lower income group people. The problems of land acquisition and low compensation are the main hurdles in the success of the Act. The National Commission on Urbanisation 1987 recommended that "The Act must remain on the statute book. All excess land must be identified and notified as surplus and can be made liable to acquisition. All surplus vacant land must be quickly released for city development, so that the owners of surplus land be encouraged to use it for house construction rather than indulge in unnecessary litigation to retain it. They may be permitted with a minimum of formality to build housing units." For an early acquisition of surplus land, owners should be paid compensation according to market value. Thus there is a need to amend the Act for social justice and equal distribution of land. This surplus land can be used by the government to provide housing for the poor.

4. Lack of Finance

Affordability is an important aspect of housing. The purchasing power of each person differs depending upon the income. Finance should be made available depending upon the repaying capacity of the individual. The new national housing policy has liberalised the housing finance than earlier for those who can repay the loan. It is available through banks and financial institutions. Lending of loans is also available for housing institutions, but they are beyond the reach of the urban poor.

5. Violation of building regulations

Violation of building regulations is a sort of a menace in the cities. These violations are normally seen in zoning, setbacks, building height, built-up area, encroachment of land and road, and unauthorised constructions. In addition to this, land grabbing is also frequently seen in urban areas. It has become very difficult to curb these violations, unless there is political will and public awareness. If proper light and ventilation are not provided in the houses, then one has to wonder what kind of planning and design is done in the construction for improved housing conditions. Liberalised and specific building regulations without political relaxations would be extremely useful to curb these tendencies and create healthy housing environment.

C. NATIONAL HOUSING POLICY

The National Housing Policy was formulated in 1992, and incorporated in the Eighth Five Year Plan (1992-97). The basic objectives of this policy are:

1. To assist all people, and in particular the houseless, the inadequately housed and the vulnerable sections, to secure for themselves affordable shelter through access to developed land, building materials, finance and technology.

2. To create an environment for housing activity by various sections by eliminating constraints, and by developing an efficient and equitable system for the delivery of housing inputs.
3. To expand the provision of infrastructure facilities in rural and urban areas in order to improve environment of human settlements, increase the access of poorer households to basic services, and to increase the supply of developed land for housing.
4. To undertake, within the overall context of policies for poverty alleviation and employment, steps for improving the housing situation of the poorest sections and vulnerable groups by direct initiative and financial support of the State.
5. To help to mobilise the resources and facilitate the expansion of investment in housing in order to meet the demands of housing construction and upgradation and augmentation of infrastructure.
6. To promote a more equal distribution of land and houses in urban and rural areas, and to curb speculation in land and housing in consonance with macro-economic policies for efficient and equitable growth.
7. To promote vernacular architecture and to preserve the nation's rich heritage in the field of human settlements.

The National Housing Policy identified four core areas to implement the proposals. They are supply and management of land, rural housing, legal and regulatory framework and housing finance. The major tasks to be undertaken under these are:

(a) *Land management:* Creation of an appropriate legal and regulatory framework to increase supply of land through measures such as land reforms, review of slum improve- ment laws to provide for conferment of occupancy rights, revision of Master Plan standards, building by-laws and infrastructure standards to reduce cost of land and construction, amendment to Land Acquisition Act for quick acquisition of land in public interest, amendments to Urban Land (Ceiling and Regulation) Act to remove inhibiting effects of legislation on enhancement of supply of land, imposition of punitive vacant land tax, amendment to rent control laws to promote investment in rental housing, building-up an effective information system of land and registration in the interest of efficient management of land,

and procedural simplification measures including building approval and completion certificate procedures, flexible collateral requirements and introduction of secondary mortgage system.

(b) *Rural housing:* Promote use of local building materials and technologies and create an environment for primarily self-help housing.

(c) *Infrastructure development:* Directing the activities of public agencies towards development of infrastructure which is inextricably linked to the issue of supply of serviced land, modify norms of infrastructure provision to make them more affordable in the context of the present state of the economy, encourage involvement of private developers in infrastructure development, enhance the power and fund raising capacity of urban local governments to take up the task of developers in infrastructure development, enhance the power and fund raising capacity of urban local governments to take up the task of development and maintenance of infrastructure in a more organised manner and seek to enhance budgetary provisions and institutional finance.

(d) *Urbanisation pattern:* Promoting balanced pattern of urbanisation to reduce population pressure on metropolitan and large cities, supporting development of industrial growth centres, special attention to the development of the small and medium towns as a part of integrated regional plans, and steps for reducing the migration to larger cities.

(e) *Housing finance:* Evolving over a period of time, by non-subsidised housing finance system recognising the inter-linkages of the housing finance system with the financial sector and of the housing sector with the rest of the economy, expand the flow of funds from both the formal and informal sources, promoting various instruments for resource mobilisation like secondary mortgage market as a part of housing finance networks.

(f) *Flow of funds:* Encouraging cooperatives and other community based organisations to take up various shelter related activities, creating environment for developers to invest in various forms of housing and land development, prepare public sector agencies to act as promoters and facilitators rather than builders.

D. HOUSING AGENCIES

There are two types of housing agencies in India. They are:

1. Public sector or Government housing.
2. Private sector housing.

1. *Public sector housing:* There are several government agencies which take up mass housing. Some of them are State Housing Boards, Slum Clearance Boards, Development Authorities, Municipal Corporations and State Industrial Infrastructure Development Corporations. Apart from these many government departments and public sector undertakings take up housing exclusively for their employees. The government mass housing is normaliy divided into different income groups like High Income Group (HIG), Middle Income Group (MIG), Low Income Group (LIG) and Economically Weaker Sections (EWS). Housing agencies like housing boards offer complete houses or flats for sale and other agencies like Development Authorities offer plots for sale. The allotment of houses and plots is decided by draw of lots or by auction.
2. *Private sector housing:* Private sector housing is dominated by individual housing. There are number of co-operative housing societies constructing houses or providing plots for construction of houses to their members. Recently, due to the encouragement given by the government for housing, private developers and builders are offering plots, independent houses and flats for sale in cities.

Government housing is largely criticised for poor quality and services. They are constructed to certain specific standards without any interaction with the residents, whereas in private housing an individual resident is given importance. Thus private housing meets the individual requirements, whereas in government housing an individual has to adopt to the allotted house or flat. There may be many housing agencies, but good housing is still beyond the reach of the poor. In Indian society house is a status symbol. A rich man never wants to own a low-cost house, and a poor man wants a house like that of a rich man. Affordability is a mysterious question to answer because it does not depend on the income alone. People are ready to construct houses beyond their incomes by borrowing for posterity and status in the society. It is extremely difficult to meet the desired expectations of the people.

E. HOUSING FINANCE INSTITUTIONS

There are various housing finance institutions promoting housing activity in India. Some of the important institutions are discussed below:

1. **National Housing Bank (NHB):** The most important step taken for the flow of housing finance is to set up the National Housing Bank. The bank situated at New Delhi, started its operations from the year 1988. The major objectives of the bank are:
   (a) mobilise resources for the housing sector, specially to help the low-income groups;
   (b) promoting housing finance institutions at local and regional levels;
   (c) provide financial, technical and administrative assistance to such institutions.

   The bank has been set up with an equity of one billion rupees, but Reserve Bank of India and other financial institutions make special additional contributions. The bank proposes to mobilise additional finance by floating innovative schemes to attract deposits, and act as catalyst for land development activities throughout the country. The National Housing Bank has already started significant impact on housing finance institutions. It has definitely made housing finance easy for those who can afford housing with reasonable incomes.
2. **Housing and Urban Development Corporation (HUDCO):** HUDCO was set up in 1971 to meet the needs of the housing agencies for long-term financing in the country. The corporation gives loans only to housing agencies and not to individuals. It has different interest rates ranging from 5 to 15 percent. About 55 percent of finance is allocated for low-income groups and economically weaker sections, which makes 85 percent of housing going to EWS and LIG in an year. It has been observed that most of the EWS and LIG houses pass to the upper income categories. The project delays push up the construction cost making it out of the reach of the deserving group. Thus the benefits allotted for the poor are going to the higher income groups is one of the main criticisms against HUDCO.
3. **Life Insurance Corporation of India (LIC):** LIC makes significant contribution to housing in the country. About 11 percent of LIC lending goes to housing. It gives loans to the

State Housing Boards, HUDCO and other government authorities. It also gives loans to individuals and the interest rates range from 7 to 15 percent. LICs individual loans cater to the needs of middle and upper income groups residing in urban areas. In 1988 LIC set up a Housing Finance Company with equity participation from other financial institutions like the Industrial Credit and Investment Corporation of India (ICICI), Industrial Finance Corporation of India (IFCI) and Unit Trust of India (UTI). LIC is trying to boost its lendings to individuals through this channel.

4. **Housing Development Finance Corporation (HDFC):** It was started in 1977 for long term housing loans as a private sector institution. HDFC interest rates depend on the amount of loan rather than on the income of the borrower. Even though it lends directly to individual borrowers, the lending schemes are not within the reach of the poor.
5. **Commercial Banks:** The lending policies for housing by the government through commercial banks are liberalised in 1988. The amount of loan that can be borrowed was enhanced. Interest rates are reduced for small loans. The period of loan repayment was increased from 10 to 15 years. The Reserve Bank of India allowed the banks to fix instalments for repayment of the amount. Smaller amounts can be paid in the earlier years and larger amounts in the later years, so that housing loans can fall within the affordability limits of the lower income groups. Where mortgage of property is not feasible, banks have been allowed to take other forms of security. In the case of those individuals who have raised money from other sources, banks are allowed to provide supplementary finance. Banks can now lend for land acquisition and development also. They have also been instructed to give loans for repairs, additions and alterations of buildings. Thus there is sufficient encouragement from the government side to improve the housing stock of the country through commercial banks.
6. **Housing Co-operatives:** Co-operative housing is a very good form of housing unless people come together to pool the resources. There should be sufficient encouragement from the government side also. There are number of difficulties in co-operative housing like lack of long-term finance, poor construction management, lack of suitable land, lack of services etc., The government should come up with firm legislation to

encourage co-operative housing. In India many experiments are successful in co-operative sector. For example, the production of milk. All possibilities of encouraging co-operative housing should be explored. Thus it can bring people together to meet one of their basic needs.

F. NEIGHBOURHOOD CONCEPT

1. **The Concept:** The Neighbourhood unit is not based on any sociological theory. It is based on the following assumptions to create a physical environment.
   (a) A child need not cross traffic streets on the way to school.
   (b) A school within easy walking distance from home.
   (c) A housewife can walk to a shopping centre to obtain daily household goods.
   (d) Convenient transportation to and form the work.
   (e) A playground is located near the home.
   (f) Population of a neighbourhood unit shall range from 3000 to 12000 approximately.
   (g) Arrangement of space depends upon the number of families to be accommodated.
   (h) Unit of measurement of required space is calculated based on the number of persons to be accommodated.

It represents a unit of the population with basic common needs for educational, recreational and other service facilities. Clarence A. Perry defined this concept in specific terms and Clarence Stein conceived the design concept of a neighbourhood unit. The neighbourhood unit or some equivalent is normally used for physical planning of urban areas. (see Fig. 7.1)

2. **Case Study: Layout of a section in Gandhi Nagar, capital of Gujarat State.** The regular grid iron pattern of main roads surround the sector. Each sector measures one kilometer by three-fourth kilometer with an area of 75 hectares or 185 acres. Each sector accommodates residential communities of about 15000 population with necessary facilities like schools, shopping complex, playgrounds and parks. In the layout none of the plots are exposed to the main roads. All residential streets end up as cul-de-sacs avoiding passing movement of vehicles. A cycle track and pedestrain walk-way passes through the centre of the sector. All internal roads are shaped in such a way that speed of vehicles is always under control. All service

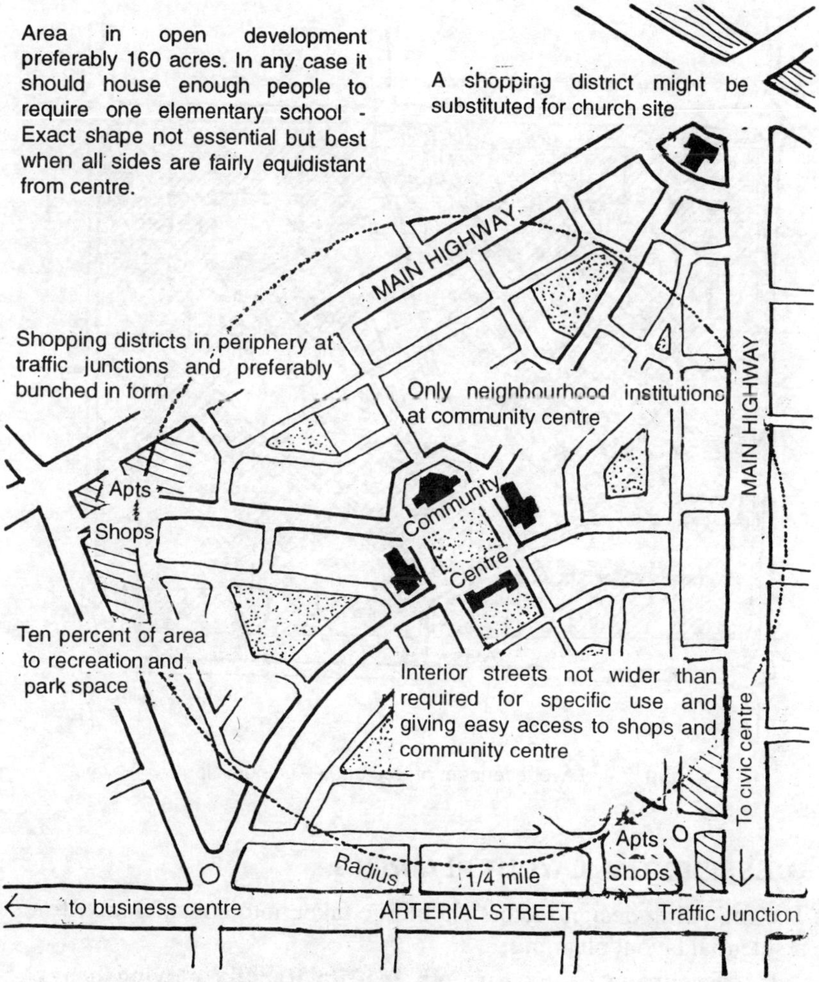

Fig. 7.1 Neighbourhood Concept (by *Clarence Perry*, 1920)

facilities are provided in the centre of the sector which is easily accessable from the residential areas. (see Fig. 7.2)

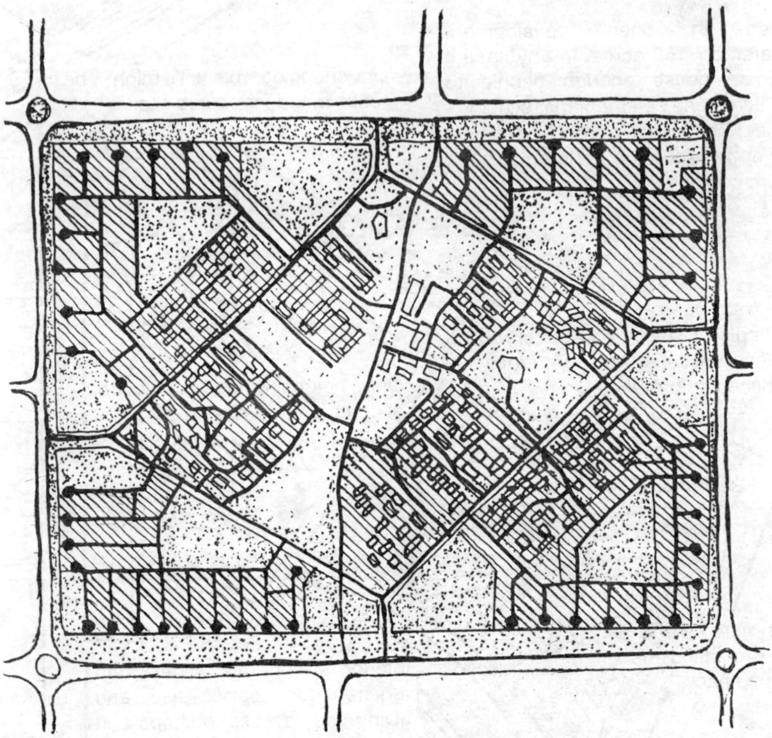

Fig. 7.2 Layout concept of Sector 9 — Gandhi Nagar

G. RESIDENTIAL LAYOUT PLANNING

The following design factors should be taken into consideration for residential layout planning:

1. **Discourage heavy through traffic:** Rapidly moving heavy traffic on local residential streets causes undue accidents and also increases the total cost in the shape of pavement construction and maintenance.
2. **Plan for extension of major streets:** When major traffic streets are not planned as part of the layout, plots may be sold and houses built in the path of a future highway. Thus the development of a through street is blocked and opening of the street later becomes expensive.

3. **Traffic should flow towards thoroughfares:** When traffic does not flow towards main thoroughfares, it causes an unnecessary use of local streets in order to reach the main traffic ways. This excessive use of residential streets increase the expenditure due to pavement construction and maintenance.
4. **Minor streets should enter the major streets at right angles:** Streets should intersect each other as nearly at right angles as possible, and the number of streets converging upon a single point should be kept to a minimum. When minor streets join the thoroughfare at raking angles, visibility is affected for both motorists and pedestrains. Drivers are likely to turn with great speeds without seeing.
5. **Avoid planning dead-end streets:** Normally dead-end streets are planned against rail-road rights-of-way or some natural barriers like hills or permanent properties. This results in slum development or misuse of land with unauthorised constructions. When there is a possibility of the street going on through in future, the plot at the end of the street may be reserved for a given time and not sold or built. If it develops then the street connection will not be necessary, the plot can become a building site and complete the design of the neighbourhood. When the conditions make it impractical to avoid a dead-end street, it should be terminated by a turn-around. This circle should have a diameter of atleast 100' and have atleast the depth of one plot from the boundary line of the site.
6. **Streets should fit contours of land:** When the levels of the site vary considerably, streets should be laid out to conform to the natural contours. General observations of high and low ground are enough to determine the location of streets. If the land is rough, a topographical map should be made to obtain complete ground conditions. If streets are laid out to fit the contours of the land, it will avoid steep gradients and reduce construction costs. A layout plan based upon the topography of the site gives a better designed development and economical installation of utilities. In locating streets consideration should be given to the size and shape of plots and blocks to obtain the best use of the land.
7. **Short blocks of plots are uneconomical:** Short blocks increase initial construction costs because of the large number of cross streets and increase traffic hazards and travel time. Better shaped plots are secured and those facing the state highway are

protected by a park strip. The plotting of residential blocks upto 1300 feet in length by two plot depths wide, bounded by streets adjusted to topographic and traffic requirements is economical.

8. **Long blocks of plots need cross-walks near centre:** The use of cross-walks through long blocks for direct access to nearby community facilities is desirable for convenience. Such pedestrain ways near the middle of all the blocks exceeding 1000 feet in length is recommended. When a shopping centre, school or park is located in such a way that the residents are forced to take circutous routes in order to reach their destination, then it is desirable to provide cross-walks in shorter blocks of 750 feet in length. This reduces the walking distance.
9. **Plan commercial sites:** Local shopping centres are definite assests to the community. They should be located within safe and convenient walking distance for the residents with adequate off-street delivery and parking facilities. Commercial structures should be located at suitable centres adjoining a major thoroughfare and accessable from connecting residential streets. They should be designed together as a group. Based on the shopping habits of the residents, a detailed analysis should be made to calculate the amount of land required for commercial sites.
10. **Provide sites for social services:** If the layout is large, then sites should be provided for schools and religious places like temple, mosque, church etc. These sites should be centrally located for the convenience of all the residents. Adequate space should be provided for the parking of cars and two-wheelers. The selection of convenient sites for these services will help in increasing the saleability of the plots.
11. **Parks act as community areas:** Areas that are difficult to develop into economical dwelling sites are often adopted for recreational use. A well located park will help to sell remotely situated plots also. Parks are definite asset to a community. Children and adults can enjoy outdoors with safety. The natural features of the parks can be seen and enjoyed by surrounding residents.
12. **Plan wider corner plots :** Every residential plot within a neighbourhood should be spacious to provide free area on all sides of the dwelling to be constructed. It is recommended that corner plots be given extra width for side street setback requirement. In the case of a normal corner plot the width

should be 10′ wider than interior plots. Normal plot sizes can be assumed as 60 × 30 feet or 60 × 40 feet.

13. **Make plot lines perpendicular to street:** To obtain maximum advantage from all plots, it is suggested that the plot lines should be kept perpendicular or radial to street lines. If this is not done, there is a tendency to build houses without facing the road. This creates an unattractive street picture and many times causes the front of the one house to face the side or rear of neighbouring house. If a maximum use is to be made of every square feet of the plot area, it is important that the plot should be well shaped. If lines are not perpendicular to the street, sharp angled corner will result. These are difficult to utilise and give an undesirable appearance.
14. **Plan plots facing desirable views:** In planning a layout the advantage of any natural or created beauty spot should be taken. Plots should be so faced that houses look towards the park rather than face side streets. It should be seen that the plots do not overlook neighbouring rear yards, face undeveloped and restricted property or exposed to the adverse effects of heavily travelled streets and adjacent non-conforming landuses. Each plot in a layout should not only constitute a good house site, but take full advantage of desirable natural features such as views, slope of the land, sunlight, prevailing wind, shade of trees and adjoining public spaces.
15. **Preserve natural features of site:** It is recommended that whenever possible all natural features of a neighbourhood should be preserved to add beauty to the layout. In many cases valuable tree growth is cut and hillocks are removed to fill lower ground. Quite often this is an unnecessary expenditure and only results in the destruction of the site. A more desirable neighbourhood can be created when roads are located to fit the existing contours of the land and preserve the native tree growth. The curving of streets to fit contours of the land and the saving of valuable trees add to the beauty of a development and reduce construction cost.
16. **Deep plots are wasteful:** Deeper plots in a residential layout does not increase its saleability. This type of plotting decreases the number of plots in a layout. Residential plots of over 150 feet depth are usually undesirable. For economical layout, plots of 30 feet to 40 feet in width should not exceed 130 feet in depth. Back to back plots from 100 to 120 feet in total depth of

two plots is satisfactory for single family dwellings. Plot sizes should be made after a careful study of local conditions and analysis of the cost relationship of services, road construction and land development.

17. **Plan plots of adequate width:** The well being of a neighbourhood and the economic soundness of a project depends on the manner in which the land is divided into plots. The width of these plots should not be reduced beyond a minimum requirement for building coverage, light and air. The question of plot width should be considered from the point of view of local regulations, the topography of the site and the type of dwellings. Practical building sites require plots of atleast 30 to 40 feet width to provide adequate setbacks for light, air, driveways and to avoid crowding.
18. **Avoid sharp angled plots:** Plots having sharp pointed corners are wasteful of land because the wedge shaped areas have no utility. Such plots also constitute poor building sites. Sharp angled plots can be avoided by planning streets to intersect at right angles and by making side plot lines perpendicular or radial to street lines.
19. **Street plots against adjacent non-conforming uses:** Residential plots should be arranged in such a way that they will not be seriously affected by a non-conforming use of adjoining property. Objectionable properties can be blocked off by screen planting or the plots should not have the front towards the objectionable use. It is suggested that wherever possible the layout boundary line should be along the rear side of a plot rather than the centre of a street. The appearance and value of a building site is improved when it faces a street having plots on the other side. Correct location of plots and zoning regulations protect against adjacent objectional property uses.
20. **Protect residential plots from major street traffic:** When residential plots are located on a major thoroughfare, it is suggested that the through traffic should be separated from a local service road by 20 feet wide tree planting strip. A 20 feet wide local service road should be located inside this planting protecting the residences against the noise and dust of traffic and street dangers to children. Thus it will increase the saleability of the plots and the planting of trees and shrubs will add to its attractiveness.

H. SLUM HOUSING

Housing the urban poor is an important duty of the government in a welfare state like India. For politicians, they form an assured vote bank during the elections. Thus their interests and demands cannot be ignored in a democratic country.

Whenever we think and talk about slums, we hear that architects are worried about their housing problems; engineers are worried about their services like water supply, drainage, roads and electricity; sociologists are worried about their social habits and customs, and economists are worried about their economic contribution. Thus the problems of slums in India are cast on epic scale in damaging the healthy growth of urban areas. To be practical, one cannot do away with them because we cannot remove the entire poverty of the country. We must accept that slums are a way of life in our cities. The positive way to solve the problems of slums is to improve the living conditions and stop further deterioration of the environment.

Lewis Mumford, well known urban theorist, says "There are two methods by which problems of uncontrolled urban growth are tackled. The direct method is to clear the areas of blight and house the affected population in a decent environment. This is commonly referred as 'Slum Clearance' which means not only cleaning slums but also properly rehabilitating the dishoused population. The indirect method is to control incomes, redistribute land to peasants, increase employment opportunities in small towns and create new settlements with employment opportunities."

1. **What is a slum:** According to Slum Area (Improvement & Clearance) Act, 1956, enacted by the Central Government of India, a slum has been defined as "Any predominantly residential area, where the dwellings which by reason of dilapidation, overcrowding, faulty arrangement of design, lack of ventilation, light or sanitary facilities or any combination of these factors, are detrimental to safety, health or morals"

   The 'Slum Improvement Scheme' contemplates the grant of financial assistance by the Central Government to State Government and Union Territories for slum clearance and improvement projects. The two important principles on which the scheme is based are:

(a) There should be minimum dislocation of slum dwellers and efforts should be made to rehouse them as far as possible on the existing sites of the slums and/or sites nearby in order to ensure that they are not uprooted from their fields of employment.

(b) In order to keep dov.ı rents within paying capacity of slum dwellers, the emphasis should necessarily be laid more on provision of minimum standards on environmental hygiene and essential services rather than on construction of any elaborate structure. Environmental Improvement of Urban Slums (EIUS) and Urban Basic Services (UBS) are the two programmes aimed at improving the quality of life of the urban poor under the Eighth Five Year Plan (1992-97). EIUS aims at provision of basic amenities like water supply, drainage, community baths and latrines, improving roads and streets lighting. This scheme is under state sector.

The Urban Basic Services (UBS) scheme is a social programme aimed at assisting mentally retarded and handicapped children, rehabilitating alcoholics and drug addicts and helping restrict children. This scheme also includes provisions for strengthening of urban local bodies, non- governmental organisations and other related works with an organisation for monitoring and evaluation. These two schemes are integrated and co-ordinated with other schemes like Nehru Rozgar Yojna (NRY) and liberation of scavengers.

The following case studies throw ample light on the slum improvement programmes practiced in India, particularly in metropolitan cities.

2. **Case Study: Calcutta bustee improvement programme:** 'Bustee' is used as a name for a special type of slum development. It contains huts. Each contains usually eight to ten cubicles, which are rented to separate families. They are the only available shelter that low-income people can afford. The tenant provides an essential service and he is called the 'thika tenant' who pays a land rent and resident in his own hut. The bustee is responsive to the needs of the population and provides a destination for the in-migrant. An important consideration in planning for the bustees is that they generally house a transient and not a stable population.

The Calcutta Metropolitan Planning Organisation proposed a major programme for the improvement of the bustees. It recognises that they cannot be cleared but improvements in the standard of living can be made at reasonable cost.

It was proposed to use tubewells to provide adequate supply of clean and safe water for the daily needs of bustee residents. Community water-tap for every 100 persons and two baths for every 100 persons were proposed. A sanitary sewer system was proposed. Sanitary latrines at a standard of 4 per 100 people provides one latrine for each hut. Storm water drain below the pavement to provide safe and clean paths. Street lights at regular intervals and at crucial location where walkways cross or turn. The tanks would be cleaned and improved.

A basic part of the concept is that the 'landowners' interests are purchased by a combination of bonds and cash so that the land becomes an urban land bank for the future development of the city. As clearance of bustees becomes financially possible within the city, land will be available and the profits from the reuse of the land will occur to the public. This programme calls for the vigorous undertaking of an urban community development programme.

If uncontrolled slum formation is to be prevented in the future, it is necessary to devise a programme to provide mass housing. Such a programme cannot look to government subsidies to meet its requirements but should depend upon the people to pay for their own shelter. It means that cost of housing born by low-income people must form the essential component in any mass housing programme. The government funds should be allotted to provide an urban environment, where the in-migrants are introduced to urban living without bad effects. Calcutta proposed this type of scheme under the 'low-cost temporary urban settlement programme'. Community facilities were also provided in temporary buildings.

These areas were intended to look like improved bustees with better community facilities and superior to the slums. The idea that these areas would be temporary was an essential part of the overall concept. The difficulties of moving the slum area people is well known. This programme is based on the assumption of an on-going development programme. This will ensure a constant supply of relocation housing, always within a short distance of the existing housing. Apart from the concept of temporary housing is the assumption of continuous growth of the city. The sites for temporary housing would be at the fringe of the city, which would be required for permanent construction. If temporary occupancy of land on the urban fringe by low-cost housing is followed by the use of the same land for permanent urban construction, then it is possible to solve many problems of urban growth.

The structures proposed for the low-cost temporary urban settlement programme are partly finished, so that they can provide flexible use of interior space, which is an advantage over the pucca slum clearance housing projects. Slum dwellers due to their low-incomes have to make the maximum use of their living space. Permanent flats does not allow adjustment to the wide range of family sizes and incomes of the slum dwellers but the temporary shelters would be flexible for their use. It would permit the development of workshops, cottage industries, schools and animal shelters within the project areas. It would allow a family to acquire as much space as his income and family permits.

This process of low-cost temporary urban settlement requires careful planning. At present, the new migrant to the city comes alone and leaves his family in the village until he is settled. He goes to friends from the same village in a particular bustee and stays with them. It is unlikely that these migrants can be attracted to the low-cost urban settlement areas directly. The long-term bustee residents who have lived more than twenty years in a particular bustee are also reluctant to move to any new location. In the beginning, the people most likely to be attracted to the new areas are the residents of one to ten years and did not establish permanent attachments to the bustee. So in the beginning, it will be necessary to attract people to the new areas by extensive publicity and by taking groups of potential 'thika tenants' to the sites to see the areas. An organised effort is necessary. Once the social character of a particular settlement area is established, it will receive new migrants with the residents already in the project area.

3. **Case Study: Chennai Slum Clearance Scheme:** They have experimented with two low-cost housing schemes. They are 'open plot development' and 'transit housing scheme'. The later consists of large buildings of about eight units each made of country wood frames covered with woven coconut matting and low brick walls. These units are used to house families from the slum areas during the time that the permanent tenements are being built on the original site. The usual duration of a family stay in the transit housing is about one year. Then they move to their tenement unit, normally on the site they occupied earlier as squatters. Transit camps are considered to be short-term housing, so no environmental facilities are provided on a permanent basis.

The latrines are of concrete construction. The water supply is carried from tubewells and taps located on nearby streets. The paths are not paved and there is no lighting. As a result, the transit camps provide a very low standard of housing, which is not better than that found in the slum areas. There is no rent charged in the transit camp. The reason for not improving the site to a level of the environmental standards used in the open plot areas is the desire of the government to make it absolutely clear that transit camps are only temporary locations for short-term occupancy.

Open plot development, on the other hand, is considered permanent housing. They provide 1000 sq. ft. per family at an over-all density of twenty five units per acre with 20 × 30 feet mud platform. A concrete lavatory and bath in one corner of the plot, so that one lavatory and bath unit containing four lavatory-bath pairs can be placed at the corner of four lots and serve four families. In addition each family receives raw materials in the form of bamboo, thatch etc., and some money to be used for the employment of skilled labour in the construction of the unit. For these units, the families are charged nominal rents. However, only half the rents are actually collected.

These open-plot units were constructed on the basis of combined State and Central financing, with a very high level of subsidy involved because of land costs and facilities. As most of the open-plot schemes are located on the periphery of the city, the rent must be very low to compensate for transport inconvenience involved. The open-plot units are not sold on a hire-purchase basis because it is felt that it would lead to resale of the plots to persons for whom the plots were not intended. The open-plot developments were built as a part of a large scheme that included approximately 1000 open plots and 1000 tenements.

The open-plot rent collection is done by the State Housing Board and the property is retained by the State. They are not maintained by the State, it is upto the rentee to repair his hut, bath or flush latrine.

This open-plot development scheme seems to be popular with the residents. They feel that they have more space than in the tenements. The rents are lower and they prefer the feeling that the structure is their own. However it is very expensive as it is heavily subsidised and rent collection is poor.

4. **Case Study: New Delhi Jhuggi-Jhonpri scheme:** In New Delhi, approximately 20,000 families have been moved to

resettlement sites at the rate of about 2000 families per month. Though the sponsors of the project within the Municipal Corporation of Delhi do not think the programme has made any appreciable reduction in the number of squatters and other slum families in the city. It is an appreciable effort.

When the decision is made to move on a particular site within Jhuggi-Jhonpri scheme, municipal corporation trucks along with demolition gangs and police execute the move quickly, taking each family along with its possessions and the building materials of their present hut to the new site. They are usually allocated 25 sq. yds. plot. The family then erects their own shelter on the plot assigned.

The family is given a one year lease by means of a site allocation slip. The rent of the site is fixed at a low-price, but infact, rent collection is so hapazard and difficult that money realised in this way fail to even cover the cost of administration. Frequently, the tenant sells the rights of a site to another party not eligible for this scheme. This practice is particularly true in areas with bigger sites. The family then moves back into slums of the city.

Housing constructed on the 25 sq. yds. plots is primarily of a mud brick nature. However, some concrete and brick structure have also been built. Site coverage is upto 75 percent. Community facilities are on a shared basis. One latrine per five families and one bath per six families. These facilities are in pucca structures. Water is supplied through tubewells. Most of the housing has three common walls with its neighbours.

A large number of commercial and semi-industrial uses are carried on within the project sites. There is a site management office at each area with an authorised strength of over ten persons. In practice, there are many vacancies on the management staff and the overall management of the projects is very lenient. There is no programmed effort to tie social services or urban community development activities into the programme.

Many people consider Jhuggi-Jhonpri scheme to be an inadequate solution to slum problems. It has proved conclusively that this type of housing can be provided on a massive scale if land is available. It has proved that the slum inhabitants will accept this type of housing. The distant sites selected have caused hardship and many families returned to the city slum. Its drawbacks are glaring but can be rectified. The lack of management can be overcome by trying alternative proposals. The distance to the city and places of employment can be overcome through good mass-transit facilities.

5. **Case study-4: Mumbai Slum Improvement Scheme**: In Mumbai multi-storeyed tenements are proposed for housing slum dwellers. Rehabilitation of slum dwellers can be carried out by owners or developers or co-operative societies of slum dwellers on the same plot. The following are 15 conditions:

(a) FAR shall be maximum 2.5.

(b) Names of the eligible slum dwellers on the land shall be certified by the concerned officer.

(c) All eligible slum dwellers residing on the plot shall be accommodated on the same plot as for as possible.

(d) Area for social infrastructure shall be cleared and made available for development by the concerned authority.

(e) Each slum dweller family shall be given a tenement of carpet area of 16.75 sq. m. including toilet but excluding common area.

(f) The maximum density should not exceed 5000 units/ hectare on the basis of FAR of one.

(g) In any scheme of redevelopment of affected slum dwellers, the area shall not exceed which existed prior to the development of the property.

(h) The scheme would provide 5% of the net plot area for commercial uses.

(i) Design of building for rehabilitation would be approved by a competent authority.

(j) A multipurpose room with size upto 12.5 sq. m. and minimum width of 2.4 m. Cooking space with a minimum size of 2.4 sq. m. and minimum width of 1.2 m. should be provided.

(k) A combined toilet permitted for more than one tenement with minimum area of 1.85 sq.m. and minimum width of one meter should be provided.

(l) Plinth height of 30 cm.

(m) External walls of 115 mm.

(n) Pathways: 1.5 m. upto 20 m. length; 2 m. upto 30 m. length; 2.5 m. upto 40 m. length and 3 m. upto 50 m. in length.

(o) In the case of notified slums on private lands, the Commissioner of Mumbai, with the consent of the owner may invite quotations from developers/owners for redevelopment in terms of surplus tenements as provided in the regulations.

In such cases, the owner would expect a return based on the balance land potential. This potential would be the permitted FSI in that scheme minus the actual FSI consumed in the slum. In the quotations, it would be presumed that developer would have taken into account this aspect. Therefore, while evaluating the quotations necessary calculations should be done for proper evaluation of the bids. In case, the consent of the owner is not received within the stipulated time such land can be developed according to the scheme after following acquisition proceedings.

These experiences have shown that management of the projects has proved to be extremely difficult in cities and the low level of rent collection is a clear indication. There is a feeling which is frequently pointed out by the officials is that lowest-income people seem to feel that because it is government housing scheme they should not be required to pay rent. This makes an impossible management situation, which must be rectified if there is to be a successful housing programme for lowest-income group.

The Above experiences of major metropolitan cities stand as guidelines for slum clearance and housing. As long as poverty is a way of life in India, we must accept slums in the urban areas and try to improve their living conditions by various schemes.

MODEL QUESTIONS

1. Describe the importance of housing.
2. What are the housing problems in India?
3. What are the major features of the National Housing Policy in India?
4. Which are the major housing agencies in India?
5. Which are the major housing finance institutions in India?
6. Describe the neighbourhood concept with a case study.
7. What design factors are taken into consideration for residential layout planning?
8. What is the importance of slum housing?
9. Describe briefly the slum improvement programmes undertaken in the following cities:
   (a) Calcutta (b) Chennai (c) New Delhi (d) Mumbai

8

Traffic and Transportation

(A) IMPORTANCE OF TRANSPORTATION

There is a need to understand the terms traffic, transport and transportation before understanding their importance in our society. Traffic means movement of people and vehicles. Transport means movement of people and goods from one place to another place. Transportation means the entire activity involving traffic and transport. It is used in broader sense embracing all related activities.

All the roads in old Indian towns were laid for pedestrain walking and movement of animal drawn vehicles like bullock carts and tongas. With the rapid pace of urbanisation, the number of cars, lorries, buses, autos and two-wheelers increased rapidly creating traffic jams, accidents and parking problems. Modern cities need better highways to link the cities and improved traffic regularisation. The parking problem within the cities is also acute which needs immediate attention. With the changing life styles in cities, faster modes of transport are preferred by the people. The economic prosperity increased the car ownership in the recent days and it has become a business necessity to reach destinations. The large variety of vehicles on the roads are creating traffic jams and parking problems, which are difficult to manage.

To solve the traffic and transportation problems, a comprehensive package of measures is needed. Increasing concentration of economic activities in few cities should be discouraged. Employment generation and economic activity should be encouraged in small and medium towns to discourage people migrating to large cities. However, this does not solve the existing problems in the cities. Transportation system within and between the cities should be improved by providing improved road conditions, traffic regulation, better parking facilities and good highways. Inadequate traffic facilities means not only loss of time and energy but also loss of economic development. There is a need for smooth flow of traffic by using or widening the existing roads and construction of new roads, flyovers and other traffic regulation measures.

(B) NATIONAL TRANSPORTATION POLICY

Most of the transportation proposals and schemes are guided and aided based on a National Transportation Policy. So, the National Transportation Policy of India and per Eighth Five Year Plan (1992-97) is quoted below for comprehensive understanding.

"Transport sector bears a close and complex relationship with all other sectors of the economy. While it tends to act as the prime mover of the development process, it must also respond to development process, if the latter has to be smooth. Socio-economic planning engenders structural shifts in the economy, widely influencing the pattern of movement of people goods and therefore, the nature and the quantum of demand for transportation. Transport planning has, thus, to be integrated with overall development plans.

Creation of transport infrastructure require time. It is necessary to anticipate the demand on the transport system ahead of socio-economic changes. In view of the long gestation involved, transport planning has to be seen in perspective longer than the Five Year Plan periods. Often, the capacities created during one plan period are the results of the investments made in earlier plans. Two issues, therefore, stand out—first, the need to preferably complete all the ongoing works to derive the maximum benefits from the earlier investments and secondly, to make investments keeping in view the longer time-frame perspective.

i) **Urban Transport:** Increasing urbanisation and the growth of personalised transport in the cities are resulting in acute congestion on city roads, besides causing environmental pollution. The emphasis has to be on the growth of public transport, which also has to be improved substantially. In the metropolitan cities, an integrated mass Rapid Transport System needs to be evolved.

Provision of transport facilities has to be integrated with Iand use planning which is particularly important for small and medium cities. It is also essential to prepare perspective transport plans for all cities so as to avoid fragmented, costly and often partial and ineffective solutions.

The transport problems of urban areas and especially those of metropolies, have not received due attention in the past. Meanwhile, the traffic has continued to multiply with the result that the urban transport infrastructure in almost all large cities is on the verge of a breakdown. In the absence of reliable transport, people are compelled to resort to private vehicles, which has aggravated congestion, pollution and energy intensity. There is no single agency to plan, coordinate or execute transport policies and programmes in urban areas.

It may be worthwhile to consider the creation of a financial institution for funding urban transport projects on soft terms to explore involvement of private/joint sector agencies in the development of transport systems. The research and development priorities during the Eighth Plan include—development of Urban Bus and introduction of energy efficient transit systems. The participation of the Ministry of Railways in developing mass rapid transport system in mega cities appears to be crucial. A comprehensive study of urban transport is also long overdue and is proposed to be undertaken during the Eighth Plan."

(C) IMPORTANT TRANSPORT COMPONENTS

The following are the important components of any transport.

1. Carrier or Vehicle.
2. Driver or Crew.
3. Right-of-way or Channel of movement.

The performance of all the above three determine the efficiency of the mode of transportation. The terminals and servicing points are also very important.

1. Carrier: Vehicle characteristics which need to be taken into consideration are length, width, weight, manoeuvrability, turning radius and horse power. Most of the vehicles are not more than ten feet high. The length between the front and rear wheels is known as axial length and the actual body length is known as total length. When the vehicle is fully loaded, it is known as 'ladden weight' which includes its own weight. 'Unladden weight' is the weight of the vehicle without any load. If the unladden weight is deducted from ladden weight, then it is known as 'pay load' of the vehicle. The number of axles depends upon the type of work carried out by the vehicle. A car has two axles and the trailer has four or six axles.

Manoeuvrability shows how best the vehicle can be manoeuvred or operated with ease. Here the ingenuity of the manufacturer is revealed. Easy manoeuvrability makes it an attractive vehicle for purchase and it helps easy movement on the roads. The turning radius of a vehicle depends on the weight, length and manoeuvrability. Turning radius is easy for light vehicles and difficult for heavy vehicles. The vehicles on Indian roads can be broadly classified into four categories:

(a) Private vehicles: Cars, Two-wheelers, Jeeps and Vans.
(b) Public vehicles: Buses.
(c) Hired Vehicles: Taxis, Three-wheelers and animal drawn carts.
(d) Goods vehicles: Lorries, Tankers, Three-Wheelers and animal drawn carts.

2. Driver: Normally fear of accident creates a behaviour in a driver. There are also other means of controlling a driver behaviour by legal rules and regulations like punishment and fine. The perception and reaction time of the driver is very important. After a persons eye registers a given happening, a period of time lapses before muscular reaction occurs. This period is called 'reaction time' and it differs between two persons.. Another interval of time called 'perception time' is required before reaction can begin. Under alert conditions perception time appears to be between 0.2 and 0.3 seconds. An alert driver reacts to situation quickly. It depends upon the age also. With increasing speed more alertness is required, so speed controls are essential to avoid accidents. There is specialised training for drivers to get acquainted to the traffic rules and road conditions. There are severe punishments in case of grave violations. All these measures should be able to control the behaviour of the driver for safe driving.

3. Right-of-way: In the past, the land acquired for right-of-way used to be narrow. Thus when it was felt necessary to widen a road or a street, then developed property along one or both sides of the road or street has to be purchased at high cost. Some times the same property was purchased at different times at different higher rates. To avoid such situations, it is felt necessary to acquire rights-of-way of roads, which are wide enough for future expansion. It is recommended that the width of land acquisition should include all necessary elements like ramps, walls and border areas. The channel of path should be wide enough with hierarchy of roads for easy plying of vehicles. The segregation of vehicular and pedestrain traffic is preferred.

(D) CHARACTERISTICS OF TRAFFIC

1. The nature
2. Volume
3. Speed

1. The nature: The nature of traffic plying on the road may consist of slow and fast moving vehicles. Slow moving vehicles are bullock carts, push carts and bicycles. Fast moving vehicles are scooters, motorcycles, cars, trucks, buses etc. Most of the cities in India carry both slow and fast moving vehicles. The traffic carrying capacity of a road or street can be divided into the following:

(a) Basic
(b) Possible
(c) Practical

(a) *Basic:* It refers to any street or road, where maximum number of passenger cars are moving or crossing a point in an hour (no. of cars/one hour) under most ideal traffic and road conditions.

(b) *Possible:* It means maximum number of vehicles that can pass given point or line under prevailing road conditions in an hour.

(c) *Practical:* It is normally less than the possible capacity under the prevailing practical road conditions.

Thus it is possible to estimate or measure the nature of traffic.

2. Volume: The volume of traffic is measured as the number of vehicles that pass a given line or point in the given time. It is measured in Passenger Car Unit (PCU). An index number is assigned to a vehicle taking all the characteristics into account. A passenger car is compared with other vehicles. For example if passenger car is equal to 1 PCU then if 100 cars can ply on a road then it is 100 PCU. If a bus is introduced on the same road, then the number of cars may reduce to 94, so 100 minus 94 is 6 PCU. Thus 6 PCU is equivalent to 1 bus. The number of cars a vehicle can substitute is known as PCU of that vehicle. This PCU value can change at junctions and straight roads. It is not an absolute but relative value.

3. Speed: Speed of a vehicle is very important for movement of traffic. Existing speed is not important but proposed speed is important. Speed limits are indicated depending upon many factors of the roads. Traffic surveys spreading over atleast two or three days are undertaken and its average is worked out. The survey can be conducted on a working day, holiday, Sunday and in rural areas on a shandy day. The maximum number of vehicles plying at particular period of time is known as peak hour traffic.

(E) TRANSPORTATION PLANNING PROCESS

There is a basic approach to all forms of transportation planning. This approach may be divided into four distinct phases:

1. Survey
2. Analysis and model building
3. Forecasting
4. Evaluation

The first two phases should bring out two important aspects. First, the existing travel demand and second, satisfying this demand with the existing transport facilities. To understand these aspects, survey and analysis is made of the existing travel demand. Then it is related to the existing urban environment. This study allows model building, which can be used in the forecasting phase.

In the third phase, forecasting uses the relationships in the analysis and model building stage to make estimates of the future demand. It requires a plan for testing. Information on the population and the proposed transport facilities in an area is needed. It is essential to note here that the techniques of landuse and transportation planning can differ from one situation to another situation for a given set of policies and conditions. It is the expertise of the planner to choose a suitable set of policies and transport facilities for a given situation.

In the fourth phase, evaluation takes into consideration, the results of the two previous phases to see whether the defined social, economical and operational objectives are satisfied. Many a time, more than a set of policies and transport facilities meet the desired objectives. It is a common practice to test a series of different assumptions before producing a preferred plan.

The above four phases are discussed in detail below:

1. Survey: The definition of the study area is very important for survey. Large scale studies take up important strategic transport facilities such as motorways, major routes, rail and road services. Small scale studies take up travel characteristics more in detail.

The main objective of a transport model is to predict the number of trips that will take place by different modes of transport. Then to predict the origins and destinations of these trips to decide the route which will be choosen between origin and destination. To describe the origins and zones. The size of these zones depend upon the details required. If destinations of journeys, the study area is divided into number of traffic zone is small, the model will be more accurate but the cost increases because the number of zones will be more. In the country side, the zones can be of larger size.

The data basically collects information on the origins and destinations of the journeys. There are many ways to find out the travel patterns. For smaller studies, registration number plate surveys, roadside interviews or pre-paid postcards can be used. For larger urban studies, household interviews may be conducted for collecting more information easily and cheaply. Apart from household interviews, roadside and public transport interviews may be conducted at selected points called as 'screenlines' to check and adjust the proposed transport model.

Separate inventories are prepared for the road and public transport system. Detailed information is collected on the facilities in each network. Then plan drawings are prepared for each network of the major transport systems. They are coded as input for the traffic model. For roads, data is collected on daily and hourly traffic volumes, average vehicle occupancies, the proportion of light and heavy commercial vehicles and speed and traffic flow relationship and Public transport networks require more information such as fare paid, walking and waiting time, frequency of service, and walking and waiting time at interchanging stations.

In each traffic zone information is collected on type and intensity of landuse, details on population quality and other information on trip generation.

2. Analysis and model building: Data analysis is necessary to design existing facilities such as large scale traffic management schemes or the routing and scheduling of the bus system. It gives an understanding of the relationship between travel behaviour and the urban environment.

Model building is the most important part of transportation planning because it can forecast future travel demands. The transport model is divided into four stages. These are:

(a) Trip generation or the decision to make a journey.
(b) Trip distribution or the selection of a suitable destination.
(c) Trip assignment or the actual journey undertaken on a transport facility by a particular route.
(d) Model split or the method of travel used for the trip.

(a) Trip generation: It is an examination of the relationship between the number of trips made. Early studies were confined to a numerical description of origins and destinations by zone. With increased stratification of journeys, better understanding of the relationships between generation and planning parameters can be worked out. Other parameters, which determine trip generation are household income, vehicle ownership, intensity of landuse and distance of the origin from the central area.

(b) Trip distribution: It analyses trips between zones. In the early models, simple growth factor methods were used. These models used

data on the base-year trip patterns but did not take into account other effects on the demand for travel. However, the number of trips from one zone to another depends upon same function of the distance between two zones. Growth factor models were replaced by synthetic models of trip interchange. The term interchange is used because existing trip pattern is used and the surveyed trip origins and destinations are not used directly in the model.

The most widely used models are 'Gravity Model' and 'Opportunities Model'. Gravity model says that trips are distributed between destinations according to the attractions of the destinations and the difficulty of travelling to the destinations. The Opportunities Model says that the probability of a trip ending in a given zone can be predicted.

(c) Trip assignment: It is the process by which the route taken by a traveller between two zones is determined. It is normally assumed that a trip between two zones can be determined from the network based on the minimum time or cost route between two zones. Sophisticated computer programmes are developed to calculate these minimum time or minimum cost routings.

(d) Model split: It is the method of travel, public or private transport, used for the trip. Model split is integrated in the transport model at various stages between trip generation and trip assignment. There are basically two approaches. One, at the trip generation stage and the other at the trip assignment stage. When it is related at the trip generation stage, the model split does not take into account route characteristics. When it is related at the trip assignment stage, the model split ignores the effects of choice of mode on the distribution of journeys. Model split choice depends on three things—first the properties of the journey, second the properties of the traveller and the last properties of the transport system.

When a complete transport model is prepared, various internal data checks are carried out. Any discrepancies are corrected at this stage. After a satisfactory model is prepared, it shall be used to forecast future travel demands.

3. Forecasting: At this stage, it is necessary to obtain as much information as possible for the design year concerning the travel behaviour. In particular, forecasts are required regarding planning parameters, population, employment and income distribution. These parameters may need sub-models to develop proper forecasts. The main feature, which affects future travel in the survey area is the location and nature of the future employment expected in the area. It is very difficult to estimate changes in industrial and commercial sectors employment. Future income and expenditure patterns should also be considered because changes in personal incomes affect trip generation patterns. Particularly, the car ownership will depend upon the rate of economic growth. Another important factor is the future transport system adopted. The landuse and transport networks are already planned and established in the urban development plans, so these should be taken into consideration.

4. Evaluation: Evaluation may be made in four stages. First numerical evaluation is necessary at all stages of the forecasting process. Computational or coding errors should be checked. Second, the accuracy of the resultant forecast should be assessed. This is essential to all subsequent evaluation. Third, operational evaluation should be carried out to check if a proposed network adequately satisfied the forecast travel patterns. Fourth, the best network may be decided based on the given budget limitations with maximum benefit to the community by minimising the cost of travel. Cost-benefit studies are used to guide investments. Costs include the capital, land and maintenance costs. Benefits are measured by savings in operation costs, journey time and reduction of accidents.

(F) SURVEYS OF TRANSPORTATION PLANNING

1. Defining the study area.
2. Origin-Destination surveys.
3. External-Cordon surveys.
4. External-Internal cordon surveys.
5. Post-card surveys.
6. Cordon-screenline surveys.
7. Commercial vehicle surveys.
8. Home questionnaire surveys.

1. Defining the study area : The boundary of the study area is known as external cordon. In this, major parts of the developed area and those parts, which are likely to be developed within the planned period of study are included. Residential areas adjacent to the main area may also be incorporated into an extended study area, if they rely on the major centre for employment or shopping. The most important factor to be considered when locating external cordon line is that they should be selected in such a way that they are suitable with previous or projected studies of the region.

The first task after defining the external cordon line is to subdivide the internal area of the study into small units, usually referred as 'zones'. This is done taking origin, destination, trip making, population, employment etc., into consideration. The external area is also broken down into zones. These external zones will become as larger as they are from the study boundary because the influence of other areas on the traffic pattern in the study area decreases with distance from the study area.

An initial need of a zone is that it should contain a homogeneous activity. Activities are closely related to type of landuse. A compromise has to be made, so that most zones have a predominance of one landuse. Special attention should be given to residential zone areas. Households of similar type should be grouped in one zone. At times it may be useful having sub-zones also for large office complexes or shopping centres.

A general consideration is that the size of zone should not be so small that the data collected is statistically unreliable. The zone boundaries must also be in harmony with the transport network configurations. For example, a zone may completely enclose one bus stop or railway station.

Having divided the area into zones, they should be discussed with local planning authorities. This is to ensure that proper account is taken of future changes in landuse proposed by the various planning authorities. At this stage, 'Screenline' should be defined on the zoning map and should coincide, if possible, with zone boundaries. The purpose of the screenline is to check on data collected in the interview and cordon surveys. They should be located in such a way that the survey area is split into equal areas so that few main routes are interrupted.

2. Origin-Destination surveys: In urban areas alternate paths are often available and individual drivers choose the most favourable paths. Improvements on particular routes will draw drivers from other routes. Street capacity, condition and directness of route affect traffic volumes. Traffic counts may not give a clear picture of the needs. Thus in urban areas, origins and destinations are very important than volumes on specific routes in long-range planning. The basic purpose of O-D studies is to determine the trip ends (Origins and Destinations) of individual persons or vehicles. For data gathering the area is sub-divided into geographical zones and sub-zones, and all trip ends are identified in these units. The zones are selected to conform to topographic or other barriers that control travel routes.

3. External-Cordon surveys: O-D interviews are held in a statistically determined number of dwellings, normally, between 20%

in cities of 50,000 to 4% for those over 1,00,000 population. The interviews note down the origins and destinations, and methods of transportation by each member of the family on the previous day. Interviews are guided by the counts at the cordon stations and bus, truck and taxi movement guided from company records.

4. External-Internal cordon surveys: For population of 50,000 and above an internal cordon surrounding the CBD (Central Business District) in addition to the external cordon is recommended. Interview data and techniques correspond quite closely to those described in external-cordon surveys like noting the origin, destination, trip purpose, route to be followed, intermediate stops, parking places, vehicle ownership and garage locations. At the stations on roads crossing this cordon line, a statistically determined percentage of vehicles are stopped and the drivers are interviewed.

5. Post-card surveys: Return paid post-cards are mailed to registered owners of all vehicles in the survey area. Spaces are provided on the return post-card for information about the driving done on a designated day. Although it provides less information than other methods, it can be done cheaply. Only 25% of the owners may reply and the results are difficult to verify. In some cases post-cards for O-D studies may be distributed to motorists at bridges or other points where traffic is confined to a few routes. Sometimes this method is quite reliable. In other areas, where drivers are concerned about the implications of the survey, results may be badly distorted.

6. Cordon-Screenline surveys: In large scale transportation studies, it is customary to divide the study area into a series of major areas known as sections, usually bounded by screenlines or cordons. A sample of all traffic crossing those screenlines is interviewed to provide further information on trip patterns throughout the study area.

7. Commercial vehicle surveys: Addresses of commercial vehicles are collected from a landuse survey. These addresses are then contacted and the drivers of a stratified sample of the vehicles operated from each depot are asked to record their movements. Another way of obtaining the sampling base is to use local vehicle excise records. In this case, the sampling unit becomes the vehicle itself rather than the vehicle operator. Because of the number of commercial vehicles and the difference in trip pattern followed by different commercial vehicle operators, a relatively large sample size may be required.

8. Home questionnaire surveys: In this method, an explanatory letter is sent in advance. The interviewer collects only the household information and leaves forms for the residents of the households to complete their travel information for the following day. After a day or two, the interviewer collects the forms and checks them.

(G) TRAFFIC CONTROL AT THE INTERSECTIONS OR JUNCTIONS

An intersection or junction is a place where two or more roads meet. Intersections can be of various types. Normally, the following methods are adopted in controlling the traffic at intersections.

1. Using a warning sign like a hump or speed-breaker.
2. Manual control by a traffic policeman to regulate the traffic.
3. Channelisation of traffic.
4. Traffic rotary or roundabout or island to slow down the traffic, when the volume can be controlled.
5. Automatic traffic signal lights with calculated time to regulate the traffic.
6. The interchanges or grade separators, in case of those intersections which cannot be controlled by the above five methods.

1. Using a warning sign: This is normally used where the traffic volume is less. On busy traffic roads, it does not work smoothly as it delays the movement and will not regulate the traffic as much as it is needed. This method is mainly adopted to reduce the speed of the vehicle where the traffic volume is less and pedestrain movement is more. The hump or speed-breaker compels the driver to slow down the speed of the vehicle to avoid any possible clash with other vehicle or person.

2. Manual control by a policeman: Normally traffic policemen are employed at the intersections, when the traffic volume can be controlled manually either with hands or with signal lights. This method is useful, where the traffic volume is not very high and it can be controlled by a person. At some intersections the traffic volume is high only during the peak hours like morning during office hours and evening during marketing etc. At such intersections instead of automatic traffic signals, a policeman can regulate the traffic for smooth flow.

3. Channelisation of traffic: Channelisation has the following advantages:

(a) Vehicles can be confined to definite paths. The accidents are more likely when drivers have free choice of routes creating conflicting movements.

(b) The angle between intersecting streams of traffic can be made more favourable. When cross traffic meets at flat angles the accidents can be head-on collisions. It has been established that the intersection of traffic stream at about right angles (75° to 105°) is most favourable. (see Fig. 8.1)

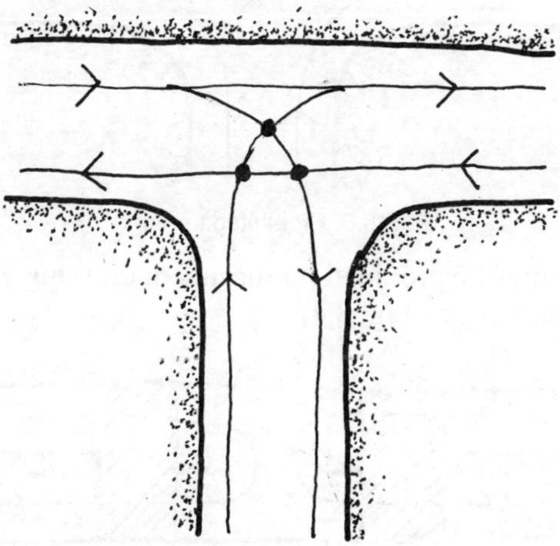

Fig. 8.1 Right-angled intersection

(c) Drivers can be forced to merge into moving traffic streams at flat angles and proper speeds.

(d) Speed control can be established over vehicles entering an intersection. One method is to bend the traffic stream, another method is to funnel the vehicles into a narrowing opening. This makes the driver feel hammed-in and reacts by reducing his speed. (see Fig. 8.2)

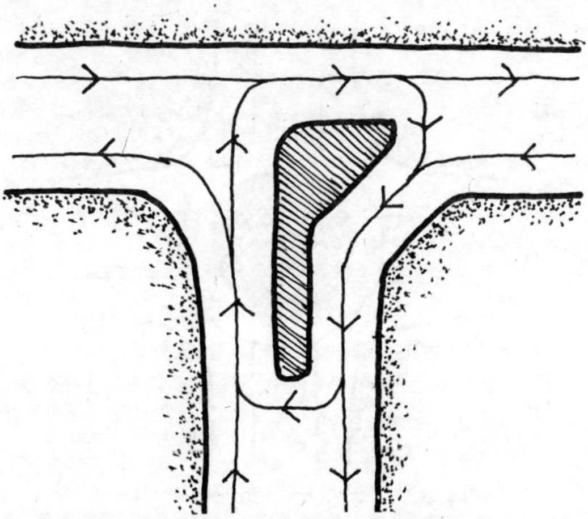

Fig. 8.2 Speed control by channelisation

(e) Prohibited turns may be prevented. (see Fig. 8.3)

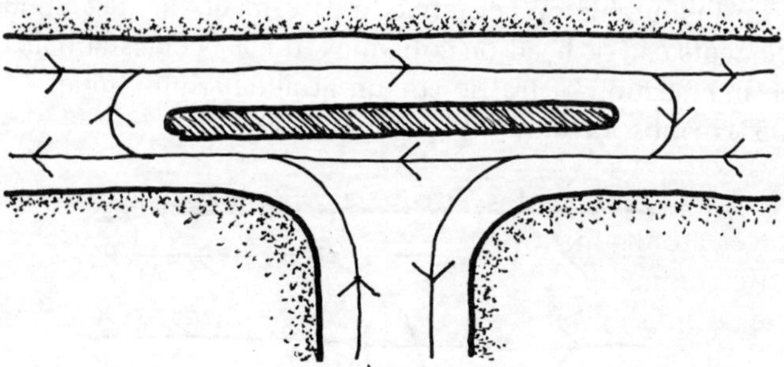

Fig. 8.3 Prohibited turnings

(f) Refuge may be provided for turning or crossing vehicles and for pedestrains. (see Fig. 8.4)

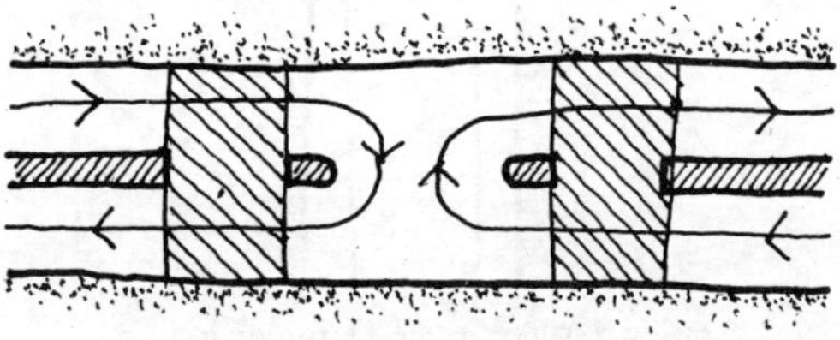

Fig. 8.4 Pedestrain & vehicular refuge

(g) Points of conflict may be separated in such a way that the driver faces only one decision at a time. This reduces confusion and accidents.

4. Traffic rotary or roundabout: A rotary intersection called as 'Roundabout' emerges from one-way road around a central island. (see Fig. 8.5)

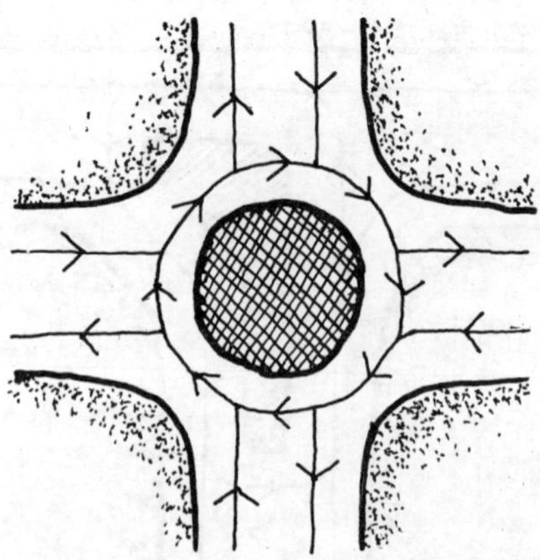

Fig. 8.5 Traffic roundabout or island

The advantage of the traffic rotary is that it reduces the speed of the vehicles while taking the turning, either right or left, particularly the right turn where the chance of conflict is more. In this method the vehicle moving straight merges with the traffic coming from the other side and diverges in the middle and merges in the end before leaving the rotary. These merging points are known as 'weaving sections'. Four weaving sections are formed because of this process. The advantages are the moving vehicle while going straight merges with the traffic coming across avoiding the possible conflict created in a free intersection and also the speed of the vehicle is considerably reduced. The disadvantage of right turning and the danger of conflict with the vehicles coming across on the other side is also reduced due to the reduction in the speed of vehicle and weaving sections. These traffic rotaries are useful when the volume of traffic is moderate and not heavy. The traffic rotary need not be a circle, it can be ecliptical in shape depending on the volume of traffic on each road. Rotaries are not being used today except in special instances because they require relatively large area for development, the extra travel distance within them, the speed reduction of all entering vehicles and the limited capacity of the weaving sections. It is found possible to handle greater volumes of traffic combining channelisation and traffic signal controls.

5. Traffic signals: Traffic signals are usually indicated in three colours red, amber and green. Red indicates stop for the moving traffic, amber indicates that driver can start his vehicle meanwhile the pedestrain traffic can cross the road completely and green indicates the vehicles to move ahead. The time taken between red and green signals is indicated by amber to protect the moving pedestrain traffic crossing the road. Traffic signals are usually adopted where traffic volumes are large at the intersections. Traffic signals are meant not only for vehicles but also for pedestrain movement. The space used for pedestrain movement on the road is marked by zebra lines near the intersection, where the vehicles are usually forced to stop.

Before installing the traffic signals for both pedestrain and vehicular movement a survey should be conducted to know the time intervals between the red, amber and green signals. If the pedestrain movement across the road near the intersection is more, a subway is adopted than the traffic signal. Traffic signals are synchronized for smooth movement of traffic and does not cause any obstruction like traffic rotaries. Traffic signals may not be able to control heavy volumes of traffic, at some intersections, then interchanges or grade separators are used for smooth flow of traffic.

6. The interchanges or grade separators: In this method, a new separate road is constructed on the existing road to free the traffic without any collision or conflict. The interchanges can be of various types. The simplest interchange is to have a fly-over. (see Fig. 8.6)

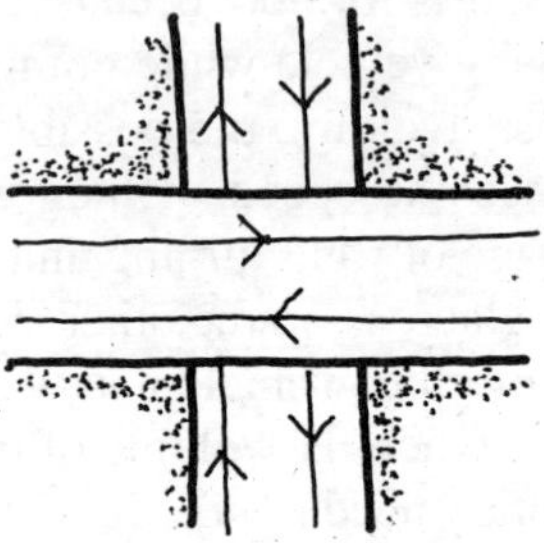

Fig. 8.6 Prohibited turnings

There are other types of interchanges like cloverleaf and diamond shaped interchanges. The most common is the cloverleaf interchange. (see Fig. 8.7)

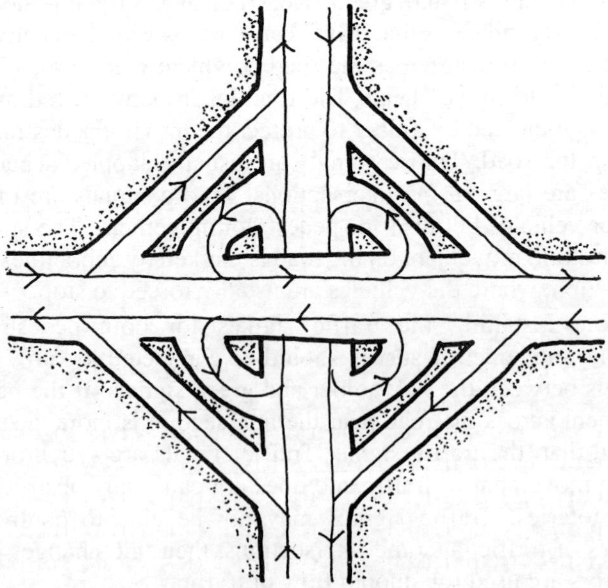

Fig. 8.7 Prohibited turnings

In this type of intersection the movement is free without any obstruction because of the fly-over above. The movement of traffic is always towards the left. Even for the right turn, the vehicles should climb a ramp on the left side to join the stream above. This method of intersection takes more space and longer distances to be covered by the driver. However grade separators solve many of the problems of traffic movement for smooth flow at good speed.

(H) PARKING

Vehicles parking has become a major problem in the cities. Using various vehicles like cycles, two-wheelers, three-wheelers, lorries, buses and cars has become common for movement of people and goods. In cities, people prefer to use a vehicle than walk to their destinations. The availability of vehicles has made people commute to long distances for various purposes. Pedestrain walking is limited to short distances. General vehicle parking habits of the people can be broadly classified into three categories:

1. Parking within premises
2. Short-time parking
3. Long-time parking

1. Parking within premises: Vehicles parked within the premises normally include independent houses, residential and commercial complexes. Vehicles parking in all these types of buildings is guided by local building bye-laws. Construction of residential and commercial complexes is permitted, only if they meet the required parking norms. Whenever the parking is inadequate, vehicles are parked on the roadside. Visitors parking is also neglected in the rules compelling them to parks on the roadside. Such roadside parking often obstructs flow of traffic creating traffic jams. Parking norms should be periodically revised depending upon the vehicle ownership of the people. Violation of parking norms should be dealt severely.

2. Short-time parking: Normally, short-time parking takes place on the roadside by visitors to attend to some work, shopping and recreation. The parking time varies from few minutes to one hour. Adequate parking lots should be provided at proper places for such parking on the roadsides and in the lanes without obstructing free flow of traffic. Nominal parking fees is collected to discourage people from long-term parking in such places. Short-time parking is not a major problem, but it requires proper planning and traffic regulation.

3. Long-time parking: Long-time parking varies from few hours to one or two days. People need such parking near railway stations, airports, stadiums, auditoriums, cinema theatres and commercial complexes. Normally, these parking facilities are charged. Premises like cinema theatres, auditoriums, stadiums and commercial complexes should show adequate parking norms before approval of the building plans to the local authorities. In spite of such parking provisions, inadequacy of parking space is felt due to the increasing vehicle-ownership of the people. Multistoreyed buildings are constructed at some central areas of the city to meet the increasing demand of parking space. Long-time parking is going to be a big problem in the coming years with the rapid increase of vehicle ownership, particularly with the raise of car-ownership of the people.

To solve the vehicle parking problems, good mass transportation system should be developed in the cities. People should be discouraged to use personal transport to commute to their work-place. Efficient bus and rail transport can mitigate many of the acute parking problems.

(I) CASE STUDY: HYDERABAD TRAFFIC & TRANSPORTATION STUDY 1988.

Based on the expected travel demand for the City-Region strategy, recommendations are made to improve the traffic and transportation facilities with the population growth rate. They are briefly summed-up below:

1. Improvement of traffic flow

(a) At 66 intersections physical improvement plans are suggested. These include realignment of approaches, widening of carriageway, realignment of drainage, traffic islands, paint markings, relocation of bus bays, sign boards etc.

(b) At 111 important junctions traffic signals are suggested. On 7 major corridors signal co-ordination is proposed.

(c) At 18 major intersections grade separators are proposed.

(d) On the 7 corridors mid block improvements in the form of carriageway improvements, pavement widening, bus bay relocations, paint marks etc., are suggested over a length of 55 km.

(e) Traffic paint markings and signs are to be installed on all the major arterials totalling to a length of 50 km.

(f) At 6 rail/road crossings where heavy delays occur grade separators are proposed.

(g) To facilitate the heavy pedestrain movement in the city, footpaths of width 2m to 5m. on either side of the carriageway are to be improved along the major roads.

(h) To meet the demand of passenger flow between north-south parts of the city 5 new bridges are suggested across river Musi.

(i) To cater for the needs of high bicycle flow a parallel bicycle network is suggested.

(j) To safeguard the pedestrains at intersections, measures like pedestrain subways at 4 locations, sky-walk at Secunderabad railway station and signal intersections are suggested.

2. Improvement to Intermediate Public Transport (IPT) services: To strengthen the IPT services, parking terminals for cycle-rickshaws at 19 locations and for auto-rickshaws at 18 locations are suggested. These include black topping of the parking area, shelter, phone etc.. with other amenities.

3. Integration of urban region: With a view to contain the growth of the city, it is suggested that the following cities are to be encouraged to grow by locating basic industries nearer to them.

(a) Warangal
(b) Nalgonda
(c) Mahboob Nagar
(d) Tandur
(e) Zahirabad
(f) Nizamabad
(g) Karimnagar

To discourage the densification of Central Business District (CBD) in the city, service centres are proposed in the following zones for development.

(a) Ramachandrapuram
(b) Medchal
(c) Ghatkesar
(d) Vanasthalipuram
(e) Rajendranagar

4. Road network: To augment the existing network, new roads of about 385 km. length are proposed. The present roads in the Hyderabad region is of a length of about 365 km. which is to be upgraded to highway standards. To enable the development of Hyderabad region and integrated highway network connecting other growth centres, an additional road network of 3100 km. is suggested.

5. Transit service improvements: To improve the bus transport facilities in the city 1000 buses should be added to the present fleet within 10 years in stages. On the present network about 200 bus bays are to be constructed and 4 new regional bus terminals are to be built for effective city regional integration. In order to improve the operational efficiency of the city bus routes, route rationalisation has been suggested. To achieve a balanced regional growth an efficient regional bus network is suggested. For this purpose 2000 buses are to be added to various district depots in the Hyderabad influence region.

This may need 10 depots to accommodate 50 to 100 buses over a period of time throughout the region at a distance of about 40-50 km. and the rest being operated from other regions.

6. Track guided system: To transport large number of people on dense corridors, two alternative strategies are suggested.

(a) If the railways agree to share their right-of-way for local traffic, inner circular railway with radials inclusive of Light Rail Transit (LRT) system is proposed.

(b) If the railways do not agree to operate the local trains, then independent Light Rail Transit (LRT) system is suggested.

It is also suggested to run trains during peak hours in east-west direction on broad-gauge track from Warangal to Tandur for regional communication.

7. Goods transport management: To discourage goods traffic plying on the city streets the following truck terminals and parking lots are suggested.

(a) Major truck terminals.

(b) Mini truck terminals.

(c) Truck parking lots.

It is suggested that large number of wholesale markets within the city be shifted to 5 different locations near to 5 service centres.

8. International airport location: To accommodate expected domestic and international air travel, a new site for the international airport has been suggested in Nadergal Zone.

9. Traffic education: Realising the importance of traffic education a booklet containing the explanation of standard road signs, markings, signals, police signs, driver signs etc., is prepared.

Hyderabad has a very poor hierarchy of roads. All are residential roads with through traffic and shopping. Shops and other business establishments directly open to the major roads and highways. Narrow residential streets are often choked with heavy through traffic. These problems cannot be measured with any mathematical technique. Another important factor is the excessive dependence on private transport. The available public transport is not able to meet the demands of the people. To solve Hyderabad traffic problems sustained efforts to educate people and policy makers is needed.

MODEL QUESTIONS

1. What is the importance of transportation in cities?
2. What are the major features of the National Transportation Policy in India?

3. What are the important transport components?
4. What are the characteristics of traffic?
5. Describe the transportation planning process.
6. What are the various surveys undertaken for transportation planning?
7. What are the measures to control traffic at junctions?
8. What are the essential steps suggested in the Hyderabad Traffic and Transportation study 1988?

9

Landscape Design

(A) IMPORTANCE OF LANDSCAPE DESIGN

Nature always formed a part of human existence. The trees, shrubs and green grass are part of human life. The growth of human civilisation began to change the environment causing damage to the nature slowly. The destruction of wooded forests for human survival is one of the major destructive activities against nature. The crowded cities with increasing growth of population and industry did not care for proper preservation of natural landscape. Planned tree planting with well laid out open spaces make cities congenial for living. Planned urban landscaping is intended to give good appearance, provide shade and comfort, prevent dust collection, act as wind breakers, serve as visual barriers and above all provide fresh air to breathe. The landscape development depends upon the climate and soil conditions of the area. The number of trees in a town has a direct impact on the living atmosphere of the citizens. Trees need light and space to grow. Scarcity and absence of trees is an indication of poor living environment. Roads and streets looks barren and artificial without trees and plants. Playgrounds, gardens and recreational spaces have their own value in a city. As cities get more and more crowded, the importance of landscaping gets increased. Expanding cities pushed natural surroundings to the countryside, and citizens are deprived of the various moods of nature during different seasons. Intelligent landscape development can make cities pleasant and citizens to become environment friendly. Proper tree plantation in the cities can improve general climatic conditions, moderates solar radiation, controls temperature, reduces wind speed, provides shelter, reduces air and noise pollution, useful for soil conservation and protects wildlife.

(B) NATIONAL BUILDING CODE OF INDIA 1983 — A GUIDELINES

1. **Greenbelts and Landscaping**: Greenbelts and iandscaping including plantation of shrubs and trees help to certain extent in enhancing the environmental quality.

   Planting of trees in streets and in open spaces should be done carefully to take advantage of both shades and sunshine without handicapping the flow of natural winds. Their advantage for abating glare and for providing cool and/or warm pockets in developed areas should also be taken.

   Where relief from noise is to be provided by means of greenbelts, these may be of considerable width and be landscaped. The extent of relief that may be derived from the above may be estimated only after considering other environmental factors. Strong leafy trees may be planted to act as noise baffles. Shrubs or creepers may also be planted for additional protection between tree trunks, artificial mounds and banks should be formed wherever practicable.

2. **Norms for planting of shrubs and trees**: Suitable provisions may be made for greeneries including plantation of shrubs and trees as a part of environmental protection in general. This aspect shall be taken care of from the initial stage of town and country planning, zoning and planning of development of particular area and group housing. Finally, this aspect shall also be taken into account in planning individual building of different occupancies. A guide for the quantum of plantation of shrubs, trees and other greenery in different occupancies and community spaces is given below:

(a) **Residential areas**

1. For smaller plots (less than 200 sq.m.) and EWS housing, slum area etc., for every 50 families create one small community space of about 100 sq.m. where clumps of trees may be planted so as to provide shade and improve the quality of environment.
2. For bigger plots (more than 200 sq.m.), 10 percent of open space is to be left unpaved for greenery with atleast two small/medium trees upto plot area of 500 sq.m. An additional one tree for every 100 sq.m. area of plot or part thereof for above 500 sq.m. plots. Hundred trees per hectare of total land area and 40 percent of the permissable open space to BE covered by greenary.

Landscape proposal shall be got approved from the local Authority along with the building plan for group housing schemes.

(b) Educational and Institutional areas

1. 125 trees per hectare should be provided.
2. 50 percent of the permissable open space should be provided for greenery

(c) Industrial areas

1. For plot sizes 300–1000 sq.m. 5 trees for 300 sq.m. plot area and 2 trees for every additional 100 sq.m. area should be provided.
2. For plot sizes 1000 sq.m. above, 150 trees per hectare and 20 percent of the permissable open space should be provided for greenery.
3. For industrial plots, it is advisable to have peripheral plantation to minimise pollution especially air and noise pollution.
4. Large polluting industry should be separated from the neighbouring residential area by a thick green belt which should occupy an area of about 15 percent of the industrial area.

(d) Other occupancies: For other occupancies namely assembly, business, mercantile, the quantum of greenary shall be planned taking the development as a whole. However, a minimum of 50 trees shall be provided per hectare; 25 percent of the permissable open space should be covered by greenary such as shrubs, grass and suitable landscape.

(e) Roads: For roads in a Development Plan, trees shall be provided on either side of the road or on both sides depending upon the width of the roads, the location of building along the road side and other considerations. However, minimum one tree for every 10 m. should be provided.

1. The types of plants, the distance between trees/plants from the building and the distance between plants shall be carefully worked out keeping in view the structural safety and aesthetic requirements of buildings.
2. Trees shall be numbered area-wise, plot-wise and road-wise by the concerned authority and they shall be checked periodically.
3. Cutting and pruning of trees in public as well as private areas shall be suitably regulated. Trees shall be cut only after obtaining the permission of the authority designated for this purpose.

(f) **Landscape design process**: Landscape design process can be divided into four stages:

1. Data collection stage
2. Preliminary design stage
3. Final design stage
4. Post design stage

1. Data collection stage: Landscape survey information comprises all available factual data of the site including sections, diagrams and survey schedules. Aerial survey can help data collection in large landscape projects. Records should mention the date and source of data.

Data should include climate, Geology and soils, Hydrology and drainage, Vegetation, Natural habitat factors, Landuse, Social, Economic and Demographic factors, Structures, Roads and Services, Archeological and local history, Access and Communications, Pollution factors, Legal and Planning aspects and any other special data.

2. Preliminary design stage: Schematic diagrams should be prepared for interpretation of clients requirements. Sketch plans should be based on schematic diagrams. Feasibility study may be made on site data. These drawings should be numbered and dated for preliminary consideration. The approved preliminary drawings should be checked against the proposals of other specialists.

3. Final design stage: The preferred preliminary drawings should be developed for the final design. The drawings should be legible and concise with sufficient information for implementation and preparation of bills of quantities. Layout drawings should be clear for execution. Complex layouts need separate plans for various work aspects such as site clearance, underground services, hard and soft landscape works etc. Separate plans should be based on a Master Plan of the layout. This Master Plan Layout should be retained for additional aspects of the work and for any major revision. The drawings may include Final Layout, Location Plan, Site Plan, Services Plan, Planting Plan and other details.

4. Post design stage: During the construction, a set of drawings should be recorded and kept with all changes in design. After completion a set of drawings showing the actual construction should be prepared. For maintenance after the construction, drawings should show the locations and frequency of maintenance operations for the long term implementation of the design intentions. This information can be in the form of drawings or notes attached to the plans.

(D) Case study: Landscape design of Chandigarh

Landscape design of Chandigarh is unique because it is the first new town in India to be fully planned from the beginning. It is a fair opportunity to integrate landscape design in the overall town planning. The natural landscape features of the site were preserved and enhanced with design in Chandigarh. No city can have a·rigid landscape design because of inward and outward expansion of the city for various activities. In the process, the natural features are destroyed for construction but some broad guidelines can be made for conservation of existing landscape while planning for expansion of activities. Projects could be taken up within these broad guidelines by preserving the existing landscape. Each city is endowed with some major natural features, for example Bombay has beautiful seaside, Goa has beautiful beaches and Bangalore has beautiful ponds and lakes, which can be preserved and enhanced in the landscape design.

1. Existing natural features of the site: The major landscape features of Chandigarh are:

a) The site is situated at the foothills of the Shivalik hills at 1300 feet height above sea-level. The site has agricultural fields and 26 villages. It has a slope of 1 in 100 feet from north-east to south-west for natural surface drainage.

b) The seasonal streams, Patiali-ke-Rao on the north-west and Sukhana Choe on the south-east formed the boundaries of the site. A rain-water drain runs through the heart of the city

c) The city site has mango grooves, peepal, banyan and various fruit trees besides many ponds, mounds and small drains.

2. Landscape design concept: A hierarchy of green spaces were created from private gardens to the public parks. These green spaces were intended to form an integral part of the city. The city's landscape was not changed as far as possible to fit the grid-iron pattern of the city. Retaining the natural topography of the site formed the basis for the landscape design of Chandigarh. A Landscape Advisory Committee was set up to lay down the basic principles of landscape design and implementation. Classification of trees was made based on their form, foilage, shape and type of flowers. It formed the base for all tree plantation in Chandigarh. A Tree Preservation Order was passed in 1952 to stop felling of existing trees. Le Corbusier identified important places for tree plantation. Some of the major feature's of Chandigarh landscape design are:

a) Each sector in Chandigarh was provided with a hierarchy of green spaces ranging from private gardens to public parks. Artificial green mounds were created in the Capital Complex with the excavated earth. These mounds were covered with different plantations. Two big water ponds were designed by the architect as a part of the capital complex, one in front of the Assembly and the other in front of the High Court. Existing mango groove trees around the capital complex are preserved. Trees are also planted on either side of the road approaching the capital complex.

b) Four ponds are provided in the city centre, but no green spaces were planned in the industrial area. A green-belt of fruit trees were planted to protect the residential neighbourhoods from industrial pollution.

c) A Leisure Valley was planned along the existing rain water drain to have a central green space in the heart of the city. With series of gardens it extends from north to south of Chandigarh city. It includes Bougainvillea Park, Flower Garden, Rose Garden, Children Garden and series of different other gardens.

d) Another major green space is the Golf Course, which is comparatively the best maintained among the green spaces.

e) Sukhana Lake is another major landscape feature. It has an area of three square kilometers. It is a rainfed lake by damming the Sukhana Choe. Its catchment area lies in Shivalik hills. The beautiful setting made it a tourist attraction.

f) Trees were planted in single rows, double rows or in multiple rows. The landscaping scheme provides high trees to separate the roadway and a variety of shade-trees for pedestrain path. The shopping streets were planted with a variety of trees to give different character to each sector. The traffic intersection islands of the main road have been beautified with attractive landscape designs.

g) Chandigarh's landscape is incomplete without the mention of 'Rock Garden'. In a corner of the city, Nek Chand began in the mid-sixties his creative work with rocks and stones found in the Shivalik foothills, and other discarded materials of the city to create his own world of fantasy. For many years it remained unknown to the world. The city administration opened in 1976 the 'Rock Garden' as it became known, to the public. The rock garden still continues to grow as a reminder that creativity knows no bounds. It is a major tourist attraction of the city.

MODEL QUESTIONS

1. What is the importance of landscape design?
2. What are the landscape design guidelines as per NBC 1983?
3. Describe the landscape design process.
4. What are the major features of Chandigarh landscape design?

10

Urban Conservation

Urban conservation philosophy is centered around the relationship between man and his built-environment. Urban conservation is a new thought in our cities. It is an idea developed in Europe. The large scale dynamic changes in the landuse of metropolitan cities led to this kind of thinking of conserving historic structures. There are many arguments for and against this concept. Some of them are briefly summed-up below:

(A) Pro-conservation Arguments

1. Historical justification for conservation is the easiest to uphold. History is vital to an understanding of the present because it records and generalises from past events relevant to the future. Artefacts from the past provide material evidence of the past civilisation and architecture.
2. Another argument is that we must learn from the past, re-examine our design processes and begin to re-inject the development programme with creative planning. Conservationists use their knowledge of past design as a basis to criticise monotonous new buildings and particularly the building of the modern movement in architecture.
3. One more argument relies upon the identity, association and psychological needs of the local population of the city or town.
4. With the depleting energy sources, the extended use of the existing building stock for renewed uses saves the energy spent on new development is another argument for conservation.

(B) Anti-conservation Arguments

1. Conservation inhibits progress and change, both in material and imaginative sense, when these are essential to our way of life.
2. The conservation of buildings of inefficient design for new

economic use prevents the building of new housing or work-places mearly because powerful minority group regard old buildings as intrinsically good. Meanwhile because of conservation many people must continue to work in cramped and unsuitable conditions.

3. New buildings will be expected to fit in older neighbourhoods by virtue of the use of traditional materials and vernacular details. Architects consider this kind of stipulation as a severe inhibition to their creativity.
4. Planners have undertaken the impossible task of acting as aesthetic judges. Our descedants might have very different ideas of what was beautiful and what was ugly.
5. Another strong argument against conservation is that we feel ourselves to be no longer the men of the cathedrals, palaces and tribunes but those of the great hotels, the railway stations, the immense streets, big ports, posh markets, straight roads and beneficial demolitions.

(C) Identification of Heritage Buildings

Normally the following factors are taken into consideration for identification of heritage buildings for conservation.

1. **Type of building**: The original purpose for which the building was constructed followed by the present use.
2. **Date**: The date and period of construction as accurately as possible.
3. **History**: Historical importance of the building.
4. **Architect/Patron**: The concerned architect and his builder or client.
5. **Plan and Arch. style**: Identification of the architectural style and actual plan of the building.
6. **Materials**: The materials used in construction should be written in order from bottom to top like foundation, walls, roof, interior etc.
7. **Facades**: Detailed description of the frontage of the building from bottom to top.
8. **Interior**: Significant interior design features to be conserved.
9. **Subsidiary features**: Subsidiary features like gates, grills, railings etc.
10. **Other Information**: Information related to the building and its surroundings, which is not listed above.
11. **Source**: Source of information gathered from should be given for reliability.

(D) Case Study: Hyderabad Urban Conservation Study 1984.

In Hyderabad capital city of Andhra Pradesh state, Hyderabad Urban Development Authority (HUDA) took up an urban conserva- tion study of Hyderabad and identified 165 buildings for conservation.

1. Major features of Hyderabad Urban Conservation Study:

(a) Guidelines in selection of the buildings:

1. The age of the building.
2. Architectural excellence or style of any particular period.
3. Relevance to the social and economic history of the city.
4. Association with well known persons or events.
5. Its value as a part of a group of buildings.
6. Its reuse potential and suitability for conservation through recycling.

(b) The distinguishable architectural styles:

1. Qutb Shahi. (see Fig. 10.1)
2. European. (see Fig. 10.2)
3. Temples.
4. Qutb Shahi revival.
5. Regional Mughal variation (general).
6. Regional Mughal variation (wooden devdis).
7. City Improvement Board or Osmanian style.
8. Indo-European. (see Fig. 10.3)
9. Vernacular.
10. Other styles.

The three most dominant architectural styles are Qutb Shahi, European and Indo-European styles.

(c) Typology of buildings:

1. Religious (mosques, temples, churches, tombs)
2. Monumental structures (gateways, towers etc.,)
3. Palaces and complexes
4. Buildings with internal courtyard (devdis & havelis)
5. Pavilions
6. Small buildings in rows (roadside groups etc.)
7. Individual buildings

(*d*) Out of 165 buildings identified for conservation 31 percent are owned by government and 69 percent are owned by private people; 10 percent are unoccupied; 64 percent of the buildings are between 50 to 100 years old and 19 percent are more than 100 years old.

EXAMPLES OF DOMINANT ARCHITECTURAL STYLES

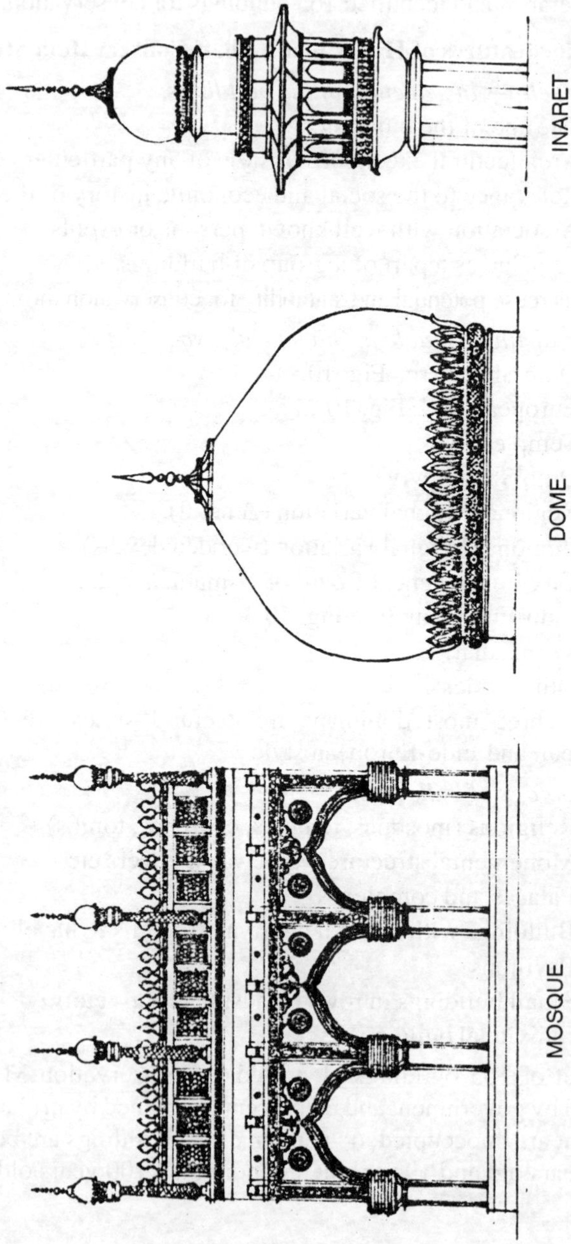

Fig. 10.1 Qutb Shahi Style (not to scale)

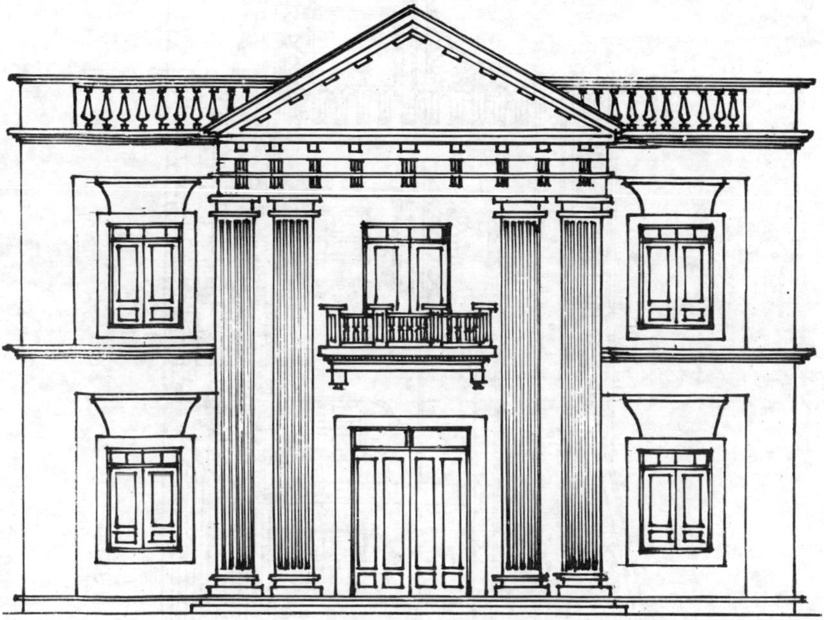

Fig. 10.2 European Style

(e) Special areas identified for conservation:

1. Conservation areas (immediate surroundings of protected monuments and important listed buildings)
2. Design zones (new areas requiring design control)
3. Neighbourhood improvement ideas (areas requiring specific improvement of buildings, facades and services)

(f) Measures suggested for conservation:

1. Imaginative grants or loans scheme to interested individuals, religious, public and government institutions.
2. Exemptions on income tax, estate duty, gift tax and wealth tax.
3. 'Free trade zones' by extending total or partial exemption from sales tax and entertainment tax
4. Constitution of high level 'Landmarks commission' for co-ordination.

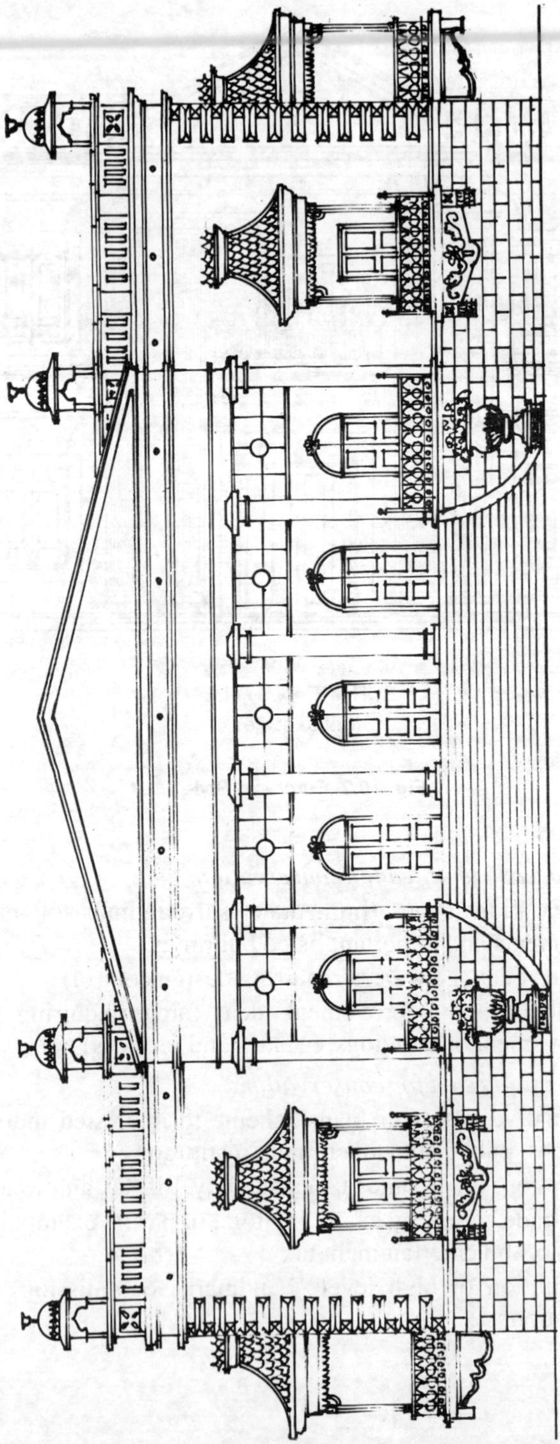

INDO-EUROPEAN STYLE
(not to scale)

Fig. 10.3 Indo-European Style

5. Revolving fund at Central and State Government levels to receive donations.
6. Urban conservation laws.
7. Demonstrations projects.

The first legislation in India was made by Govt. of Maharashtra by identifying more than 600 buildings and precincts in Bombay and declared them as 'Heritage Buildings and Precincts.' They were included under 'Development Control Rules for Greater Bombay' for conservation.

Later, Govt. of Andhra Pradesh brought a legislation to protect 'Heritage Building and Precincts' in Hyderabad. Under this legislation, 152 heritage buildings and 9 heritage precincts were notified for conservations.

With rapid social and technological changes in our cities, the landuse is frequently changed by addition or demolition or alteration. In the process, many precious heritage buildings are pulled down to meet the money greed of the builders. Such a trend may create a void between our present and past values leaving us lost and uninspired. Under these circumstances, urban conservation assumes significant role in city development.

MODEL QUESTIONS

1. What are the pro and anti urban conservation arguments?
2. What factors are taken into consideration to identify the Heritage Buildings?
3. What are the major features of Hyderabad Urban Conservation Study 1984?

11

Planning Standards

(A) The Basic Framework

1. The basic objective of suggesting various norms and standards for urban development plans formulation is to provide a basis for taking decision. The suggested norms and standards are indicative and can be suitably modified depending upon the local conditions. Variations in the norms and standards, as applicable to small and medium towns and large cities have been given. Variations in respect of urban centres located in hill areas have also been provided at appropriate level.
2. Norms and standards have been provided for:
   a. Distribution of land use,
   b. Infrastructure, further classified as:
      i) Physical infrastructure including:
         Water supply
         Sewerage
         Drainage
         Electricity, and
         Solid waste
      ii) Social Infrastructure covering:
         Education
         Health
         Soco-cultural Facilities including:
         — Religious Sites
         — Community Room
         — Community Hall and Library
         — Recreation Club
         — Music, Dance and Drama Centre
         — Meditation and Spiritual Centre
         — Socio-cultural Centre

— Museum and Art Gallery
— Cinema/Theatre

Distributive Services including:
— Petrol Pump
— Milk Booth, and
— LPG Godown

Miscellaneous Facilities including:
— Dhobi Ghat
— Cremation Ground
— Taxi Ground, and
— Bus Stops

Other Facilities and Services including:
— Communication
— Postal Service
— Security Service, and
— Fire Protection Service

iii) Commercial Facilities covering:
— CBD
— Sub-city Business District
— District Centre
— Local Shopping Centre
— Convenient Shopping Centre
— Informal Shopping and Weekly Markets, and
— Service Centres

iv) Recreational Facilities covering:
— Parks and Open Spaces
— Sports Centre and Play Grounds
— Botanical and Zoological Parks
— Water Bodies/Other Natural Features, and
— Places of Tourist Interest

c. Traffic and Transportation

(B) Distribution of Land Use

The land use distribution norms are dependent upon the following basic norms for densities and work force :

1. Developed Area Average Densities

Settlement Type	Persons per hectare (pph) in	
	Plain Areas	Hill Areas
Small Towns	75-125	45-75
Medium Towns	100-150	60-90
Large Cities	100-150	60-90
Metro Cities	125-175	—

2. Work Force

(a) Work force participation 33% of total population

(b) Industrial workers as percentage of total work force:

Small and medium town	20
Large cities	25

(c) Industrial workers density 100 pph to 125 pph

3. Proposed land use Structure of Urban Centres in Plain Areas

Landuse Category	Percentage of Developed Area			
	Small	Medium	Large Cities	Metro Cities
Residential	45-50	40-45	35-40	35-40
Commercial	2-3	3-4	4-5	4-5
Industrial	8-10	8-10	10-12	12-14
Pub. & Semi-Public	6-8	10-12	12-14	14-16
Recreational	12-14	18-20	18-20	20-25
Transport & Communication	10-12	12-14	12-14	15-18
Agriculture & Water Bodies	Balance	Balance	Balance	Balance
Total Developed Area	100	100	100	100

4. Proposed Land Use Structure in Hill Towns

Land Use	Percentage of Developed Area		
	Small Towns	Medium Towns	Large Cities
Residential	50-55	48-52	45-50
Commercial	2-3	2-3	4-5
Industrial	3-4	4-5	5-7
Public & Semi-Public	8-10	8-10	12-15
Recreational	15-18	15-18	16-20
Transport & Commn.	5-6	5-6	6-8
Ecological	8-10	8-10	8-10

(C) Infrastructure

1. Infrastructure is the basic requirement of urban life and its adequacy and accessibility are two important ingredients and key contributors in the upgradation and enrichment of quality of urban life which is the primary objective of any planned development effort. The extent and the nature of problems faced by different towns vary by size, geographical conditions, local natural resources, state/regional differentials in the resource availability and the policies, resource base of local authorities and several such factors directly or indirectly affecting the population of cities/towns.
2. Social amenities and infrastructure fall under the social welfare objectives of the urban development programme, as distinct from economic development objectives and especially in context of the rapidly developing liberalised and competitive economic scenario.
3. The city planners, urban managers and administrators are required to make special efforts to devise innovative strategies in order to ensure their wider coverage and equitable distribution for the society as a whole and the vulnerable sections of the urban society in specific. Thus, this is an effort to suggest the norms and standards for different components of infrastructure with respect to their hierarchy, locational and spatial attributes, affordability, socio-economic compatibility and manageability.

(D) Physical Infrastructure

The standards are applicable for hill as well as non-hill town/cities.

1. Water Supply

S. No.	Aspect	Size of Town: Small (< 50,000)	Medium (> 50,000)	Large and Metro (> 10 lakh)
1. Standards				
	a) Domestic			
	i) Absolute Min.	70 lpcd	70-100 Upper limit above 100,000	135 lpcd—it can be reduced up to 70 lpcd
	ii) Desirable	100 lpcd	135-150 lpcd	150-200 lpcd—Upper limits for metro cities income areas the standards to lpcd

(Contd.)

b) Non-Domestic

i) Institutional	Refer Table 0.2		
ii) Industrial	Refer Table 0.3.		
iii) Fire Fighting	1% of total demand		
iv) Public Purpose	10-15 lpcd	20-25 lpcd	30-35 lpcd

Suggested Policy Interventions

- Involvement of NGO's for awareness programme on optimal utilisation and saving water.
- Involvement of community to develop their own systems of supply.
- Equitable distribution, every individual household shall get atleast the minimum including those living in squatters.
- Cross-subsidisation for weaker sections.
- Efforts should be made to reduce the water losses in transmission and distribution. The contingency provision of 15-20% to be made to account for the losses.

2. Water Requirements for Institutional Buildings

Sl. No.	Institutions	Litres per head per day
1.	Hospital (including laundry)	
	a). No. of beds exceeding 100	450 (per bed)
	b). No. of beds not exceeding 100	340 (per bed)
2.	Hotels	180 (per bed)
3.	Hostels	135
4.	Nurses homes & medical quarters	135
5.	Boarding schools/colleges	135
6.	Restaurants	70 (per seat)
7.	Airports & seaports	70
8.	Junction stations & intermediate stations where mail or express stoppage (both railway and bus stations) is provided	70
9.	Terminal stations	45

10. Intermediate stations (excluding mail and express stops)	45 (could be roduced to 25 where bathing facilities are not provided)
11. Day schools/colleges	45
12. Offices	45
13. Factories	45 (could be reduced to 30 where no bathing rooms are required to be provided)
14. Cinema, concert halls and theatres	15

Source: Manual on Water Supply, CPHEEO, Government of India.

3. Water Requirements for Industrial Units

Industry	Unit of Production	Water Requirement In Kiloliters per unit
Automobile	Vehicle	40
Distillery	Kilolitre (proof alcohol)	122-170
Fertilisers	Tonne	80-200
Leather	100 Kg (tanned)	4
Paper	Tonne	200-400
Spl. quality paper	Tonne	400-1000
Straw Board	Tonne	75-100
Petroleum Refinery	Tonne (Crude)	1-2
Steel	Tonne	200-250
Sugar	Tonne (cane crushed)	1-2
Textile	100 Kg (goods)	8-14

Source: Manual on Water Supply CPHEEO, Government of India.

4. Sewerage

1. The treatment of sewerage is essential to check the decay in the environment as well as to provide hygienic conditions for the population. Besides the sewerage from households, the waste from industries also needs attention. The sewerage is estimated at the rate of 80% of the water supply in any area.
2. The small and medium towns may be encouraged for adopting

low-cost sanitation technologics with the technical assistance by the local bodies and involvement of NGO's in actual implementation of such programmes. The newly developed areas shall be considered for the provision of community level septic tanks based on economic and environmental considerations with a flexibility in planning for the extension of regular sewerage facility in long term. The large and metro cities shall be provided with regular sewerage treatment facilities at zonal/city level. The squatter settlements may be provided with a facility of 1 toilet for 4 to 5 families based on the concept of low cost and low water consumption, the maintenance of such community toilets to be looked after by the community and the voluntary organisations together. For the existing developed areas without sewerage network the individual households or a group of households may be encouraged for adoption of low-cost sanitation systems.

5. Drainage

The drainage system for any city/town is governed mainly by natural drainage course and topography. Besides on the impact of region level of development, its climate and hydrological consideration, the discharge is calculated that guides the requirement for provision of additional drain as well as upgradation of existing drains.

6. Electricity

Based on the estimated requirements of power supply as per the Master Plan for Delhi, the consumption works out to be about 2 KW per household at the city level and includes domestic, commercial, industrial and other requirements. The actual estimation of power requirements can be made based on the industrial development (type and extent), commercial development, domestic and other requirements. The provision of one electric sub-station of 11 KV for a population of 15,000 is recommended as a general standard for all categories of towns/cities.

7. Solid Waste Disposal

The production of solid waste in an urban centre is a function of the socio-economic profile of the population and activities in the area. The insufficient conservancy services in most of the urban centres tend to leave the garbage spread on the road sides or open spaces leading to unhygienic living conditions. The garbage is removed by the municipal bodies and dumped at the sanitary landfill or in some cases it is converted to compost especially in small towns. The generation of waste varies from about over a quarter of kilogram in small towns to about half a kilogram per capita in large and metro cities.

(E) Social Infrastructure

- The provision of these amenities in any size town/city shall consider the regional bearings as small towns cater to the requirements of surrounding villages, medium size towns cater to small towns and villages and so on in the hierarchy of settlements in the region for the higher level facilities. Especially in case of large and metro cities, certain apex level facilities significantly cater to regional demand in addition to the city demand.
- This affects the general level of satisfaction and further strains the facility infrastructure. In order to efficiently cater to the city and regional demands, alternatives which could be considered may be to provide:
  — Amenities for 25% additional population overall as a cushion, or
  — Exclude such apex level facilities from the total estimated needs provision.
- It is common knowledge that the local level facilities once provided at considerable cost, tend to lose their efficiency owing to neglect, inefficient management, lack of funds for upkeep, encroachments and at times misue. It is imperative to encourage local community participation in management of local level facility units, even if created fully or partly by public funds. The idea is that the user community should have a stake in proper functioning and maintenance of the facility.
- It is also observed that a number of lower level social amenity units particularly in regard to education and health infrastructure are operating in private residential premises due to both non-availability as well as deficiency in number of designated sites. The potential of such practices shall be assessed to find out the actual needs, which shall be reliable input for arriving at realistic norms, as also for providing adequate number of sites for such facility units.
- In residential areas where exclusive sites for social amenities units are not available, local level facilities only (*viz.* nursery

and primary schools, dispensary, etc.) may be allowed to operate from residential use premises on condition that specific controls and guidelines are adhered too.

- The possibilities for multiple use of social amenities may also be considered especially for the areas with deficiencies of certain facilities depending upon the compatibility of the activities and acceptance of the society.
- In distribution of infrastructure, population plays the guiding role and, therefore indication of population served by a facility or service has been given. In some cases depending upon the regional requirements, a higher order facility becomes necessary in a lower order settlement. No attempt has been made to classify them by size of town, that is, small, medium town or large city.

1. Educational Facilities

a) Pre-primary to Secondary Education

i. Pre-primary nursery school 1 for 2500 population

Area for school	0.08 ha

Pre primary/nursery school to be located near a park

ii. Primary school (class I to V)

Strength of the school	500 students
Area per school	0.4 ha
School building area	0.20 ha
Play field area with a minimum of 18m × 36m to be ensured for effective play	0.20 ha

iii. Senior secondary school (VI to XII) 1 for 7,500 population

Strength of the school	1000 students
Area per school	1.60 ha
School building area	0.60 ha
Play field area with a minimum of 68m × 126m to be ensured for effective play	1.60 ha

iv. Integrated school without hostel facility (Class I-XII) 1 for 90,000-1 lakh population

Strength of the school	1500 students
Area per school	3.50 ha
School building area	0.70 ha
Play field area	2.50 ha
Parking area	0.30 ha

v. Integrated school with hostel facility
1 for 90,000 - 100,000 population

Strength of the school	1000 students
Area per school	3.90 ha
School building area	0.70 ha
Play field area	2.50 ha
Parking area	0.30 ha
Residential hostel area	0.40 ha

vi. School for handicapped 1 for 45,000 pop.

Strength of the school	400
Area per school	0.50 ha
School building area	0.20 ha
Play field area	0.30 ha

b. Higher Education - General

i. College
1 for 1.25 lakh population

Student strength of the college	1000–1500 students
Area per college	4.00 ha
College building area	1.80 ha
Play field area	1.80 ha
Residential including hostel area	0.40 ha

ii. University campus

Area of the university campus	10.00 ha

iii. New University Area 60.00 ha

c. Technical Education

i. Technical education centre (A)
1 such centre provided for every 10 lakh population to include one industrial training institute and one polytechnic 500 students

Strength of the polytechnic	400 students
Area per centre	4.00 ha
Area per ITI	1.60 ha
Area for polytechnic	2.40 ha

ii. Technical centre (B)
1 provided for 10 lakh population to include 1 Technical centre and 1 coaching centre

Area per centre	4.00 ha
Area per technical centre	2.10 ha
Area for ITI	1.40 ha
Area for coaching centre	0.30 ha

d. Professional Education

i. New engineering college
2 numbers to be provided in urban extension
Strength of the college 1500–1700 students
Area per college 60.00 ha

ii. New medical college
2 sites of 15 ha each in urban extension
This includes space for specialised general hospital

2. Health Care Facilities

a. General hospital
Hospital for 2.5 lakh population capacity 500 beds
Initially the provision may be for 300 beds
Area for hospital 4.00 ha
Area for residential accommodation 2.00 ha
Total area 6.00 ha

b. Intermediate hospital (Category-A) 200 beds
1 hospital for 1 lakh population capacity
initially the provision may be for 100 beds
Area for hospital 2.70 ha
Area for residential accommodation 1.00 ha
Total area 3.70 ha

c. Intermediate hospital (Category-B)
1 hospital for 1 lakh population capacity
80 beds initally the provision may be for
50 including 20 maternity beds
Area for hospital 0.60 ha
Area for residential accommodation 0.40 ha
Total area 1.00 ha

d. Poly-clinic with some observation beds
1 for 1.0 lakh population
Area 0.20 to 0.30 ha

e. Nursing home, child welfare and maternity centre 1 for 0.45 to 1 lakh
Population 25 to 30 beds
Capacity 0.20 to 0.30 ha

f. Dispensary
1 for 0.15 lakh population
Area 0.08 to 0.12 ha

3. Socio-Cultural Facilities

a. Community room

One for 5,000 population Area 660 sq. m.

b. Community hall and library
   One for 15,000 population
   Area 2,000 sq.m.

c. Recreational club
   One for 1 lakh population
   Area 10,000 sq.m

d. Music, dance and drama centre
   One for 1 lakh population
   Area 1,000 sq.m

e. Meditation and spritual centre
   One for 1 lakh population
   Area 5,000 sq.m

f. Socio-cultural centre. One for
   10 lakh population
   Area 15 ha.

4. Distribution Services

a. *Petrol pump*

- One petrol pump for 150 ha. of gross residential areas in residential use zone
- One petrol pump for 40 ha. of gross industrial area
- Two petrol pumps in each freight complex
- Two petrol pumps in each district centre
- One petrol pump in each community centre

b. *Milk distribution*

One milk booth for 5,000 population. The standard recommended as per the Delhi Master Plan is adequate.

c. *LPG godowns*

One LPG gas godown for 40-50 thousand population is sufficient for any size of town. The major concern for its storage and distribution is the location which shall be away from the residential areas.

5. Police

Planning norms for police, civil, defence and home guards and fire shall be as under:

a. *Police station—1 for 90,000 population*

Area inclusive of essential residential accommodation 0.05 ha additional to be provided for civil defence and home guards. 1.5 ha

b. *Police post—1 for 0.4 to 0.5 lakh*
population (not served by a police station)
Area inclusive of essential residential
accommodation 0.16 ha

c. *District office and battalion*
1 for 10 lakh population
Area for district office 0.80 ha
Area for battalion 4.00 ha
Total area 4.80 ha

d. *Police line*
1 for 20 lakh population 4.00 to 6.00 ha

e. *District jail—1 for 10 lakh*
population
Area 10.00 ha

f. *Civil defence and home guards*
1 for 10 lakh population
Area 2.00 ha

6. File

1 fire station or sub-fire station within
1 to 3 km to be provided for 2 lakh population
Area for fire station with essential
residential accommodation 1.00 ha
Area for sub-fire-station
with essential residential accommodation 0.60 ha

(F) Commercial Activity

1. Hierarchy of Commercial Centres

Hierarchy of commercial centres is a function of the hierarchy of planning units in an urban centre. Normally an urban centre has some or all of the following, depending upon its size :

Planning Unit	Class of Settlement			Popn. served	Hierarchy of Commercial Centre
	S	M	L		
Housing cluster	×	×	×	1000–4000	Cluster Centre
Sector	×	×	×	5000–20000	Sector Centre
Community	×	×	×	25000–100000	Community Centre
District	–	×	×	125000–500000	District Centre
Sub-city	–	–	×	25 lakh–50 lakh	Sub-city Centre
City	–	–	×	50 lakh +	City Centre

S: Small town M: Medium towns L: Large cities

× Indicates the availability of the planning unit and the hierarchy of the commercial centres.

Since every settlement has a town/city centre, for small and medium size towns one of the community centre or district centres, as the case may be will serve the function town centre.

2. Area of Commercial Centres

	Area per 1000 persons sq.m.	No. of shops
Cluster centre	220	1 for 110 persons
Sector centre	300	1 for 200 persons
Community centre	500	1 for 200 persons
District centre	880	1 for 300 persons

3. Distribution of Shops by Type

Type of Shops	District	Community	Sector	Cluster
Formal Shops (total)	1250	365	55	24
General Retail	1200	295	35	16
Fruit & Vegetables	Not specified inclu-ded in general retail	40	6	3
Service & Repairs	50	30	13	5
Informal Shops	370	110	22	13
General Retail	355	88	14	8
Fruit & Vegetables	Not specified included general retail			
Service & Repairs	15	9	5	3
Total shops (formal and informal)	1620	475	77	37

a. Distribution of Activities

Activities	Hierarchy of Commercial Centre				
	City and sub-city centre	District centre	Community centre	Sector centre	Cluster centre
1	2	3	4	5	6
1. Shopping (retail service, repair)	×	×	×	×	×
2. Limited wholesale	×	×	–	–	–
3. Informal shopping	×	×	×	×	×

(*Contd.*)

4.	Commercial Offices	×	×	×	×	–
5.	Cinema	×	×	×	–	–
6.	Hotel	×	×	×	–	–
7.	Guest House	×	×	×	–	–
8.	Nursing Home	×	×	×	–	–
9.	Service Industries	×	×	×	–	–
10.	Auditorium	×	×	×	–	–
11.	Museum	×	×	–	–	–
12.	Library	×	×	×	–	–
13.	Science Centres, Art/ Craft/Music/Dance School	×	×	×	–	–
14.	Weekly Markets (on close days)	×	×	×	×	–
15.	Local Govt. Offices	×	×	×	–	–
16.	Bus Terminal	×	×	–	–	–
17.	Fire Station	×	×	–	–	–
18.	Police Station	×	×	–	–	–
19.	Telephone Exchange	×	×	–	–	–
20	Electric Sub-station	×	×	×	×	×
21.	Post and Telegraph	×	×	×	–	–
22.	Petrol Pump	×	×	×	–	–
23.	Conveniences	×	×	×	×	×
24.	Residential	×	×	–	–	–

× Activities to be provided in the commercial centre.

4. Norms for Informal Sector Activities

a.	Retail Trade	No. of informal commercial units
	Central Business District Sub-Central Business District District Centre Community Centre Convenience Shopping Centre	3 to 4 units per 10 formal shops as specified in the norms separately
b.	Government and Commercial Offices	5 to 6 units per 1000 employees
c.	Wholesale Trade and Freight Complexes	3-4 units per 10 formal shops
d.	Hospital	3-4 units per 100 beds
e.	Bus Terminal	1 unit per two bus bays

(Contd.)

f.	Schools	
	Primary	3-4 units
	Secondary/Senior Secondary/Integrated	5-6 units
g.	Parks	
	Regional/District Parks	8-10 units at each major entry
	Neighbourhood Parks	2-3 units
h.	Residential	1 unit/1000 population
i.	Industrial	5-6 units per 1000 employees
j.	Railway Terminus	To be based on surveys at the time of preparation of the project

(G) Variations in norms and Standards by size of Settlement

1. Small Towns

a) For the general retail shopping requirements, the concept of street/roadside commercial activity shall be accepted as a policy with certain specific controls such as:

- no commercial activity along the NH/SH or any major district road;
- the minimum width of the street to be 12 m. where vehicular movement is permitted to a limited extent (i.e. only upto 2 wheelers or rickshaw) and the streets with a minimum width of 4.5 m without vehicular movement may be permitted for road/street side commercial activities.

b) The open spaces within residential areas or certain streets with completely controlled traffic on specific day can be made available for weekly markets to shop-keepers. The weekly markets tend to generate more waste and thus effort should be made to ensure that the cleaning of the area is arranged by the co-operation of shopkeepers. It has been generally observed that the service and repair shops emerge along the major roads and the activities are extended upto the roads in most cases, thereby affecting the smooth flow of traffic and increasing probability of accidents.

c) Thus, it is suggested that the service centres shall be provided as a planned component and the sites near the petrol pumps shall be considered. The exact requirement of the area for service centre will be guided by the following factors:

- vehicular population,
- villages falling in the influence zone of the towns or, in

other words, the service requirements of the villages in the surrounding areas.

d) The function based commercial requirements such as mandi (vegetables/grains/fruits), cattle markets or any other such specialised markets are to be planned as per the case specific requirements based on the study of the area.

e) The other important aspect that requires a serious thought is the quantum of commercial activities to be proposed but in light of the suggested policy, it is envisaged that the control shall be restricted to locational attributes and the local need based emergence in its natural growth be permitted.

f) For the newly planned schemes in small towns also, the policy of mixed land use shall be considered as accepted practice to suit the behavioural pattern of the society.

g) As already dealt in the previous section on landuse, the area requirements for commercial activities in small sized towns works out to be about 0.2 - 0.25 ha/1000 persons on an average, based on the proposed landuse which is governed by the functional character of the town.

2. Medium Size Towns

a) The growth of towns from small to medium sized town through transition phases (50,000 - 100,000) changes the requirements of commercial activities gradually and for a town exceeding a population of 1 lakh, the extensions starts developing in pockets of well-defined economic strata of the people and thus it is suggested that the areas predominantly planned for upper income groups shall be provided with the planned commercial centres (with adequate inbuilt provision for informal commercial activities wit the commercial centres) at the rate of 4-5 formal shops and 2-3 informal shops per 1000 persons. The requirements for wholesale trade will be governed by the following factors :

- location of the town with respect to large/metro cities;
- small towns and villages falling in the direct influence zone of the town for which it has to act as a distribution centre.

b) As already dealt in the previous section on land use, the area requirements for commercial activities in medium sized towns works out to be about 0.24-0.32 ha/1000 persons on an average, based on the proposed land use which, in fact, is governed by the functional character of the town and the regional imperatives mentioned above.

3. Large and Metro Cities

The average land requirements for commercial activities (based on a sample of 14 large cities) work out to be 0.4 ha per 1000 persons in a range of 0.2 to 0.6 ha/1000 persons depending on the location of these large cities with respect to metro cities. Similar requirements have also been observed in case of metro cities which are located in the influence zone of mega cities, the average land requirement for commercial activities under this category works out to be about 0.3 ha/1000 persons.

(H) Variations for Hill Towns

1. The hill areas can be broadly classified into two categories, i.e., tourist centres and non-tourist centres. The requirements of commercial activities in hilly areas are mainly limited to retail activities and that too are mainly catered by small shops in the residence in non-tourist centres. The provision of commercial facilities in tourist centres is to be reviewed for two major aspects. First, the boarding and lodging requirements of the tourists and second the informal activities near tourist spots.
2. The requirements of hotels and restaurants can be worked out only on the basis of the data on tourists and their growth trends. The informal activities at the tourist spots are mainly informal eating places and other general shops selling local specialities, but it shall be ensured that these activities do not spoil the environment around the tourist spots.

(I) Recreational Facilities

The norms for parks, play fields and other open space such as specified park, amusement park, maidan, a multi-purpose open space, botanical garden and zoological parks, traffic parks etc. are as under:

Planning Unit	Area in sq.m per person
Housing Cluster	3-4 local parks and playgrounds
Sector	3-4 local parks and playgrounds
Community	2-3 community level parks and open space
District	1 district level park and sports centre, maidan
Sub-city centre	1 city level park, sports complex, botanical/ zoological garden, maidan
Overall town/city level	10 sq.m. - 12.00 sq.m. per person

(J) Variations by size of Settlement

1. Small Towns

a) In light of the standards recommended by various bodies, it is suggested to provide 1.0 to 1.2 ha per 1000 persons for town level recreational facilities (excluding the open spaces in residential pockets) which can be distributed for different residential pockets uniformly for a population of 8,000 - 10,000.

b) As already mentioned, the open spaces are to be developed with the other socio-cultural and commercial facilities so that they can serve multiple purpose.

2. Medium Towns

The recreational open spaces shall be provided at the rate of 1.4 - 1.6 ha/1000 persons as per the hierarchy recommended in the Master Plan for Delhi. The lower income areas shall be provided with more open spaces and the area under facilities like community halls etc. can be merged with the open spaces to suit their social requirements.

3. Large and Metro Cities

a) Large and metro cities shall atleast be provided with the recreational facilities as per the standards given in the Master Plan of Delhi. The suggested standards for open spaces in large and metro cities are 1.2 - 1.4 ha/1000 persons, depending on the land availability.

b) Secondly, the older parts of large cities have normally been found highly deficient with respect to the availability of recreational spaces, thus additional provisions in the new developments to take care for the existing deficiencies also to be made. For the large and metro cities, provisions shall also be made for city level special parks such as botanical and zoological parks, picnic huts, children parks and amusement parks etc.

(K) Socio-Cultural Facilities

1. Merely the prescription of norms for the provision of socio-cultural facilities is not enough as there are certain vital issues involved with their provision which are as follows:

   a) It has generally been observed that the religious buildings come up on encroached sites and especially those meant for open spaces. In fact, just the provision of 400 sq.m. area for a population of 5,000 is not enough. It is not to say that the area is inadequate but effort should be made by the development agencies, with the assistance of NGO's in the area, to ensure that the places of worship come up as planned with the participation and preferences of the community itself.

b) The provision of housing cluster and sector level socio-cultural facilities such as community room, community hall and library shall be given following considerations:

   Socio-economic profile and behavioural pattern of the beneficiaries as for the areas with lower income group population, the maintenance and management of formal community buildings is not an easy task and even it does not match with their behavioural pattern. Thus, for lower income areas the use of such facilities shall be planned and designed for multipurpose activities which can ensure optimal utilisation. The activities such as adult education, training programmes for economic generation activities, child and family welfare programmes, etc. can be organised in such spaces besides the facility of reading room.

c) The community halls for middle and higher income areas are utilised more often for various functions, etc. compared to lower income areas where open spaces/streets are preferred for such functions.

d) In the congested areas, the schools are used for various social functions in non-teaching hours which in fact is a practice in small or even in medium sized towns, can be considered as an option.

2. As a general basis, separate religious sites (2 for 15,000 population) may be provided so that places of worship do not get established on encroached sites as is invariably happening. Further, the norms for socio-cultural facilities may be considered as under :

   a) Community hall (multi-purpose) : House Cluster Level

      The small parks/open spaces should also be developed with the community hall to suit the cultural and behavioural needs of the society.

   b) Local Community Centre : Sector Level

      (Hall, Library, Space for extra-mural activities)

   c) Recreation Club : One for 15,000 population, 2,000 sq. m.

: One for 50,000 population
0.5 ha
: One for 100,000 population
1.0 ha

d) Music, Dance, Drama Center : One for 50,000 population
e) Meditation and Spiritual Center : One for 50,000 population
f) Socio-cultural Center : One for 5 lakh population

3. Increased provision of space for socio-cultural facilities is essential in view of the increasing demand of such sites for diverse needs, creating more avenues for socio-cultural interactions and enriching the quality of built environment at neighbourhood and community levels.

(L) Miscellaneous Facilities

1. Cremation/Burial-Ground

The sites for cremation grounds shall be identified in locations which are not proximous to residential areas. It may be advisable to provide one electric crematorium for large size towns besides the provision of atleast 2 sites for 5 lakh population.

2. Dhobi Ghat

It is suggested to provide one site for 1 lakh population with appropriate arrangements for water and drainage facilities and it shall be ensured that the water bodies are not polluted as a result of such activities.

3. Taxi Stands/Bus Stops/Rickshaw Stands

The taxi stands/Bus stops shall be provided with the following considerations:

- these should not be located near the road inter-sections;
- the maximum distance of such facilities should not exceed 0.5 km from the farthest point in any residential area.

(M) Other Facilities and Services

1. Telecommunication

The norms for other facilities and services listed under communication, security, fire, postal are derived from the departmental norms which are governed by the national/state level policies. The communication sector is getting lot of priorities due to its increasing importance in the economic development and thus immaterial of the size of town. It is hoped that the standards as well as level of service will be improved in time to come. The existing standards for these services are as under:

(a). **Communication** - 10 lines per 100 population.

(b). **Fire** - One fire station for 2 lakh population within 1 to 3 km distance.

(c). **Postal services** - One post office for 10-15 thousand population.

2. Fire Protection

The fire services for small and lower category of medium size towns shall be provided taking into consideration the demands of surrounding villages also.

(N) Norms of Social Infrastructure Provision in Existing Built-up Areas

1. The norms and standards of facilities outlined in the preceding paragraphs have been proposed primarily with respect to minimum requirements of social amenities to be provided in new development areas at various levels. While the level of facilities and infrastructure to be provided should not make any distinction in their qualitative aspects between existing built-up areas vis-a-vis new development areas, in view of ground realities and other constraints, it is often observed that problems arise in implementing these norms in existing built-up areas, particularly the core areas of any town, calling for their rationalisation for effective adaptation.
2. In order to resolve these problems following guidelines are proposed for existing built-up areas:
   a) It is proposed that while Unit Norms (facility per unit size of population) of local level facilities should be kept uniform, the space norms may be considered at a reduced scale, which may range between 50-60% of those proposed for urban extension areas.
   b) In order to compensate for the shortfall in various types and levels of facilities which cannot be provided within the existing built-up area, such facilities may be provided in contiguous/proximus sectors of new development as additional provision, e.g. due to space constraints in existing

built-up area the school facility may not have ample space for playground/open spaces in the proximus new sector to compensate for its non-availability in the built-up area. Such provision shall be over and above that which may be required for the sector's own assigned population.

c) As proposed earlier also, multiple use of one facility unit should be encouraged so that optimum use of a facility could be possible. Such a step would also compensate for non-availability of individual facility units in a built-up area.

(O) Special Provision for Fringe Areas/Transitional Areas

1. It has been observed that the fringe areas, particularly the fringe rural settlements, are subject to considerable stress during the process of a city's growth. Such fringe settlements are normally not included in the programme of social infrastructure development as they lie outside the urban limits, despite the fact that they are both functionally and physically integral part of the urban area. In order to mitigate the existing deficiencies and stress conditions, and to prepare such transitional settlements and development pockets for proper integration with the planned urban areas, it is proposed that such fringe villages and pockets be identified and skeletal provision of basic infrastructure and facilities may be made. An incremental approach for upgradation of these facility units should be in-built in provision of such facilities in fringe/transitional areas.
2. While no specific norms and standards can be suggested as these will depend on the broad characteristics of development and nature of demand, the above measures, if incorporated in the total programme of social infrastructure planning, would be able to help in their integration with the urban areas as well as improve the quality of life in these fringe settlements which otherwise would grow into slums, which would result in serious implications in the quality of built environment.

(P) Norms and Standards for Transportation

1. Classifications of Urban Roads

Besides express ways and freeways, the urban roads can be classified as :

a) *Arterial Road:* Roads for intra-urban through traffic, with no frontage access, no standing vehicle and very little cross traffic and minimum roadway intersection spacing 500 m.

b) *Sub-Arterial Road:* Roads for intra-urban through traffic with frontage access but no standing vehicles having high cross traffic, high capacity inter-sections and minimum roadway inter-section spacing 300 m.

c) *Collector Street:* Streets for collecting and distributing traffic from and to local streets and also for providing access to arterial and sub-arterial roads, having free frontage access but no parked vehicles and having heavy cross traffic and minimum roadway inter-section spacing 150 m.

d) *Local Street:* Street for access to residence, business or other abutting property, having necessary parking and pedestrain movement. Free Access.

2. Design considerations of Urban Roads

a) Design Speed

The recommended design speeds for different categories of roads are:

Arterial	–	80 kph
Sub-Arterial	–	60 kph
Collector Street	–	50 kph
Local Street	–	30 kph

b) Space Standards

The space standards (land width) recommended for different categories of roads are :

Arterial	–	50 - 60 m
Sub-Arterial	–	30 - 40 m
Collector Street	–	20 - 30 m
Local Street	–	10 - 20 m

The land width is often referred as 'Right-of-way'.

c) Cross-Sectional Elements

The width and layout of urban road cross-sections depend on many factors, the chief amongst them being the classification of roads, design speed and volume of traffic expected. Some of the salient cross-sectional elements are described below :

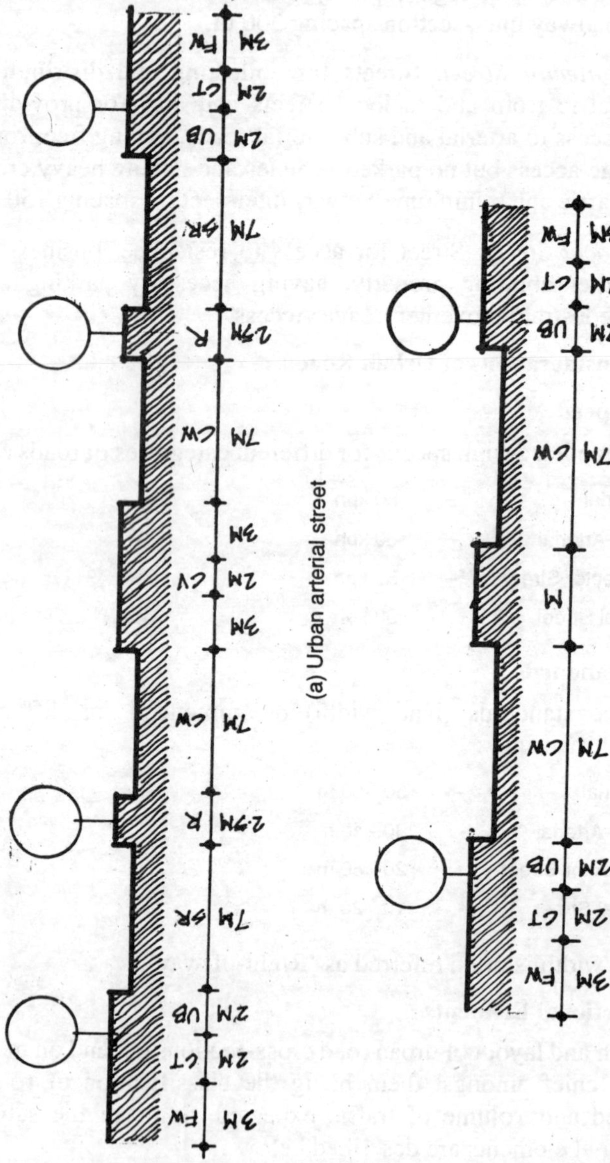

(a) Urban arterial street

(b) Urban sub-arterial street through open area

Fig. 11.1 Typical cross-sections of urban roads *(Contd.)*

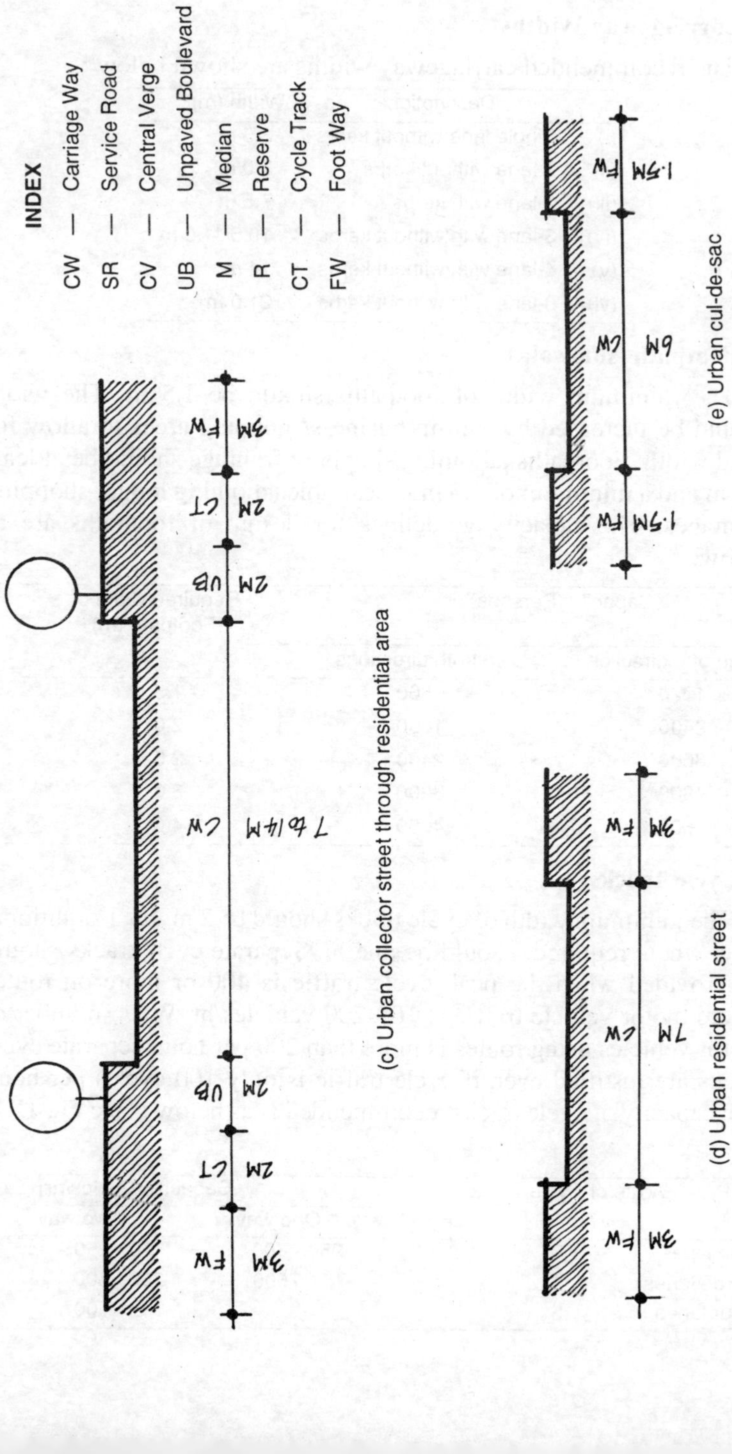

Fig. 11.1 Typical cross-sections of urban roads

1. Carriageway Widths

The recommended carriageway widths are shown below :

	Description	Width (m)
(i)	Single lane without kerbs	3.5 m
(ii)	2-lane without kerbs	7.0 m
(iii)	2-lane with kerbs	7.5 m
(iv)	3-lane with/without kerbs	10.5/11.0 m
(v)	4-lane with/without kerbs	14 m
(vi)	6-lane with/without kerbs	21.0 m

d) Footpath (sidewalk)

The minimum width of footpaths should be 1.5 m. The width should be increased by 1 m in business/shopping areas to allow for dead width. Footpaths adjoining shopping frontage should be at least 3.5 m and a minimum of 4.5 m is desirable adjoining longer shopping frontages. The capacity guidelines for design of footpaths are as below:

Capacity (Persons)		Required width of Footpath (m)
All in one direction	In both directions	
1220	800	1.5
2400	1600	2.0
3600	2400	2.5
4800	3200	3.0
6000	4000	4.0

e) Cycle Tracks

The minimum width of cycle tracks should be 2 m. Each additional lane, where required, should be one m. Separate cycle tracks should be provided when the peak cycle traffic is 400 or more on routes where motor vehicle traffic is 100-200 vehicles/hr. When number of motor vehicles using routes is more than 200 per hour, separate cycle tracks are justified even if cycle traffic is only 100 cycles per hour. The capacity of cycle tracks recommended is as below : (see Fig 11.1)

Width of Cycle Track		Capacity (Cycles/hr)	
		One way	Two way
Two lanes	3	250 - 600	50 - 250
Three lanes	4	7600	250 - 600
Four lanes	5		> 600

3. Passenger Car Units (PCU)

a. Urban roads are characterised by mixed traffic conditions, resulting in complex interaction between various kinds of vehicles. Capacity of urban roads is normally expressed in terms of a common unit, namely Passenger Car Unit (PCU). Each vehicle type is converted into equivalent PCU based on their relative interference values.

b. The relative PCU of a particular vehicle type is affected to a certain extent by increase in its proportion in the total traffic. Following table shows the recommended PCU factors for various types of vehicles on urban areas.

c. Recommended PCU factors for various types of vehicles on urban roads :

	Equivalent PCU Factors	
	Percentage composition of vehicle type in stream of traffic	
	10%	10%
Fast Vehicles		
1. Two Wheeler motor cycle or scooter etc.	0.5	0.75
2. Passenger car, pick up van	1.0	1.0
3. Auto rickshaw	1.2	2.0
4. Light commercial vehicle	1.4	2.0
5. Truck or bus	2.2	3.7
6. Agricultural Tractor Trailor	4.0	5.0
Slow Vehicles		
7. Cycle	0.4	0.5
8. Cycle rickshaw	1.5	2.0
9.Tonga (horse-drawn vehicle)	1.5	2.0
10. Hand-cart	2.0	3.0

Source : IRC Code : 106-1990.

4. Design Service Volume

a) It is recommended that normally 'C' LOS be adopted for design of urban roads. At this level, volume of traffic will be around 0.70 times the maximum capacity and this is taken as 'design service volume' for the purpose of adopting design values.

b) The design service volumes for different categories of urban roads are shown in the Table given below:

Recommended Design Service Volumes (PCU's per hour)

Sl. No. Type of Carriageway	Total Design Service Volume for different road categories		
	Arterial	Sub-Arterial	Collector
1. 2-lane (one way)	2400	1900	1400
2. 2-lane (two way)	1500	1200	900
3. 3-lane (one way)	3600	2900	2200
4. 4-lane undivided (two way)	3000	2400	1800
5. 4-lane divided (two way)	3600	2900	—
6. 6-lane undivided (two way)	4800	3800	—
7. 6-lane divided (two way)	5400	4300	—
8. 8-lane divided (two way)	7200	—	—

5. Parking

a) Equivalent Car Space (ECS) for Different Vehicles

Car/Taxi	–	1.00
Two wheeler	–	0.25
Auto rickshaw	–	0.50
Bicycle	–	0.10

b) Parking Space Requirements

1. The minimum parking space requirements for each car and truck is as follows:

   Car : 3 m × 6 m – When individual parking space is required

   2.5 m × 5 m – When community parking space is required.

   Truck : 3.75 m × 7.5 m

2. Residential

   i. Detached, semi-detached and row houses

Plot Area up to 100 sq. m.	–	No private or community parking space
Plot Area : 101 – 200 sq. m.	–	Only community parking space
Plot Area : 201 – 300 sq. m.	–	Only community parking space
Plot area : 301 – 500 sq. m.	–	Minimum 1/3rd of open area for parking
Plot area : 501 – 1000 sq.m.	–	Minimum 1/4th of open area for parking
Plot area : 1001 sq. m +	–	Min. 1/6th of space area for parking

3. Flats

One space for every two flats of 50-90 sq.m. or more of floor area.

One space for every flat of 100 sq.m. or more of floor area.

(i) For all kinds of developments excepting residential, warehouses and godowns.

One berth for initial 500-1500 sq.m. of floor area. Additional berths at the rate of one for every subsequent 1000 sq.m. or part thereof.

(ii) For warehouses and godowns

Two berths for initial 500-1500 m of floor area. Additional berths at the rate of one for every subsequent 500 m or part thereof.

4. Parking Norms for Work Centres

The parking norms for work centres as suggested by different organisations is shown below:

(ECS/100 sq. m. floor area)

	Work Centre Type	
	Commercial	Offices
Delhi Master Plan 1981	1.14	0.63
Delhi Master Plan 2001	1.67	1.67
New Delhi Redevelopment Advisory Committee 1972	2.28	1.14
Indian Road Congress, 1973	1.25	1.42
Central Public Works Departmet		1.23

Floor space per employee and employee to visitor norms

The space norm for floor space per employee adopted is :

(a) Government – 9 sq. m.

(b) Public Sector – 8 sq. m.

The employee to visitor ratio in office complexes is as 1 : 0.4.

6. Bus Terminals

a) Functions

The function of bus terminal primarily includes processing of vehicles, passengers etc. with provision of necessary facilities for their smooth flow. The terminal serves as a point and unit where necessary information to user is made available for processing. A passenger bus terminal broadly needs to perform the functions to meet requirements of the following :

- Passengers and vehicles.
- Passengers only
- Vehicles only
- Crew
- Management

The functions related to both passengers and vehicles include :

- concentration
- loading
- dispersal
- unloading

Passenger only oriented functions of the terminal include provision of :

- passenger platforms to board and alight
- waiting lounges
- rest houses/rooms
- baggage storage facilities
- basic shopping and commercial facilities
- utilities, services and amenities
- information system
- ticketing facilities
- shelter from weather
- communication and postal facilities
- eating places

b) Components

The components related to vehicles (bus) only include provision of:

- bays for loading and unloading
- idle bus parking spaces
- facilities related to maintenance
- information system for movement within terminal

The terminal components to meet the needs of crew are :

- rest rooms
- information system
- communication facilities
- eating places

The terminal facilities for the management in terms of :

- demand management on account of concentration
- incurring minimum expenditure
- development of centralised information
- ensuring better control.

c) Design Criteria

The design criteria of terminal includes determining the size of terminal and factors to be taken into consideration in planning the facilities and activities. The size of the terminal is primarily governed by the following factors :

- traffic demand
- traffic characteristics
- function of terminal
- type and sophistication of facilities

The other factors to be considered in terminal design by appreciating activity and facility inter-relationship are:

- segregation of terminal and non-terminal traffic;
- segregation of vehicular and pedestrians traffic and movement;
- segregation of traffic by type, function and direction;
- coordination of different activities in terms of functional and spatial inter-relationship;
- provision of good user and vehicular information;
- provision of necessary and identified facilities to meet requirement of all user groups;
- achieving minimum passenger and vehicular processing time;
- achieving overall functional and spatial efficiency;
- achieving smooth flow of all types of traffic to and from terminal;

d) Planning Norms and Space Standards

Norms

a)	Capacity of an intracity bus terminal	:	1.5 lakh passengers/day
b)	One bus bay for 5000 passengers per day	:	(Loading)
c)	One bus bay for 10,000 passengers per day	:	(Unloading)
d)	Peak hour load	:	10% of daily passenger load
e)	Occupancy/Bus	:	50 ideal
f)	Time taken for loading for unloading	:	6 min to 12 min 3 min to 6 min

Space Standards for parking Facilities

a) **Bus bays**

Type of parking	*Area/Vehicle*
Idle Parking	145 sq. m.
Angular	76 sq. m.
Parallel	104 sq. m.

b) **Parking of other Modes**

Car	25 sq. m.
Two wheeler	4 sq. m.
Taxi	16 sq. m.
Auto rickshaw	5 sq. m.
Cycle	1.2 sq. m.

7. Truck Terminal

A truck terminal is a highly specialised facility, designed for a specific function and operating plan in terms of the service standards it must meet, the area it serves and the volumes to be handled. It provides interface between intercity and local transportation facilities and which handle the distribution and collection of goods within the city.

The major objectives of a truck terminal are :

- To reorganise office and godown space of transport companies.
- To provide for expansion of companies.
- To reduce parking, loading/unloading instances in CBD.
- To locate the facilities for vehicle repairs, servicing, rest places, shops, etc.
- To cater to intercity movements destined to operator's godown and provide for idle parking for trucks waiting for return load.
- To function as a rest and halting place for through traffic.

a) Facilities in Transport Nagar

The main facilities for which area allocation needs to be made in transport nagar are:

1. Transport Agencies
2. Circulation
3. Parking
4. Open Space
5. Petrol Pump
6. Service Centre
7. Toilets
8. Police Station
9. Restaurant
10. Shops
11. Godowns
12. Weigh Bridge
13. Stall/Dhabas
14. Administrative Office
15. Fire Station, Post Office, Dispensary
16. Bank, Bus Station, Electric Sub-station
17. Cold Storage
18. Spare Parts Shops
19. Body Building Shops
20. Cinema.

b) Locational Factors

The following factors are generally considered while locating a truck terminal/transport nagar :

1. They should be located on main corridor of goods movement.
2. They are generally located on fringe of developed lands.
3. They should have proper linkage with other freight generating activities as well as developed areas.
4. Consideration for intra-city goods movement pattern in terms of desire of movement, modes used and distances over which movement is made should also be kept in view.

c) Broad Land Use Break-up

The broad land use break-up in a truck terminal (transport nagar) is as below :

	Use	Percentage Area
1.	Transport Operators – Office godown, loading/unloading	30.0
2.	Service Industry – Petrol pump, service area, weigh bridge, etc.	6.00
3.	Public/Semi-public – Police post, post office, telephone, first aid etc.	3.0
4.	Commercial	3.0
5.	Parking – idle, transit, other vehicles	18.0
6.	Open spaces	10.0
7.	Circulation	28.0
8.	Others	2.0
	Total	100.0

8. Integrated Freight Complex

a) Functions

The basic functions of an integrated freight complex are :

1. To provide facilities for regional and intra-urban freight movement.
2. To provide facilities for freight in transit as well as interchange of mode.
3. To provide warehousing and storage facilities and inter-link these sites with specialised markets.

4. To provide servicing, loading and boarding, idle parking, restaurants and other related functions in the complex.

b) Objectives

The functional objectives of wholesale complex-cum-truck terminal should be :

1. To provide adequate facilities for wholesale trade activities, these include :
   i. auction areas
   ii. wholesale shops and subsidiary storage capacity
   iii. packaging facilities
   iv. wholesale godowns, cold storage, etc. together with handling facilities and equipment, etc.
2. To provide adequate parking space and facilities for trucks expected to utilise the terminal. These facilities include :
   i. service/repair facilities
   ii. rest/recreation for drivers
   iii. weighing of trucks etc.
3. To provide adequate facilities for office/storage activities of trucks operating at terminal. These include :
   i. godown space
   ii. office space
   iii. loading/unloading facilities
   iv. weighing of goods vehicle etc.

Apart from the above-mentioned objectives, the complex must provide for a number of associated/ancillary facilities and services, some of which are :

1. Provision for goods movement within the complex in terms of truck movement and loading/unloading/stacking of goods.
2. Building and amenities for administration and security measures necessary for complex.
   i. Facilities like banking, postal facilities, etc. required for business transactions
   ii. Amenities for wholesalers, truckers and their employees
   iii. Areas for shops, eating houses and other service establishment
   iv. Provision of lighting, water supply and garbage, sewerage disposal.

c) Space Norms

The space norms in kg/sq.mt. for selected commodities as per Central Warehousing Corporation (CWC) is given below :

Commodity	Wt./Area (Kg/sq. m.)
Foodgrains	1054
Fruits and Vegetables	721
Hardware and Building Material	1054
Iron and Steel	904
Timber	968
Machinery	968
Auto parts	968
Textile	968
Chemicals and Fertilisers	968

d) Broad Land Use Break-up

The broad land use break-up of an integrated freight complex could be as follows :

	Use Type	Percentage of Area
1.	Wholesale Market	35.0
2.	Warehousing	8.0
3.	Booking Agencies	2.0
4.	Commercial & Public/Semi-public	5.0
5.	Utilities and Services	3.0
6.	Service Industry	4.0
7.	Parking	12.0
8.	Circulation	25.0
9.	Others	6.0
	Total	100.0

e) Area Requirements

As a general guideline, the area required for a truck terminal (transport nagar) should be reserved at the rate of one hect. per 300 tonnes of daily goods inflow into the complex. In case of integrated freight complex, the area necessary would be one hectare per 400 tonnes of daily goods inflow into the complex.

f) Modal split by Public Transport Modes

Recommended derived modal split levels i.e. share of public transport modes based on city size are :

City Size	Recommended Modal Split
Below 1 million	30%
Around 1 million	35%
1.5 million	40% Plus
3.0 million	50% Plus
6.0 million	70% Plus
9.0 million	75% plus (85% with a Mass Transit System)

In the absence of suitable modal split method, the above-mentioned modal split levels could be adopted for working out transportation system requirements of urban settlements.

g) Mathematical Techniques for formulation of spatial standards.

The Central Building Research Institute, Roorkee has evolved the following mathematical relationships for formulation of spatial standards.

1. Impact of Physical Parameters upon space standards

The impact of the value of land use percentage allocations and space requirements per 1000 persons upon gross and net densities can be determined by the following equations :

$$G = \frac{D \times .(100 - z + y)}{100}$$

where G = Gross density in persons per hectare
D = Net density in persons per hectare
z = Land use percentage allocation for amenities
y = Land use percentage allocation for circulation.

2. Impact of Economic Parameters upon Space Standards

The economic success of an amenity among a complex of amenities depends upon the overall cost of development and the paying capacity of the inhabitants. The space standard in relation to land costs, cost of development and permissible rate of interest can be calculated from the following equation :

$$D = \frac{8.3 \times C \times R}{E}$$

where D = Space standards in hectares per1000 persons
C = Cost of land or cost of development per sq.m.
R = Rate of interest per annum
E = Maintenance cost in rupees per month.

3. Location Aspects of Amenities
(Amenities, Catchment Area and Population to be served)

The population to be served by an amenity should be based upon the maximum spatial distance and density of habitation and should be determined by the following equations :

$$R = 56\ P/NZ$$

where R = distance in meter
P = population to be served
N = Net density in person/hectare
Z = Land use percentage

4. Space Requirements for educational buildings

The space requirements of nursery, primary and higher secondary should be worked out per 1000 population, keeping in view the amenities to be provided, nature of development and the socio-economic conditions of the population to be served. The space can be determined by the following equation :

$$E = \frac{A \times Q \times M}{100 \times 1000 \times F \times 100} = \frac{A \times Q \times M}{100 \times 100 \times C \times S \times 100}$$

where

R = Floor area ratio.
A = Number of children per 1000 population in the age-group pertaining to nursery or primary or higher secondary.
Q = Percentage of expected enrolment in the particular type of school
E = Site area in hectare per 1000 population
M = Gross built-up area in sq.m. per child for particular type of school
C = Coverage in percentage.
S = Number of storeys.

5. Space Requirements for outdoor Recreational Activities

The space can be determined by the following equation for total lots, play fields at primary level and play fields including parks at higher secondary level per 1000 persons.

$$A = \frac{A \times Q}{100 \times 1000} + \frac{(A1 \times R1 \times M1)}{L1 \times D1 \times 1000} + \frac{A2 \times R2 \times M2}{L2 \times D2 \times 100} + \ldots\ldots + \frac{(An \times Rn \times Mn)}{Ln \times Dn \times 100}$$

where

A = Number of children per 1000 population in age group pertaining to that amenity

Q = Percentage per expected utiliser in that age group

A1,2,...n = Area for provision and operation of amenity 1,2,...nth respectively

R1,2,...n = Average time upto which a particular batch plays on amenity R1,2....nth respectively

M1,2,...n = Percentage of users out of the total users interested in amenity 1,2...nth respectively

L1,2,...n = Load in terms of users of the amenity 1,2...nth respectively.

D1,2,...n = Duration for which amenity 1,2...nth respectively, generally remains in use.

6. Space Standards of Health Buildings

In order to find out the space requirements for health buildings, the following equations may be used:

$$E = \frac{1000 \times Q \times A}{100 \times 100} \times \frac{M}{F \times 100} = \frac{M}{C \times S \times 100} \times \frac{1000 \times Q \times A}{100 \times 100}$$

where

E = Site area in hectare

A = Percentage of population using the facility

Q = Population at risk in percentage

M = Gross built-up area in sq. m. per patient

F = Floor Area Ratio

C = Coverage in percentage

S = Number of storeys

7. Space Requirements for Shopping Facilities

The shopping requirements at different levels depend upon the expenditure pattern of the households of the residential area. The space requirements for shopping should be worked out per 1000 persons with the help of following equation:

$$E = \frac{1000}{A} \times \frac{M}{F \times 100} = \frac{1000}{A} \times \frac{M}{C \times S \times 100}$$

where

A = Population to support one shop
M = Built-up area per shop
E = Space requirements for shopping at each level
F = Floor Area Ratio
C = Coverage in percentage
S = Number of storeys.

8. Affordable Shelter — A Scientific Approach

An approach consisting of six steps for arriving at optimum housing option has been worked out as given below:

Step One : Establish the rent paying capacity for the selected groups of households and the housing demand in different urban pockets.

Step Two : Establish correlation between rent paying capacity of the different households, and the capital cost of housing in relation to rate of interest and period of amortisation.

Step Three : Apportion optimally the capital cost of housing per dwelling into the three components viz. cost of land, cost of infrastructure and cost of construction.

Step Four : Establish correlation between plot size and net land use percentage of housing, land cost and cost component of housing each dwelling arrived at in step three.
The relationship is governed by the following equation:

$$C = (10{,}000/P \times 100/Z)\ LP$$

where

C = Cost of land per dwelling unit
P = Net density in plots per hectare
Z = Land use percentage allocation in net housing
LP = Price of land in Rs. per sq.m.

Step Five : Establish correlation between costs of infrastructure (provision of amenities) and community facilities costs of infrastructure development and its component per dwelling as arrived in step three. The provision of on-site and off-site infrastructure is very important and the cost of provision affects the economic viability of the total project. The following equation is suggested to determine the cost of infrastructure per dwelling for varying parameters :

$$A = 10{,}000/D \times B$$

where

A = Cost (in Rs.) of infrastructure development per house (apportioning the total cost of development per dwelling unit)

D = Gross residential density in dwellings per hectare.

B = Cost of infrastructure development per sq.m. (taking total area under development)

Step Six : Establish correlation between built-up space and cost component per house for superstructure as arrived in step three.

The provision of plot size, land use extent of infrastructure services on minimum acceptable land for specific situation determines the cost of superstructure within the specified cost of the house assigned in step two. Therefore, the cost of superstructure should be viewed as function of several alternatives of plot area and its cost (after examining various alternatives based on above steps) so as to lead to an acceptable and affordable shelter solution within the exiting cost limits.

(*Source:* UDPFI Guidelines; Govt. of India; August 1996)

12

Urban Planning Terminology

1. **Apartment**: An apartment is a dwelling unit consisting of two or more units within the same structure.
2. **Bench mark**: In surveying, a reference point from which other heights are measured and computed. A bench mark may be any relatively permanent object.
3. **Building**: Any structure with its foundation, plinth, walls, floors, roofs, chimneys, sanitary and plumbing services, verandahs, balcony or other projections is treated as one building. Temporary structures are not considered as building.
4. **Building bye-laws**: Rules and regulations imposed by local municipality or municipal corporation for the construction of buildings.
5. **Building height**: It is the vertical distance measured for a building. For flat roofs, it is the distance from the average ground level around to the highest point of the building. For pitched roofs, it is the distance from the average ground level around to the point where the external surface of the outer wall intersects the finished surface of the sloping roof. Architectural features for decoration are excluded in taking heights. If the building does not abut on a street, the height shall be measured above the average level of the ground around.
6. **Building line**: The line upto which the plinth of a building adjoining a street may legally extend further. The building line may change from time to time as decided by the local authority.
7. **Building setback**: The distance by which any building or structure shall be separated from the boundary lines of the plot.
8. **City**: As per Census of India 1991, an urban unit having the population of one lakh and above is treated as city.

9. **Contour**: A line on a 'Topographic map' representing the height above a reference point.
10. **Coverage**: Ground area covered immediately above the plinth level by the building.
11. **Cul-de-sac**: It is a dead-end street having a turn around at the end.
12. **Development**: The works carried out like building, engineering, mining or other operations in, on, over or under land or the making of any material change in any building or land.
13. **Development area**: Any urban area or group of urban areas declared to be a 'development area' under an Act.
14. **Detached building**: A building whose walls are independent of any other building with open spaces on all sides.
15. **Dwelling:** A building or a portion, which is designed or used wholly or mainly for residential purposes.
16. **Dwelling unit**: Independent housing unit with separate facilities for living, cooking and sanitary requirements.
17. **Elevation**: It means any side view of a building in a drawing. It is also used to mention height.
18. **Facade**: Any exterior face of a building.
19. **Green belt:** It is the protected landscaped zone encircling a city.
20. **Habitable room**: A room occupied by one or more persons for study, living, sleeping, eating and cooking.
21. **Infrastructure**: It means basic service facilities used by the people like roads, bridges, water, transport etc.
22. **Master Plan**: It is an over-all, long range development plan. This term was used earlier as Master Plan of the city. Now, it is often referred as Development Plan of a city to give a comprehensive meaning to the planning of a city.
23. **Metropolitan city**: A city with ten lakhs or one million population or more is known as metropolitan city.
24. **Non-conforming use**: A building, structure or use of land existing at the time of commencement of the regulations, and which does not conform to the regulations pertaining to the zone in which it is situated.
25. **Obsolescence**: The loss in value of an asset due to change in technology, lack of demand or out-dated in use.
26. **Open space**: In urban planning, it means an area forming an integral part of the site left open to the sky.

27. **Plinth area**: The built-up area measured at the floor level of the basement or of any storey.
28. **Primate city**: A primate city dominates the surrounding region due to the concentration of economic activities and employment potential. Most of the state capitals in India can be called as Primate Cities.
29. **Region**: It is a space comprising cultural, social and economic aspects bounded by geographical or administrative boundaries. A planning region is selected for planning purposes. Regional planning is an instrument for economic development and to achieve socio-economic development of a depressed area or developable area.
30. **Real Estate**: It means land including buildings and improvements, and its natural assets such as water etc.
31. **Right-of way:** Any right of use to a strip of land. It means normally the strip of land used by a railway or roadway.
32. **Row buildings**: A row of houses with only front, rear and interior open spaces.
33. **Ribbon development**: Developers often choose to build along existing roads and highways to save money forming linear development on the outskirts of the cities called as Ribbon Development.
34. **Semi-detached building**: A building detached on three sides with open spaces.
35. **Sewerage**: It is the process of receiving and carrying off the excess water and filth of the city by sewers. A system of sewers is called as 'Sewerage system'.
36. **Storey**: It is the portion of a building included between the surface of any floor and the surface of the next floor ceiling above it.
37. **Town**: As per Census of India 1991, a town is defined as:
    (a) All places with a municipality, corporation, cantonment board or notified town area committee etc.,
    (b) All other places which satisfy the following criteria:
    1. a minimum population of 5000;
    2. atleast 75 percent of male working population engaged in non-agricultural pursuits;
    3. a density of population of atleast 400 persons per sq. km. (1000 persons per sq. mile).
38. **Urbanisation**: It is the process of increasing urban area in a geographical or administrative area.

39. **Urban agglomeration**: As per Census of India 1991, an urban agglomeration may constitute:
    (a) a city with continuous outgrowth (the part of outgrowth being outside the statutory limits but falling within the boundaries of the adjoining village or villages);
    (b) one town with similar outgrowth or two or more adjoining towns with their outgrowths;
    (c) a city and one or more adjoining towns with their outgrowth, all of which form a continuous spread.
40. **Urban renewal**: It is the process of improving the built environment by conservation, rehabilitation or redevelopment.
41. **Urban sprawl**: It means spread of urban growth outwards from the town to the suburbs.
42. **Zone:** Zone is a division of the development area for development under an Act. Zoning is the legal regulation of the use of land.

Index